William Cobbett

A topographical and political description of the Spanish part of Saint-Domingo:

Containing, general observations on the climate, population, and productions; on the character and manners of the inhabitants - Vol. 1

William Cobbett

A topographical and political description of the Spanish part of Saint-Domingo:
Containing, general observations on the climate, population, and productions; on the character and manners of the inhabitants - Vol. 1

ISBN/EAN: 9783337728670

Printed in Europe, USA, Canada, Australia, Japan

Cover: Foto ©ninafisch / pixelio.de

More available books at **www.hansebooks.com**

A
TOPOGRAPHICAL AND POLITICAL
DESCRIPTION

OF THE

SPANISH PART

OF

SAINT-DOMINGO;

CONTAINING,

GENERAL OBSERVATIONS ON THE CLIMATE, POPULATION AND PRODUCTIONS; ON THE CHARACTER AND MANNERS OF THE INHABITANTS; WITH AN ACCOUNT OF THE SEVERAL BRANCHES OF THE GOVERNMENT.

By M. L. E. MOREAU DE SAINT-MERY.
Member of the Philosophical Society of Philadelphia, &c.

TRANSLATED FROM THE FRENCH,
By WILLIAM COBBETT.

VOL. I.

PHILADELPHIA:
PRINTED AND SOLD BY THE AUTHOR, PRINTER AND BOOKSELLER, N°. 84, SOUTH FRONT-STREET.

1798.

A LIST

OF THE SUBSCRIBERS,

In Alphabetical order.

MM^{rs.}

A

ADAMS, Vice-President of the United-States of America.
ADET, Minister Plenipotentiary of the French Republic to the United-States of America.
AMERICAN (an) Gentleman. *Two hundred Copies.*

B.

BACHE (Benjamin-Franklin), Printer, Philadelphia. *Six Copies.*
BAUMEZ, Philadelphia.
BELIN DE VILLENEUVE.
BIDDLE (Clement), Notary public, Philadelphia.
BINGHAM (William), Senator of the United-States.
BLACON, Asilum, Pensylvania.
BONAMY, Albany.
BONNECHOSE, New-York.
BOUCANIER (H. E.), Philadelphia.
BOUSQUET (Augustin), Merchant, Philadelphia.
BRADFORD (Thomas), Printer-Bookseller, Philaphia.
BRANU, Philadelphia.

BRECK, Son (Samuel), Philadelphia.

C

CAMBEFORT, Elizabeth-Town, Jersey.
CAMPBELL (Robert), Bookseller, Philadelphia.
Three Copies.
CAREY (Mathew), Bookseller, Philadelphia.
Six Copies.
CAZENOVE (Théophile), Philadelphia.
CHAMPION (Edme), Paris.
CHEVALIER, elder, Philadelphia.
COATES (Samuel), Merchant, Philadelphia.
COLLINS (R. Dr Nicholas), Minister of the Suedish church, Philadelphia. *Two Copies.*
COLLOT (Général Victor), Philadelphia. *Two Copies.*
CORDEIL (Lewis), Philadelphia.
COUGNAC-MION, Elizabeth-Town, Jersey.
COURBE, New-York.

D

DALLAS (Alexander James), Secretary of the Commonwealth, Philadelphia.
DARTIS, Philadelphia.
DECOMBAZ, Bookseller, Philadelphia.
DELAFOND, New-York.
DELAHAYE elder, Havre.
DELANY (Sharp) Collector of the port, Philadelphia.
DEMEUNIER (J.).
DESLOZIÈRES, (By.) Philadelphia.
DEVÈZE (Dr.), Philadelphia.
DOBIGNIE, Philadelphia.

List of the Subscribers.

DUCLOS-CARPENTIER, Philadelphia.
DUFFIELD (D. B.)
DUPONCEAU (P. S.), Attorney at Law, Philadelphia.
DUPONT DE GAULT, Wilmington, Delaware.

E

ÉLIOT, Philadelphia.
ESTÈVE, Wilmington, Delaware.

F

FAVARANGE,
FRENCH (a) Gentleman.   *One hundred Copies.*
FREIRE (Chevalier) Minister of Portugal to the United-States.   *Two Copies.*

G

GALLINE, Philadelphia.
GARESCHE (Jn.), Philadelphia.
GARESCHE DUROCHER, Wilmington, Delaware.
GATERAU, Philadelphia.
GAUTIER LA GAUTTRIE, Philadelphia.
GAUVAIN (Peter), Philadelphia.
GERVIN (J.) St-Lucia.
GOUIN DU FIEF, Philadelphia.
GOYNARD (Peter), New-York.
GRAMMONT (Rossignol), Philadelphia.
GRANDPREY, Baltimore.
GUILLEMARD (J), Philadelphia.
GUYMET, Philadelphia.

J

JAMES (Tho. C.), Philadelphia.

K

KING (Rufus), Senator of the United-States.
KNOX (General), St-Georges, Maine.
KRASENSTERN, Officer of the englifh navry, Halifax.

L

LABARRE, New-York.
LABORIE.
LA COLOMBE (Lewis), Philadelphia.
LADEBAT, Elizabeth-Town, Jerfey.
LA GRANGE (J. E. G. M.), Philadelphia.
LA ROCHE (Dr.), Philadelphia.
LA ROCHEFOUCAULD - LIANCOURT, Philadelphia.
Two Copies.

LA ROCQUE, Philadelphia.
LATOUR DU PIN, Albany.
LAVAUD, Philadelphia.
LETOMBE, Conful general of the French Republic, Philadelphia. *Three Copies.*
LINCKLAEN (J.) Cazanovia, New-York.
LINE (A), Philadelphia.
LISLEADAM, Philadelphia.
LOGAN (Dr.), Penfylvania.
LOIR, (J. B.), Philadelphia.
LORENT.

M.

MAILLET, New-Heaven.
MAZURIÉ (Joseph), Merchant Philadelphia.
MORSE (Dr. Joseph), Charleston, Massachussets.
MOZARD, Consul of the french Republic, Boston.

N

NAIRAC, Philadelphia.
NOAILLES (General), Philadelphia.

P

PALYART (J) Consul-general of Portugal, Phiphia.
PICKERING (Thimothy), Secretary of State, Philadelphia.
PROUDFIL (James), Philadelphia.

R

RANDOLPH (William), Virginia.
RICARD (General).
RICE (H & P), Booksellers, Philadelphia.
ROCHAMBEAU (General.)
ROSS (Dr. Andrew), Philadelphia.

S

SAXON (Jn.), Attorney at Law, Rhode-Island.
SCHWEIZER (J.), Philadelphia.
SIMSON, Merchant, Philadelphia.   *Two Copies.*
SONIS, Philadelphia.

SONNTAG (W. L.) Merchant, Philadelphia.
STEPHENS (Thomas), Bookfeller, Philadelphia.
Two Copies.

STEVENS (Dr, E.)., Philadelphie.
SWANNUICK, Member of the Congrefs.

T

TALLEYRAND-PÉRIGORD, Philadelphia.
TANGUY DE LA BOISSIERE, Philadelphia.
TERRIER DE LAISTRE, elder, Trenton, Jerfey.
THURNINGER, Philadelphia.
TOD (W. H.), Attorney at Law, Philadelphia.
TREGENT, Philadelphia.

V

VAN-BERCHEL, Minifter of Holland, Philadelphia.
VAUGHAN (John), Merchant, Philadelphia.
Two Copies.

VOLNEY, Philadelphia.

Y

YARD (James), Philadelphia.

THE reader will see, by the close of the historical summary at the head of this work, that I thought it necessary, in the description of Saint-Domingo, studiously to avoid touching on any thing relative to the revolution, since 1789.

This description was nearly finished at that epoch, as far, at least, as relates to the Spanish part. I had even read some fragments of it in the public sittings of the Museum of Paris, in 1788; and its object being to represent Saint-Domingo such as I had seen it, it would have appeared whimsical in me to lay aside a true and interesting picture in order to take one that was every moment upon the change. I should have feared, in so doing, to resemble a painter, who, having undertaken to draw the portrait of a person, celebrated for beauty and other advantages, should determine, at the moment of finishing it, not to represent the original in its natural state, but disfigured with the cruel effects of a convulsive malady.

Besides, during the year 1793, when in France, I was retouching what relates to the Spanish colony of Saint-Domingo, I had continually before my eyes the dangers that had surrounded me for more than a year; the events and arrestations which had threatened

(*a*)

me with the approach of a cruel death, a death from which I have been preserved only by the influence of those very acts of my public life for which I had before been persecuted. I felt the necessity of keeping myself within a narrower circuit, for fear of being sacrificed before I had finished a part, at least, of what I had in store for the good of my country. Thinking nothing, then, of the present, but as it enabled me to draw from the past a lesson for the future, in a description of the finest colony that European industry had ever created in the New World, I was still more determined not to mix the effects of the revolution with my first plan.

While I was thus labouring for my country, I expected that those men of blood, who then ruled it, would dispose of my fate. A courage, examples of which multiplied daily, would even have rendered all dangers indifferent to me, if the sight of a wife and children without support, if that of other dear relations also, had not impressed my mind with too sad and distressing ideas, and rent my heart with the severest torture. I even caught myself sometimes sighing at the idea of death, a trifle in itself for one who has lived so as neither to wish nor fear it, but which would have robbed me of the only fruit I wished to reap from eighteen years of laborious enquiry, that of rendering it useful to mankind. In this situation, being then in one of the ports of France, waiting for an occasion to return to the colonies, I became the object of fresh persecutions, from some of the subaltern agents of tyranny, which had covered the country with scaffolds. They ordered me to Paris, to give an account of a conduct, which they well knew Robespierre had never approved, even from the epoch when we were both members of the Constituent Assembly. I was ordered, too, *to take my family with me.*

This last condition awakened in my heart feelings, the power of which can be known by a husband and a father only. I went to those who had ordered my departure, among whom were some who had terror at command, because they themselves obeyed it. I spoke with the firmness that so important an occasion inspired, and nature rendered me so eloquent, that the majority were moved; the order for going to commit my head to the executioner was changed into a permission to return to Saint-Domingo, by the way of the United States; and when an emissary of Robespierre, without doubt informed that I was escaping from him, came with a mandate express for my arrestation, in spite of the passports granted *in the name of the law,* the vessel containing all I held dear, and myself also, had been hardly thirty-five hours under sail.

Arrived in this allied country, and learning that the part of Saint-Domingo to which my profession attached me, was in the power of the enemies of France, I took the resolution of seeking a livelihood in the United States, as I ever have done, from the product of my labour.. The delicious sentiment which told me that I ought to devote myself entirely to the happiness of my family, has rendered every thing easy to me, and this family repays by its love, the labours and cares in which it partakes.

I had brought with me but a small part of my writings, and dared no longer reckon on the utility of my studies. But, with a horror against blood-shed, has re-appeared a system which gives protection to all who love their country, and are happy in finding an occasion to serve it. This beneficent protection, to which I had a right, has produced with respect to me, a most delightful effect, in bringing me safe all my materials, all that my fatigue, a considerable expence, and an indefatigable zeal, have been able to collect in the space of twenty years. Blessed forever be this return to an order of things, that renders our love for our country no longer a crime!

A motive very natural to a writer having led me more than once to run over different parts of my manuscript, and perceiving but a very distant hope of publishing the history of Saint-Domingo, I wished to see if I could not make some alterations in it, which facts posterior to the revolution seemed to dictate; but in reading over some pages with this intention, I met with a real difficulty to interweave what I had already written, and what I wished to add, and so I was still brought back to my first opinion.

How did I congratulate myself on this perseverance when the news of the cession of the most considerable part of Saint-Domingo from Spain to France, arrived at Philadelphia, made me believe, that the publication of the description of the Spanish part of that island would be interesting to the public!

ADVERTISEMENT.

The Spanish colony of Saint-Domingo was the first founded by Europeans in America. Under this point of view it must give the first traces of the European genius, receiving councils, from situations and events, till then unknown. It must show the proof of the transplantation of the ideas of the Old World, in the New, and of their naturalization, more or less perfect in this foreign land. It should, by its priority to all the other European colonies, formed under the torrid zone, have presented, in its administration, principles for other nations to adopt in their turn, with modifications more or less sensible, and produced by the influence that each of them receives from its particular manners and character. In a word, the Spanish colony of Saint-Domingo, is the first mark that the Europeans impressed on a vast part of the globe, and with so many recommendations united, it certainly ought to attract the attention of the *philosophical* observer.

And, what time can be more proper for the exhibition of this picture than the moment when the original is going to disappear? Indeed, the cession of the Spanish part has already, in destroying the administration, and with it the greatest part of those things which served to mark the character of the colony, rendered it impossible to discover, in what now subsists, what has subsisted; in future it can be known but from report. It must be then sought for in the remembrance of those who have known it, and endeavour to come, by the means of what it has yet in its physical existence, to the knowledge of the spirit which animated it, and hazard a conjecture, if it not been happily painted when it formed a whole, when each of the features, which characterised it, could be studied at leisure and traced from nature; and this is the picture, which I dare call a faithful one, here presented to the public.

This description of the Spanish part must, then, be read, without ever forgetting that it was written entirely independent of every thing the French revolution may have produced; because, generally speaking, it was written before that epoch; because this idea has never been lost sight of in what has been since added, and because I had ever to speak of things anterior to the revolution.

I have carried the respect for my own motives so far in this instance, that I have not made any alteration in that part of the work, relating to the question, whether the cession of the Spanish part would be advantageous to France or not. My opinion on this subject, as on all others on which I have written, is the result of internal conviction. My sentiments are not a law, and if they deserved to have the force of one, what surer guide, for me at least, could I be required to follow, than my conscience? My conscience has forbidden me to bend my thoughts to occasional events. And if those disastrous times still existed, when every unpleasing truth was criminal, it would be much easier for me to hold my tongue than falsify my principles. It is the esteem of mankind that I seek; I know how to do without their approbation.

The fame principles will be my guide in the publication of the *Defcription of the French Part of Saint-Domingo*, if encouragement and other circumftances fhould enable me to commit it to the prefs. They are alfo my guide, and ftill more ftrictly fo, in my *Hiftory of Saint-Domingo*, that unfortunate ifland, the paft fplendor of which will aftonifh future ages. It is in tracing this hiftory that I recollect, almoft at every line, that the hiftorian exercifes the power of a real magiftracy, and that he ought to throw down his pen with affright, if he forgets, for a fingle moment, that, at a future day, pofterity may have no other teftimony than his to direct its judgment, on facts and individuals; and that, if this teftimony deceives, he is chargeable with irreparable injuftice; unlefs, indeed, pofterity detecting the partiality of the hiftorian, cites him, in his turn, before its awful tribunal, and ftigmatizes his name, by placing him among the perjured witneffes.

I fhall clofe this advertifement, which became neceffary from feveral motives, by a wifh, which has never ceafed to animate my heart, fince the moment, now long paft, I devoted myfelf to the ftudy of whatever concerns the colonies, and which is, that my enquiries, my facrifices, and my labours, may be of utility to mankind in general, and particularly to my own country.

ADVERTISEMENT.

Notwithſtanding the pains I have taken to be exact in the hydrographical particulars contained in this deſcription, and in the map, which makes part of it, and which has been traced under my inſpection, I do not offer them as mathematical truths, but only as the trueſt that have yet been obtained with reſpect to Saint-Domingo.

HISTORICAL SUMMARY

OF THE

EVENTS AND TRANSACTIONS,

RELATIVE TO THE BOUNDARIES BETWEEN THE SPANISH AND FRENCH COLONIES IN THE ISLAND OF SAINT-DOMINGO.

1630.

THE adventurers, that medley of individuals from almost all the nations of Europe, being augmented in number by the new-arrived French, whom the Spaniards had driven from St. Christopher's, go from the little island of the Tortue, where they had begun to settle, and erect little huts called *Ajoupas* or *Boucans* (places to cook meat) on the island of Saint-Domingo, which they then called the *Great-Land*, from a comparison with the Tortue.

1632.

The Freebooters and Buccaniers drive the Spaniards from the Tortue.

1638.

The Spaniards maſſacre almoſt all the French colony.

1639.

Such was the boldneſs of the adventurers, that they retook the Tortue.

1640.

There were already ſome French ſettlers ſcattered along the northern coaſt of Saint-Domingo, from the peninſula of Samana to Port-de-Paix, and united in little ſettlements for the purpoſe of hunting of the oxen, that were become wild.

1641.

Le Vaſſeur, an officer of the garriſon of the iſland of St. Chriſtopher, ſent by the commander Poincy, lieutenant-governor-general of the French iſlands in America, takes the command at the Tortue, where Willis, an Engliſhman choſen chief by the adventurers of his nation, had uſurped a deſpotic authority.

1663.

Mr. Deſchamps de la Place, commanding for the king at the Tortue, and on the coaſt of Saint-Domingo, in the abſence of Du Rauſſet, his uncle, begins the ſettlement of Port-de-Paix, before which the Buccaniers had one in the little island *à Boyau* or *of the Buccaniers*, situated in the middle of the bay of Bayaha, now Fort-Dauphin.

1664.

D'Ogeron, the successor of Mr. Deschamps de la place, forms a habitation at Port-Margot, which Le Vasseur, who had first landed there, had originally named the *Refuge*.

1670.

The French, encouraged by D'Ogeron, begin to settle in the plain of Cape-François.

1674.

D'Ogeron augments the settlement of Samana, which the Spaniards had attacked, without being able to destroy it.

1676.

At this epoch, when Pouançay, the nephew of D'Ogeron, succeeded him, some of the French had carried their settlements along the sea-side, from Port-de-Paix to the river of the Rebouc, and possessed the island of the Tortue, and the peninsula of Samana.

1678.

Peace of Nimeugen, between the French and Spaniards.

1680.

Don Francisco de Segura, Sandoval and Castille, president of the Spanish part, writes, the 10th July, and sends the Licentiate, Don Juan Baptiste Escofo, to Mr. de Pouançay, to notify to him the conclusion of peace, and to propose to him to fix the boundaries between the colonies of the two nations. The envoy finds the French penetrated as far as the river Rebouc, which he crosses with Mr. de Longchamp, who was settled on the bank of the river, in a canoe belonging to his habitation. Mr. Longchamp and other Frenchmen accompanied the envoy on the road towards the Cape, where Mr. de Pouançay was, and where the envoy arrived in the latter end of the same month of July.

The interpreter at this conference was Mr. Demas Jonchée, captain of the ship the St. Bernard, who had seen the Licentiate Escofo at St. Yague, and who conducted him on his return, as far as the bay of Mancenil.

An instrument was drawn up, by which the Rebouc was fixed on as the line of demarcation.

1684.

The Spanish president who wrote to Mr. de Cussy the governor, to announce to him the peace of Ratisbon, which was concluded the 15th of August, having complained that the French encroached, Messieurs the Chevalier de St. Laurent and Bégon, administrators-general of the islands, and who were then at Saint-Domingo, proposed to him to acknowledge again, that the boundaries set off from the Rebouc on one side, and ended at the cape of the Béate on the other.

Don André de Roblès, the president, rejected this proposal, and the Spaniards began themselves to destroy the wild cattle, which brought the Buccaniers a-hunting, for the sake of their skins, which they sold.

1687.

On the west of the Rebouc, the Spaniards attempt to form settlements, which the French, having one hundred and fifty horsemen under the command of Mr. Carron, an inhabitant of Bayaha, go and burn.

1688.

In the month of May, fifty Spaniards carry off two Frenchmen, caught hunting in the immense canto of Bayaha. Two hundred and fifty French pursue them, but too late.

The president, Don André de Roblès, answers, on the 3d. Oct, to the complaint of Mr. Cuffy, that Bayaha is in the Spanish territory, but that he has, however, ordered the two Frenchmen to be set at liberty.

The president complains, in his turn, that some French have settled at Samana.

1689.

War being declared between France and Spain, the former plant their standard on the western side of the Rebouc, and place out-posts there.

1690.

The French, under the command of Mr. Cuffy, attack and take St. Yago, and find no Spanish outpost till they come to the hatte of the governor of St. Yago, on the east of the Rebouc.

1691.

The Spaniards lay waste, burn, and pillage a part of the Cape, and then return within their territory.

1695.

The Spanish, joined by the English, lay waste the country as far as Port-de-Paix.

1697.

The peace of Ryswick, declaring that the possessions of the two powers shall remain as they were before the war.

1698.

The Spaniards, profiting by the peace, settle on the west of the Rebouc, certain enclosures, under pretext of keeping the cattle there, which they came to sell to the French.

Don Pedro Morel, meſtre-de-camp, ſent to the Cape to bring back Madame de Graſſe, who had been conducted to Santo-Domingo after the taking of Port-de-Paix in 1695, is ordered by the Spaniſh preſident to induce Mr. Ducaſſe, the governor, to draw back his out-poſts ſix or ſeven leagues, as far as Bayaha. Mr. Ducaſſe anſwers, that the preſident has no reaſon to complain concerning his out-poſts, as they are not beyond the boundaries,

In the month of September this year, the king, by letters patent for the eſtabliſhment of the Saint-Domingo company, grants it all the commerce of the iſland, from Cape-Tiburon to the river of Neybe *incluſively*. The company itſelf afterwards makes conceſſions there.

1699.

The 6th of February, the preſident, Don Severmo de Manzaneda, ſummons Mr. Ducaſſe to draw back his advanced poſts as far as Caracol. Mr. Ducaſſe ſends to him Mr. Duqueſnot, attorney-general of the ſovereign council of Petit-Goave, to convince him of the ridiculouſneſs of his pretenſions.

Mr. Duqueſnot agrees, that, 'till the deciſion of the two courts, the out-poſts on both ſides ſhall be drawn back to four leagues from the Rebouc.

Mr. De Galiffet, become governor by the departure of Mr. Ducaſſe for France, gives permiſſion to hunt, but never beyond the Rebouc; and he places an out-poſt at *la Porte*, the point which is now the boundary between Dondon and St. Raphaël.

1700.

The Spaniards encroach. Mr. De Galiffet writes to the president in the month of July. The president answers the 5th of September, denies the agreement made with Mr. Duquesnot, maintains that the French have never had any out posts beyond the river Jaquezy, and that, in 1684, Don André Robles refused to acknowledge the *Guyaubin*, or the Rebouc, as the boundary.

Mr. De Galiffet does away these errors the 27th of October; he offers the testimony of all those who have been stationed at the Rebouc during the preceding peace, and defies the president to prove, that, at that time, there was a single Spaniard settled on the west of the river.

This year appeared an engraved map of the island of Saint-Domingo, by N. De Fer, geographer of the king of Spain, according to which the boundaries begin at Porte-de-Plate on the north coast, cross the island, and end at the mouth of the Neybe.

1701.

October the 7th. The president summons the French to draw in all their posts as far as Caracol, on the confines of Limonade, or, at least, as far as the river Jacquezy, making protests at the same time.

November 2d. Mr. De Galiffet sends an answer, supported by the declaration of Mr. Duquesnot himself, and, in his turn, summons the president to observe the agreement, made with the attorney-general.

1705.

Accession of Philip V. of the House of Bourbon, to the throne of Spain, which settles the disputes about the boundaries.

1706.

Don Guillermo Morfil, appointed president of the Spanish part, lands at the Cape, whence he sets out for his government. Mr. De Charitte, then chief of the French part, gives him a numerous guard of honour, and accompanies him in person as far as the Rebouc. The Spanish militia receives the president on the other side of the river.

1710.

The Spaniards, who had been permitted to form four or five hattes on the French side of the Rebouc, having manifested certain pretensions, the governor of the Cape, with a sufficient force, repairs to the spot, and informs them, that his suffering them to remain there is an act of pure favour.

1712.

The French settlements, even on this side the Massacre, are laid waste by the Spaniards, who exercise many cruelties.

Those of the town of St. Yago make an incursion of the same kind.

The governor and inhabitants of St. Yago, in an address to the king of Spain, dated 30th July, accuse the French of invasions and violences.

1713.

In the month of March, the court of Spain directs its ambassador at Paris to demand orders for the demolition of all the French habitations at Bayaha; and the same court writes, the 14th July, to the president of the royal court at Santo-Domingo, to oblige the French to evacuate all that they have usurped, since the accession of Philip V.

1714.

France proposes to Spain to appoint commissioners to fix on the boundaries.

Towards the end of the year, the president of the royal court at Santo-Domingo, dispatches Don Ramire, governor of Azua, to the Count of Blénac, governor-general, then at Leogane, and Don Pedro Morel, governor of St. Yago, to the governor of the Cape, to summon them to withdraw all the French settled beyond the river Marion: that is to say, as far as the spot where Fort-Dauphin now stands.

Mr. Blénac refuses to yield to this unjust demand. The general and the intendant order an examination to be made before Messrs. Beaupré and Durocher, notaries at the Cape, when twenty-four witnesses (one of whom, named Bigot, was ninety-three years of age), attest, that the French have been possessors, for sixty years past, of all the country lying to the west of the Rebouc.

1715.

The duke of St. Aignan, the French ambassador at the court of Spain, is directed by his court to maintain the examination of 1714, and to propose commissioners once again. He is answered, that information is expected from Santo-Domingo. But, on the 20th of May, the king of Spain sends instructions to the president, to leave the French in possession of what they had when he mounted the throne, and to send such information as might enable the court to name commissioners.

1719.

In consequence of the declaration of war between France and Spain, Mr. de Chateaumorand, the governor, and afterwards Mr. Sorel, who succeeded him, at this epoch, proposed to the Spanish president, Don Fernand Constant Ramirez, to observe a neutrality in the island of Saint-Domingo, to leave the dispute of the boundaries undecided, not to suffer the Spaniards to cross the Rebouc, nor the French to go beyond Capotille.

The Spaniards place an advanced guard-house at

the point where the little river Montcuffon falls into the Artibonite. Mr. de Paty, commandant of the weft, orders it to be burnt.

1721.

The Spaniards kill four Frenchmen in the fouth, under pretext of invafion of territory; but the prefident requefts, in the month of February, that this unhappy affair may not deftroy the harmony that exifts between the twe nations at Saint-Domingo.

1724.

The court of France fends an order, 10th July, to the count of Robin, chargé d'affaires in Spain, to leave the fubject of the boundaries afide, becaufe it is more convenient to treat on the fpot.

Minguet, (whofe name is juftly celebrated at Saint-Domingo), returning from the conqueft of Carthagena, had obtained from Mr. Ducaffe, 11th September 1693, a vaft tract of land at Dondon. The Spaniards after having long vexed him, had at laft congratulated themfelves in finding in this gentleman an excellent Efculapious; but certain grants lately made at Dondon alarmed them. The prefident complained to Meffrs. de la Rochalar and Montholon, the general and intendant, who anfwered him, that it was no more than the fame fpot, originally granted to Minguet. After this the governor of Hinche, and the juftice of the fame place, came and fummoned the inhabitants to retire.

Messrs. de Chastenoye and Duclos, governor and *ordonnateur* of the Cape, went to Dondon, in the month of October, accompanied with a detachment of militia; here they had an interview with Mr. Miesse, the governor of Hinche, at the house of Signor Saint-Yago de Ribera, and it was agreed that the French inhabitants should remain, except two, concerning whom it was agreed that further inquiries should be made.

1727.

The Spaniards come and erect a guard-house, even on the eastern bank of the river Dajabon, or the river of the Massacre.

1728.

Fifteen Spaniards, under the command of an officer from the guard-house, erected in 1727, go to the canton of the Trou-de-Jean-de-Nantes, in the dependancies of Ouanaminthe, and destroy two French settlements, carry off some slaves, and one of the inhabitants bound.

Mr. de Chastenoye goes from the Cape to the Spanish advanced guard-house, finds that it was an enterprize of the officer, and complains to the president. As he returned he learnt that the French inhabitants went armed, in order to avenge themselves on the Spaniards; nor were they appeased, till the commandant, Juan Gerardino de Gusman, acknowledged his error.

In the month of August, an order was sent to the Marquis of Brancas, French ambassador at Madrid, to renew the proposals for the appointment of commissioners to fix the boundaries.

1729.

Mr. de Nolivos, commandant for the king in the western cantons, made his annual visit round the frontiers of the Cul-de-Sac, Mirebalais, and Artibonite: when he arrived at the little river Montcusson, he found a hut where there lived an Isidre negro, who, desiring a grant of land, took, in order to obtain it, a certificate from Mr. Hardouineau, commandant of the Mirebalais, the 28th July.

The Spaniards, who saw this certificate, took umbrage at it. The commandants made the alarm be founded from Hinche to Azua. The people flew to arms, they marched to the frontiers from the Cahobe (of Acajoux or Mahogani), and from the Vérettes. They even wound a man, *Etienne Trouvé*, an inhabitant of Mirebalais, with a musket shot.

The 8th of August, the president, Mr. de la Rocheferrer, wrote to Mr. de la Rochalar, the governor, to propose to him to appoint commissioners on both sides, in order to avoid greater evils.

In consequence of this, Mr. Nolivos was dispatched, and he had a conference with Don Gonzalo Fernandez de Oviedo, auditor-general of war, at the house of Mr. Hardouineau. The Spanish plenipotentiary said, that he would answer in writing; retired into his territory, and wrote, that the disputed land, from which Mr. Nolivos withdrew an advanced-guard, belonged to the Spaniards.

173

The 6th of May, president Rocheferrer writes to Mr. de la Rochalar, and complains that, since four or five years, some French have been settling at the Fond-de-Capotille. He requests that they may be ordered to remove, and threatens to employ forcible means. The governor-general answers, that it was sacrificing a great deal to the love of peace and harmony, to stop on the west of the river of the Massacre, when the French had a right to go as far as the Rebouc. But Mr. Buttet, lieutenant-general of the king at Fort-Dauphin, having made inconsiderate expressions on the subject of the boundaries, and having determined two inhabitants to settle beyond Capotille, the Spaniards, in the night of the first of September, came, four hundred hundred in number, destroyed three plantations, and burnt the houses.

On the 14th, in open day, Mr. de Chastenoye, governor of the Cape, came with a detachment of two hundred men, and destroyed the same number of plantations in the Spanish territory, but without setting fire to any thing. After this reprisal, the two governors, of the Cape and of St. Yago, agree that the river of the Massacre shall be looked on as the provisionary boundary.

The 25th of December, the minister approved of the whole of the conduct of Mr. de Chastenoye, and again directed that the settlers should not go beyond the Massacre, 'till the boundaries had been fixed by commissioners, named by the two powers.

1732.

Mr. de Chastenoye informs the Spanish president that he will not suffer, as his predecessors had done for some years past, the justice of St. Yago to come, at each change of the presidency, and summon the inhabitants of Maribarou, Bayaha, le Brulage, l'Acul-des-Pins, and the Trou-de-Jean-de-Nantes, to retire.

1733.

In the month of October, Don Alphonso Castro y Mezo accuses the French, in a letter to his court, of devastating the Spanish territory, of killing some of the inhabitants, of wanting to seize on the little island of the Massacre, and of continuing to fortify Fort-Dauphin.

1735.

The 29th of April, the Spanish minister sends this complaint to the French ambassador at Madrid. The court of France answers by once more proposing to appoint commissioners.

Quarrels for the little island of the Massacre-river.

1736.

The Spaniards not only prefume to fettle, as they had done in 1719, on the borders of the Mirebalais, but they even place an advance-guard on the weft of the river Seybe, a hundred fathoms nearer the French.

Mr. de Fayet, the governor-general, marches with fome regulars and militia, demolifhes the guard-houfe, and pitches a camp on this part of the frontiers. However, he agrees in the month of March, with Don Nicholas de Guridi, who comes to his camp, that the Spaniards fhall keep poffeffion of the difputed territory, and that an advanced-guard fhall be placed on each fide, 'till the boundaries are finally fixed by the two crowns.

1737.

The king, by his inftructions to Mr. de Larnage, difapproves of the condefcenfion of Mr. de Fayet.

The Spaniards enter on the French territory, in the dependancies of the Gonaïves; the governor-general orders Mr. Maupoint, commandant of Saint-Mark, to verify the fact. The commandant names Mr. Jean Baptifte Roffignol de la Chicote, captain of militia horfe at Artibonite, who, on the 8th of May, finds, at the provifion habitation of Minguet, a hatte occupied by two Spaniards, though it is proved that, two leagues further on, there ftill exifted fome ruins of the fettlement, where Minguet (already mentioned in the article of

1724) had refided twenty-one years. A crofs and a French flag were placed on the fpot where thefe ruins were.

The Spanifh colony is put in movement: the militia of Hinche are affembled, as alfo thofe of Banique and St. John; but this affemblage is not followed by any overt-act.

1741.

The Spaniards make incurfions at Dondon, whence they drive feveral inhabitants, and eftablifh an advance-guard in the canton of the Baffin-Cayman.

1747.

Another incurfion is made at the Marre-à-la-Roche, in the parifh of Dondon, where the invaders carrry off five negroes, and the overfeer of Mr. Mauny de Jatigny.

1750.

The 13th of October, fifteen Spaniards armed, lay wafte the plantations of Mr. Loyer, on the weft of the Maffacre, and threaten to burn the habitations of Meffrs. Lambert Camax, and Perrault.

The 29th of October, Mr. De Conflans makes a complaint on this fubject to the prefident of the Spanifh part.

1752.

At the end of the year, the Spaniards again drive Mr. Mauny de Jatigny from the settlement he had formed at Dondon, on the territory of Minguet. Messrs. de Vaudreuil and de Laporte-Lalanne, the administrators of the colony, re-establish Mr. Mauny, by an ordinance of the 1st October, 1754; and again, in 1756, the two French chiefs, in person, take possession, formally, of this territory, in consequence of the grant, made to Minguet, in 1698, having been just then found.

1755.

The 21st of February, the Spaniards summon the French living in the canton called the Ravin of the Mulattoes, (now the parish of Valliere), to quit their settlements, if they do not wish to be driven from them by force. Mr. de Lange, major of Fort Dauphin, marches to the spot, but finds the Spaniards gone.

Mr. Vaudreuil places an advanced guard here.

1757.

Four habitations of the Ravin of the Mulattoes burnt by the Spaniards.

1761.

Disputes concerning an establishment formed at Dondon, by Mr. de Villars; but Messrs. Bart and d'Azelor, governors of the two colonies, let it remain, till they know the decision of the two courts.

1763.

The Marquis of Grimaldy, the Spanish minister, writes to the Marquis of Ossun, the French ambassador, that commissioners are going to be chosen, to settle the boundaries.

In consequence of this, Mr. d'Estaing, who was then going to Saint-Domingo, received orders from the king in blank, with power to fill them up with the names of those whom he should choose to appoint.

1764.

Mr. d'Estaing fills up with the name of the Count of Ornano, the full powers to treat on the boundaries. But the court of Spain having named no commissary, the Count of Ornano returns to the Cape in the month of June.

Mr. d'Azelor attempts to establish an advanced-guard at the Marre-à-la-Roche, at Dondon, which Mr. d'Estaing obliges him to withdraw.

1769.

Towards the end of the year, Don Nicholas de Montenegro, sub-commandant of St. Raphaël and the boundaries in that quarter, carried off Mr. de Ravel, an inhabitant of Dondon, with four of his negroes and his effects. A demand was made of the person of this inhabitant, who was actually on the Spanish territory; but he remained in the prison of Santo-Domingo till the month of June 1771, when an award of the king of Spain set him at liberty, in imposing on him a fine of a hundred dollars.

1770.

Mr. de Montenegro makes an incursion at Dondon with an armed force.

Mr. de Vincent, the king's lieutenant at the Cape, is sent to Santo-Domingo, by Mr. Nolivos, where he concludes with the president, on the 4th of June, a treaty, the 5th article of which, the only one that relates to the boundaries, expresses that, in case of a dispute between the two nations with respect to the boundaries, the respective commandants of the advanced-guards on the frontiers, shall give mutual information of the same, and shall meet on the spot, to verify the object of dispute, and to settle it amicably, till the governors-general have concerted together, and given their orders. Mr. d'Azelor added to this article, that the commandants should visit their frontiers, in order to know well their situation and boundaries.

1771.

The end of March, Mr. Montenegro wishes a French mulatto, named Beligout, who had taken shelter in the Spanish part, to be permitted to settle on a portion of the land of Mr. Mauny.

On the 31ſt of May, Mr. Montenegro, at the head of fifty men, came to the canton of Canary, a pariſh of Dondon, and carried off the overſeer of Mr. Mauny, and a negro woman. He pillaged, laid ſeveral plantations waſte, and burnt the dwellings. Another habitation underwent the ſame treatment.

Mr. de Nolivos ordered Mr. Vincent to make repriſals. The latter goes, with an armed force, to the ſettlement of Don Guzman at Atalaye, takes away the overſeer and four negroes. He goes alſo to the habitation of Oſſé Panche, whence he takes four more negroes and a negro woman, but without pillaging, or burning, or any other acts of violence.

Mr. de Nolivos propoſes to exchange the captures made on both ſides, which, with difficulty, he obtains.

He goes, in the month of Auguſt, to dine at the houſe of Don Gaſpard, commandant of Dahabon, and of the frontiers. Here he finds Don Fernand de Spinoſa, commandant of St. Raphaël, and its boundaries. Meſſrs. de Vincent and de Lilancour, king's lieutenants at the Cape and Fort Dauphin, were alſo preſent. It is concluded at this conference, to adhere ſtrictly to the fifth article of the treaty of the 4th of June, 1770.

Nevertheleſs, Mr. de Nolivos ſigned, on the 3d of November, with this ſame Don Fernand de Spinoſa, in the name of the preſident Don Joſeph Solano, a treaty, by which he gave up to the Spaniards, proviſionally, the lands diſputed at Dondon; ſtipulated that the French ſhould quit them; and conſented to the establishment of an advanced-guard at the Saut-du-Canot. All which had been constantly refused since the government of Mr. d'Estaing.

1772.

The Viscount of La Ferronnays, in the interim of Mr. de Nolivos's departure to France, refused to adhere to the convention of the 3d of November, 1771, except with respect to the advanced-guard at the Saut-du-Canot. It was agreed between him and Mr. de Solano, on the 10th of February, that the execution of the said convention should be suspended for ten months, to wait for the orders of the two courts. That of France approved of the conduct of Mr. de la Ferronnays.

The 26th of November, the minister informs Mr. de Vallière, the governor-general, that the court of Spain wishes to settle, in Europe, the disputes concerning the boundaries; and he requests, in consequence, all the necessary information on the subject.

1773.

Don Joseph de Solano, threatens no longer to permit the French to receive cattle from the Spanish part, unless the affair of the boundaries is settled. By this he forces Mr. de Vallière to subscribe, a convention, which, in yielding to all the pretensions of the Spaniards, declares the boundary to begin in the north at the river of the Massacre, and to end in the south, at that of the river of the Pédernales. This convention was concluded on the 25th of August, at Port-au-Prince, to which place the Spanish president came in person.

1774.

Mr. de Vallière having given an account of this tyrannical act, and of a sort of protest, which he had thought it his duty to make, the minister approved of his conduct, the 14th of January; and the French ambassador at the court of Madrid received an order to communicate the protest in order to accelerate the conclusion of the definitive treaty of the boundaries.

1775.

February the 27th, in consequence of a complaint of the court of Spain, the minister sent an order to Mr. de Vallière to withdraw an advanced guard, which he had placed on a spot, where there was one before the 25th of August 1773.

On the 14th of August, 1774, Mr. d'Ennery arrived at Saint-Domingo, as successor of Mr. de Vallière, with an order to maintain things as they were, and to resist force by force. He conceived the design of settling the disputes, relative to the boundaries on the spot.

1776.

On the 29th of February, a treaty was signed at Atalaye, by Messrs. d'Ennery and de Solano, who named, for tracing the boundaries, and placing the pyramids that were to serve as land-marks, the Vifcount of Choifeul, and Don Joachim Garcia, lieutenant-colonel of the infantry of the Spanifh part.

These plenipotentiaries terminated their operations on the 28th of Auguft.

1777.

On the third of June, the provifional treaty became definitive by the ratification, fubfcribed at Aranjuez, in the name of their Moft Chriftian and Moft Catholic Majefties, by the Marquis of Offun and Mr. de Florida Blanca.

As this treaty is become the common title of property of the two nations, and points out what ought to be the territorial divifion of Saint-Domingo, I thought it indifpenfably neceffary to infert it here at full length.

(xxvi)

TREATY,

Concluded between the Plenipotentiaries of their Most Christian and Most Catholic Majesties, concerning the Boundaries of the French and Spanish Possessions in the Island of Saint-Domingo.

June 3d, 1777.

THE Sovereigns of France and Spain, always attentive to the welfare of their subjects, and being convinced of the great importance of establishing between the vassals of the two crowns the same union that so happily exists between their Majesties, have agreed by a common accord, to do away, as the case and circumstance may require and permit, the difficulties and obstacles, that may obstruct so salutary an end.

The frequent dissentions that have taken place, for many years past, at Saint-Domingo, between the French and Spanish inhabitants of that island, as well with respect to the possession of land, as other particular rights, notwithstanding the provisional conventions entered into by the commandants of the respective possessions of the two nations, had induced the two sovereigns to take this important object into their consideration, and to send orders and instructions, in consequence thereof, to their governors in the said island, enjoining them to endeavour, with the greatest care, and most sincere desire of success, to establish a possible harmony between the colonists of the two nations respectively; to examine by themselves the principal tracts of territory, to cause exact plans to be taken, and finally, to conclude an arrangement of the boundaries, so clear and so positive as forever to put an end to disputes, and to assure the continuation of the closest friendship between the inhabitants on each side.

In pursuance of the orders of the two monarchs, all possible information and diligence was acquired and employed, and, at last, Mr. de Vallière, commandant and governor of the French part of the island, and Don Joseph Solano, commandant and captain-general of the Spanish part, signed a provisional convention, on the twenty-fifth August, one thousand seven hundred and seventy-three; but the two courts judging that this convention did not fulfil their mutual desires, and that, the object being to do away forever, all motives and pretexts of discord, it was necessary to clear up certain points still further, dispatched new orders relative to the subject.

The governors, sincerely animated with the same desire, concluded and signed a new convention, or description of the boundaries, on the twenty-ninth of February, one thousand seven hundred and seventy-six; and they further named commissaries and engineers to make, conjointly, a topographical plan of all the frontier, from one extremity to the other, from north to south, and to place at proper distances, the necessary pillars or land-marks. This commission, as appears by the inftrument figned by the commiffioners, was executed the twenty-eighth of Auguft following.

The two fovereigns having received an exact and full account of all thefe preliminary fteps, and defiring to affix the feal of their royal approbation to a definitive arrangement, that might forever eftablifh peace and unity between their refpective fubjects, determined to have formed, in Europe, a treaty relative to the boundaries of the French and Spanifh poffeffions in the ifland of Saint-Domingo, taking for its bafis the convention of the twenty-fifth of Auguft, one thoufand feven hundred and feventy-three, the arrangement concluded the twenty-ninth of February, one thoufand feven hundred and feventy-fix, and above all, the inftrument figned by the refpective commiffaries, on the twenty-eighth of Auguft, in the fame year, one thoufand feven hundred and feventy-fix.

In order to effect the faid treaty, the two fovereigns have named the following plenipotentiaries; to wit: On the part of his moft chriftian majefty, his excellency the marquis of Offun, grandee of Spain of the firft order, field marfhal in the army of his moft chriftian majefty, knight of his orders, and his ambaffador extraordinary and plenipotentiary at the court of Spain: And, on the part of his moft catholic majefty, his excellency Don Jofeph Monino de Florida Blanca, knight of the order of Charles III. counfellor of ftate, and firft fecretary of ftate for foreign affairs. The faid plenipotentiaries after having conferred together, and made a mutual communication of their full powers, have agreed on the following articles:

Article I.

The boundaries between the two nations shall remain perpetually and invariably fixed at the mouth of the river *Daxabon*, or river of the *Massacre*, on the northern side of the said island, and at the mouth of the river *Pedernales*, or *des Anses-à-Pitre*, on the southern side, in the terms specified in the second article; observing only here, that if, in future, any doubt should arise as to the identity of the rivers *Pedernales* and *Anses-à-Pitre*, it is already decided that it is the river commonly called by the Spaniards the river *Pedernales*, that the plenipotentiaries mean to point out as the boundary.

Article II.

Seeing that the last survey, taken by the Viscount of Choiseul, and Don Joachim Garcia, in quality of commissioners, conjointly with the respective engineers and inhabitants born in the country, has been executed in the most exact and minute manner, with a perfect knowledge of the arrangement made between the French and Spanish commandants on the twenty-ninth of February, one thousand seven hundred and seventy-six, and seeing that they had before their eyes the different tracts of territory, and were fully capable of clearing up all doubts and ambiguities, that could arise from the wording of the said arrangement; and further, seeing that land-marks have been planted by a common accord, all along the frontier, and that more correct plans have been taken, in which the said land-marks are distinctly represented; for these reasons the undersigned plenipotentiaries stipulate, that the said instrument, made and signed by the said commissaries, on the twenty-eighth of August, one thousand seven hundred and seventy-six, and in which all the points, rivers, valleys, and mountains, through or over which the line of demarcation passes, are clearly and distinctly pointed out, shall be inserted in, and make part of the present articls, as follows :

DESCRIPTION of the boundaries of the island of Saint-Domingo, as fixed at Attalaya the 29th of February, 1776, by the definitive treaty, *sub sperati*, concluded between their excellencies Don Joseph Solano, knight of the order of St. Jago, brigadier in the royal army of his catholic majesty, governor and captain-general of the Spanish part, president of the royal court, inspector of the regulars and militia, superintendant of the crusade, sub-delegate judge of the revenue of the posts, and plenipotentiary of his catholic majesty;

And Victor-Therese Charpentier, marquis of Ennery, count of the Holy-Empire, field marshal in the army of his most christian majesty, great-cross of the royal military order of St. Louis, inspector-general of infantry, regulars, and militia of the French leeward ilands, and plenipotentiary of his most christian majesty.

The said plenipotentiaries having signed the said original treaty by seigniority of age, delivered, in consequence, their instructions of the same date, to the undersigned, Don Joachim Garcia, lieutenant-colonel in the army of his catholic majesty, commanding the infantry of the trained militia of the Spanish colony; and Hyacinthe-Louis Viscount de Choiseul, brigadier in the army of his most christian majesty, named as commissaries to put in execution the articles of the said treaty, which fix invariably the boundaries of the possessions of the two crowns; to erect pyramids, plant land-marks where necessary, to preclude forever hereafter all disputes that might disturb the harmony and good understanding between the two nations, and to make out, with the assistance of a sufficient number of engineers, the topographical survey, to which the undersigned refer for fuller explanation; observing that, it has been impossible to sign it, as mentioned in the treaty, by the chief engineer, Mr. Boisforêt, employed by a superior order in the functions of his office.

In execution of the said treaty the line of demarcation of the boundaries begins on the northern coast, at the mouth of the river *d'Ajabon* or *Massacre*, and ends on the southern coast, at the mouth of the river of the *Anses-à-Pitre*, or *Pedernales*, on the banks of which rivers pyramids have been erected, as marked in the plan; the two first bearing No. 1, and the two last No. 221, with the inscriptions graved in stone, *France*, *Espana*. The plan clearly explains all the rest, according to the real position; observing well that when the right or left of the line is spoken of, it is meant the right or left, according to the route followed by the commissaries; and that, with respect to the rivers and streams, the right or left, means the right or the left in going from the source towards the mouth.

In going up the *d'Ajabon* or *Massacre*, its waters and fishery in common from the line of frontier as far as the pyramid No. 2, of the little island divided by the pyramids, Nos. 3, 4, 5, and 6, conformably to the treaty, and as this line is not a tangent one to the furthest elbow of the Ravine-à-Caïman, the marsh being impassable.

The two pyramids, No. 7, mark, that the waters united into one arm between the two little islands, the river becomes in common, and forms the line, as below.

The second island is divided by the pyramids from No. 8, to No. 17, inclusively, as represented on the plan, though, in conformity to the treaty, it should be divided by a right line from one extremity to the other, which forms a fork, where the right arm of the river takes the name of *Don Sebastian*, and the other, the name of *Left arm of the Massacre*. But the particular plan that served as the basis of this article, representing the island as an elipsis, and divisible only by one right light, was so incorrect, that it became necessary to take a new one, such as it now appears in the general plan, and the island has been divided by two lines, which meet, in order to avoid doing prejudice, conformably to the fifth article of the treaty, to the effential interefts of the vaffals of his catholic majefty, whofe land would have been bereft from them by a divifion of one right line.

From the pyramid, No. 17, the river of the *Maffacre* and the *Stream of the Capotille*, form the boundary of the refpective poffeffions, as far as the land-mark No. 22. In this interval there are two pyramids, No. 18, placed on the banks of the Maffacre, which is croffed by the high road from the town of *d'Ajabon* to that of *Ouanaminthe*; two at the mouth of the Stream of the *Mine*, No. 20, and two land-marks, bearing the fame No. 21, at the bottom of the mouth, where are the fettlements of *Mr. Gafton*, and where two little ftreams join, which form that of *Capotille*. The line afcends along the deep-banked ftream on the left, as far as No. 22, where ends the plantations that it furrounds in going on to No. 23, and the top of the hill which it runs along to No. 24, on the *Piton-des-Ramiers*.

From this point the line runs to the top of the *Mountains* of *la Mine* and *Marigallega*, in following the old road of the Spanifh rounds, as far as the land-mark No. 25, at the point formed by the little favana of *Sirop*, on the plantation of the late Mr. *Laffalle des Carrières*; it continues along fome coffee grounds, furrounded with a hedge of lemon-trees, belonging to the fame inhabitant, whofe overfeer is *Mr. Maingault*, till it comes to the *Piton-des-Perches*, and then defcends in a right line by Nos. 26, 27 and 28, in the savana of the same name, on the right side of which, and by No. 29, the line ascends the *Montagne-des-Racines*, that of *Grand-Selles*, *Chocolate*, and *Coronade*, where is placed No. 30. Hence, keeping the same mountain in an open road, the line comes to No. 31, placed on the slope of the *Piton-de-Bayaha*, where the line cannot be mistaken, going over the summit of a mountain, with an open road, which runs over the top of the *Morne-à-Tenèbre*, by No. 32, over the *Piton-des-Essentes*, as far as No. 33 of *Filgueral*, leaving to the right the sources of *Grand-Rivière*, which run in the French part, and, on the left, the head, or *stream* of the *Eperlins*, which runs in the Spanish part.

From No. 33, the line continues along a well-marked road, and crosses some deep hollows, represented on the plan, till it comes to the *Montagne-Traversière*, on the top of which, and along by No. 34, it goes to No. 35, which cuts the stream, called the *Ruisseau-des-Sables*; 36, 37, on the road, in common along a *great wood*, 38 on the stream of *Ziguapo* or *Chapelets*, where by the branches of the mountain of the same name, the line comes to the top of it at No. 39, whence runs the branch, or ridge, called the *Montagnes-des-Chandeliers*, along which the line now goes, passing by the land-marks, Nos. 40, 41, 42, till it comes to 43, placed at the confluence of the *Ruisseau-des-Chandeliers* and *Grand-Rivière*, having, to the right, the valley of the river, and, to the left, the inaccessible hollow of the stream.

From No. 43, the bed of *Grand-Rivière*, is the line of boundary for the two nations, as far as the *Guard-house* of *Bahon*, where is the pyramid No. 44, and the mouth of the *stream* of this name, mentioned in the treaty, and which the commissaries could not follow from the *Montagne-des-Chapelets*, nor that of *Chandeliers*, in their western route, as a line of boundary, because it rises far in the south, in the *Mountains* of *Barrero*, *Cannas* and *Artimisa*, without forming a junction with that of the *Chapelets* and *Chandeliers*; besides, being settled with the Spanish hattes, which are very considerable, and which come out to the river, where they have their plantations, provision-farms, and ecclesiastical revenue lands. Considering, that these particular circumstances could not be known when the treaty was concluded, and to draw the line from ridge to ridge, from the left bank of the river to the mouth of the stream of Bahon, would be of no manner of use to the French nation, from the small quantity and bad quality of the land which would remain between the line and the river; and considering, besides, that it would be cutting off the water from the cattle, which would prejudice the vassals of his most catholic majesty, without benefiting those of his most christian majesty; for these reasons the undersigned commissaries have agreed, and their generals have approved of it, that, between the two above-said Nos. 43 and 44, the *Grand-Rivière* should be the national boundary, and that, in order to facilitate the communication here, the road shall be in common, crossing the river on one side as one the other, every where where the badness of theroad, or the nature of the land, or of the said river, may render it necessary.

From the guard-house of *Bahon*, the frontier line ascends the ridge which ends at the pyramid, and from its summit it goes by Nos. 45, 46, 47, 48, and 49, in winding round the present plantations of two french inhabitants, *Couzé* and *Laurent*, these being on the right, and leaving to the left the possessions of *Bernardo Familias*, till it comes to the *Guard-house of the valley*, where the land-mark 50 is planted.

From this point the line ascends the mountain called the *Montagne-Noire*, along a patrole road well known, and, half way up the side of the mountain is graven No. 51, on two rock-stones with the inscription, *France* : *Espana*. On the summit of the mountain is placed No. 52, at the beginning of the present plantations of Mr. Milscent, and the line of boundery runs along his coffee plantations, which are on the ridge, in going to the Nos. 53, 54, 55, 56 and 57, along the present plantations of Mr. *Jouanneaux*, passing by the Nos. 58, 59, to the head of one of the branches of the *Ravin-Sec (Dry-Ravin)*, and over the Piton, or hill, of the same name, to the top of the mountain, in keeping close to the plantations of Mr. *de la Prunarède*.

The Nos. 60 and 61 are at the head of the *Ravin-Sec* ; 62, 63, and 64, on the same ravin, round the present plantations of Mr. *Larivière*, and from 65 to 69 inclusive, the line is formed by the boundaries of the plantations of Mr. *Lasserre*, which are on the left of the summit of this mountain. To No. 69 the line follows a road, in common, which goes, in ascending to the top of the mountain, and winds round the plantations of Messrs. *Potier, Laleu, Gerbier* and *Béon,* wihch lie on the left with the land-marks, from No. 70 to 79 inclusive, placed at the sources of the *Ravin-Mathurin,* on the different streights of which it is formed.

From the Piton, or eminence, where Mr. Béon is settled, the line goes along an open road on the ridge, as far as No. 80, which is at the head of the *Gorge-Noire,* between the present plantations of Messrs. *Colombier, Mathias* and *Nolasco,* from the house of which last the line runs along the ridge, in descending to and ascending from certain ravins, till it comes to Nos. 81, 82 and 83, along the coffee plantations of *Dubar,* on the height, called the height of la *Porte,* which is opposite the wood of the same name, and on the top of the said heihgt, in an open road, the line descends round the plantation of Mr. *Dumar,* as far as the pyramid 84, erected at the old Guard-house of the *Bassin-à-Cayman,* on the left bank of the river.

On the right bank, opposite No. 84, is the pyramid, No. 85, where the plenipotentiaries placed the first stone, at the foot of the hill, beginning the *Mountain* of *Villa-Rubia;* the line goes now up to the top, where is placed the land-mark, No. 86, and, descending by one of the branches to No. 87, it takes the summit of the mountain on the plantations of the *baronness de Piis*, which it follows still, leaving the slope to the right towards the valley of Dondon, and to the left in the spanish part, till it comes to the present plantations of Mrs. *Collière*, which lie beyond the top of the mountain, as well as those of Mr. *Chiron*, which have all been enclosed by the land-marks, No. 88, 89, 90, 91 and 92, at which last the line begins again, and follows the ridge of the mountain, opposite the above mentioned valley, as far as No. 93, at the mountain, called the *Montagne-des-Chapelets*, and from its top, it descends to Nos. 94 and 95, in crossing the ravin which joins the plantations of Mr. *Soubira*, to come to No. 96, on those of Mr. *Moreau*, and from this point, it descends, in a right line, to the river, called the *Rivière-du-Canot*, on the left bank of which is the pyramid No. 97, at the point of the opposite branch which descends from the *Marigallega*.

The frontier line now continues, ascending, in a right line, to the top of the *Kercabras*, No. 98, and follows the ridge along by the plantations of MM. *Lécluze* and *Tripier*, as far as Nos. 99 and 100, whence it turns round the plantations of MM. de *Montalibor, Touquet, and Gerard*, by the land-marks No. 101, 102 and 103, to 104, placed at clumps of rocks on the height of *the settlement of Valero*, and below the second habitation of *Touquet and Rodanès*.

From this point, the frontier line continues, as straight as it was possible, by an open road on very rough ground, crossing *Red-Stream (Ruisseau-Rouge)*, No. 105, *and Ruisseau-Maho* as far as the land-mark 106, and then ascends, obliquely, the mountain of the *Cannas* or *Lataniers*, on the summit of which is No. 107, whence it descends to the *Ravine-à-Fourmi*, and to the pyramid 108, on the left bank, between the settlements, now given up, of the spaniard *Lora*, and those of the frenchman *Fauquet*, possessor of the land known in the treaty, under the name of *Beau-Fossé*, then the partner of *Fauquet*.

Crossing the *Ravine-à-Fourmi*, the line comes to the pyramid 109, at the right side of the branch by which it ascends the mountain of *Marigalante*, passing by the Nos. 110, 111, as far as No. 112, when the slopes on each side go, one to the french and the other to the spanish part, and here it begins to descend to get to the mountain, from whence the water runs into the river called *Rivière-du-Bois-d'Inde*, by the land-mark 113, graven on a rock; 114 placed on a branch of the mountain; 115 on the stream, called the *Ruisseau-de-Roche-Plate*; 116 on an other stream, called *Ruisseau-des-Éperlins*; 117 on a ravin; 118 on the height, called *Hauteur-Pelée-Del-Dorado*; 119 at the hollow, called *Gorge-du-Coucher*; 120 at *Brulage* of the *Montagne-Sale*; 121 and 122 in the savana of the said mountain, on the sides of the high road, and, first ascending to the top, it descends to No. 123, which is at the source of the stream, called *Ruisseau-à-Dentelles*, between the said mountain *Sale* and the mountain, called *Montagne-*

Noire-des-Gonaïves, on which the line ascends, by No. 124 to 125, where the under-signed, finding the summit inaccessible, were obliged to wind round it, through the spanish territory, to come at the opposite side, in the direction of the frontier line, which as in all other inaccessible places, was measured by the rules of trigonometry, from No. 125, passing 126 at the Piton, or Mount of the *Savana-de-Paez*, and 127 at the *Pont-de-Paez*, indicated by the treaty.

Hence the frontier line continues on towards the summit of the *Coupe-à-l'Inde*, passing by the land-mark 128, at the hill, called the *Petit-Piton-de-Paez*; 129 at a spring in the valley; 130 in the middle of the said valley, crossing the high road, called the road of *Coupe-à-l'Inde*, between two mountains running along the height to where they join again, and descending to No. 131, which is in a hollow of the said mountain *Coupe-à-l'Inde*, the ridge of which is followed by the line, passing No. 132, on a rock; 133 at the foot of a clump of inaccessible rocks, called *Hauteurs-des-Tortues*, as far as No. 134, on the height and on the side of the road, called *Chemin-de-la-Découverte*; inaccessible during the greatest part of its ridge, as far as the sources of the *Rivière-du-Cabeuil*; but notwithstanding, the Nos. 135 and 136, are placed in the *Vallée-des-Cedras*, and 137, in the *ValléePalanque*; the mountain continues to slope on one side in the spanish, and on the other in the french territory, the line goes by the land-mark 138, placed above the *Sources-du-Cabeuil*, on the mountain, called by Spaniards, *de-Los-Gallarones*.

The line now goes on above the *Sources-du-Cabeuil* and along by the land-marks 139 and 140, on the summit where the *Découverte* joins to the *Montagne-des-Cabos*, to the land-mark 141, near the plantations of *Cebère* and *Gui*; it continues along by the Nos. 143 and 144., graven on three rocks; 145, 146, by the side of the present plantations of *Poirier*; 147 and 148, on the land of *Raulin*, to 149, where it begins to descend, and comes to the first plantation of *Fiëffé* going, on the Spanish side, the top of the *Montagne-des-Cabos*, and which is bounded by the land-marks 150, 151, 152, 153, 154 and 155, in returning to take up, and follow, the ridge, as far as the second plantation, which joins that of *Cazenave*, and both these are surrounded by the Nos. from 156 to 160, inclusive.

The line, passing by No. 161, goes along from summit to summit on the ridge of the mountain (which cannot be mistaken) to the land-mark 162, at the beginning of the plantation now belonging to *Perodin*, and which is enclosed by the Nos. 163, 164 and 165, whence it takes again the ridge of the mountain as far as No. 166 along the present plantation of *Cottereau*, lying over the ridge to the left and enclosed, by the land-marks from the said 166 to 171 inclusive, hence, going along the summit of a branch of the mountain, the line comes to Nos. 172 and 173, by the side of the plantation of *Ingrand* where to summit becomes inaccessible to the greatest height of *Black-Mountain* (*Montagne-Noire*), or *Grand-Cahos*, the summit of which marks the national boundaries, as far as the falls of the river called the *Guaranas*, which joins the *White-river* (*Rivière Blanche*) at the place the French call *Trou-d'Enfer*, where, on the high road, is placed the land-mark 174.

From this place the frontier line runs along the ridge of the mountain of *Jaïti*, one slope of which is in the Spanish, and the other in the French part, as far as the summit, called the *Piton-de-l'Oranger*, which it goes straight over to the land-mark 175, graven on a rock, and along by the Nos 176 and 177, in the *flat-land* of the said *mountain*, called *Repoſoir* (*Resting-Place*), continuing along the possessions of *Hubé*, and pursues its way over the next mount to the No. 178; whence it goes, in descending along an open well-marked road, to No. 179, in the little savana of *Jaïti*, and then continues on to the great savana, where formerly was the guard-house of that name, crosses the savana, running towards south-east along by the land-marks 180, placed in the middle, and 181, at the point, going in the same direction, to the post of *Honduras*, crossing a very deep ravin, running along the branches of the mountain on the left, till it descends to No. 182, placed in the *Savana-des-Bêtes* (*Savana-of beasts*), and to 183 on the right bank of the river *Artibonite*, which it crosses at this point to come to No. 184, on the left bank, 185, on the stream, called the *Ruiſſeau-d'Iſidore*, and arrived at 186, the *Guard-houſe of Honduras*.

To go up to the summit of the mountain, called the *Montagne-à-Tonnerre*, it passes, a second time, the *Ruisseau-d'Isidore*, at No. 187, the line goes up again by Nos. 188, and 189, towards the ridge which as a well-known boundary by the division of the slopes, as far as Nos. 190, 191 and 192, to come to the rock of *Neybouc*, on the side of the high road, and on each side of which are graven the relative inscription, and the No. 193.

From the said rock at the foot of the height, called *Neybouc*, over which the line continues on, being inaccessible, the under-signed went to it along the Spanish part, to place on the summit the land-mark 194, whence the line, in an open and well-marked road, goes along the height, called the *Hauteur - de-la-Mahotière*, and along the ridge of the mountain to descend (across a hollow) to the *Ravine-Chaude*, which it crosses near its junction with the *Rivière-des-Indes*, or *Horse-shoe - River*, which the under-signed crossed for the first time, and placed, on the left bank, the land-mark 195, constrained by the badness of the passage on the right bank to traverse its straggling current, and its little islands, to come to the *Guard-house of the deep valley (Corps-de-garde-de-la-vallée-profonde)*, and to No. 196, placed on the side of the present plantations of *Colombier*.

From the said Guard-house, the under-signed, crossing the river, placed No. 192, on a rock of the first branch, and continuing to open the line, in cutting the branches and hollows of the great mountain, along by the land-marks 198 and 199, as far as 200, to the *Fond-des-Palmiſtes*, on account of the impoſſibility of following any one of them, to take at No. 201, the ridge which they ran along by Nos. 202 and 203 as far as 204, and, croſſing the hollow by Nos. 205, to come at the river *Gaſcogne*, they placed the land-mark, No. 206, on the left bank; 207, on a branch of the mountain; 208, in a flat ſpot; and all the three along by the plantations of *Mouſſet*, ſettled between river *Gaſcogne*, and the *Ravine-des-Pierres-Blanches*.

From No. 208, the line croſſes the ravin in a ſouthern direction, running along by the ſettlements of *Maucler and Guerin*, over the branches of mountain which lead to No. 209, on the greateſt height of the mountain of *Neybe*, where are to be ſeen the ponds; it follows the ſummit of this moutain, as far as No. 210, where the guides pointed out the *Bajada-Grande*, or *Grande-Deſcente* (great deſcent) adding that it was impoſſible to continue the road along the ſummit of the mountain, deſignated in the treaty as the national boundary, and deſcending along the Spaniſh part, the under-ſigned went to the foot of the *Great-deſcent*, and there fixed, on the ſide of the high road, the land-mark 211, from which, croſſing the *lake* or *Étang-Saumâtre*, and directed *on the point of the mountain, which enters the furtheſt into the ſaid lake, from the ſouthern part, near the Barguadier* (ſhipping place) *of the ſavana of the White-Ravin, or Ravin-River*, the line comes to No. 212, graven on a rock at the said point, whence it ascends towards the summit of the mountain, goes by the land-mark 213, on the road to the mountain, called *Montagne-du-Brulage*, crosses the hollow, called *Fond-Oranger*, and after rising to the opposite height, descends to No. 214, graven on a rock in another hollow, at the bottom of the settelement of *Pierre-Bagnol*, and following the said hollow arrives at No. 215, at the jonction of another hollow at the foot of the plantation of the said inhabitant.

From this point the line, going in a southern direction, cuts the mountain on which *Bagnol* is settled, till it comes to No. 216, graven on a rock where the *White-Ravin* (which has had not water since the great earth-quake), joins that which takes its rise on the land of *Beaulieu* and *Soleillet*, to preserve their present plantations, which are on both sides of the ravin, and goes over the top of the mountain *Majagual* or the *Mahots*, forming the line as far as the branch which descends to Nos. 217 and 218, in two dry streams, along the plantations of *Soleillet*.

The line now continues by the stream on the right, along a well-marked road, on the sides of which, all the large trees are marked (for want of stones fit for lands-marks), as far as the head of the Pedernales, or *Rivière of the Anses-à-Pitre*, the line marking the severals turning traced on the plan, across the branches, and coming upon the great mountain, passing by the Piton or *Brulage-à-Jean-Louis*, by the savana of *Boucan-Patate*, that of the *Discovery* and its *Little-*

Pond, to the view of the mountain of *La Flor* on the left, along the *Dark-Hollow*, the *Source of Miseries*, the settlements of the run-away negroes of *Maniel*, *difficult stream*, and *deep-stream*, then coming to the sources of the river, called by the Spaniards, *Pedernales*, and by the French *River of the Anses-à-Pitre* on the banks of which the undersigned placed landmarks, each bearing No 219, with the double inscription.

The bed of this river is the boundary of the two nations; it was followed down to its mouth, on the southern side, observing that along the first part, its waters often disappear. The inscription and No. 220 were graven on a rock in the middle of the bed of the river, which does not run at this spot; and at its mouth are exected two piramids, No. 221, on the sides, with the respective inscriptions, in sight of the two guard-houses.

The under-signed, in otder to execute this important operation with the greatest precision, have always had before them the treaty of 29th of Feb. 1776, and, except the division of the second little island, and the demarcation of the line, between Nos. 43 and 44, on account of the reasons abovementioned, accompanied with a sufficient number of men, knowing the different places along the line; besides guided by their own honour, having a sincere desire to fulfil the disire of their sovereigns, in favour of the good and tranquility of their respective subjects, having besides the example of harmony and sincerity given them by the plenipotentiaries; they have marked out the present plantations, and caused the inhabitants who had over-shot the line, on either side, to draw back, according to the stipulations of the 4th and 5th article of the treaty; the second, 6th, and 7th, of the instructions, except *Mr. Voisins*, who is mentioned as having voluntary abandoned his position. Observing that every where a mandate was published, declaring pain of death against any one, who should pull up, cary away, or remove, the land-marks or pyramids of the line, and that every one who should over-shot it, should be punished according to the exigency of the case.

The commissaries being perfectly agreed on all contained in the present description, written in the Spanish and French languages, have hereunto set their names.

Done at the Cape, 28. Aug. 1776.
Signed, CHOISEUL, *JOACHIM GARCIA.*

Art. III.

To give still more solidity to this arrangement, and prevent any doubt that might in future arise, the two plenipotentiaries will sign the same original topographical plan, which as been sent from the island of St. Domingo, signed by the viscount of Choiseul and Don Joachim Garcia, the commissaries, seeing that all the places, where the pyramids have been placed, comprehended between Nos. 1 and 221, are marked in the said plan with the respective inscriptions, *France: Espana,* it ought to be considered as a very essential part of the present treaty, to be signed by the two plenipotentiaries. It must be observed here, that, as there must be two copies of the treaty, and that there is here but one plan, to supply this want, by an equivalent formality, there excellencies, the count of Vergennes, minister for foreign affairs of his must christian majesty, and the count of Aranda, ambassador of the catholick king, are to sign the other plan, which is at Varseilles, and which also has been sent there from St. Domingo, having been signed by the same commandant and commissaries, and with the same formality as that which is here.

Art. IV.

To prevent every sort of contestation on the use of the waters of the river *Daxabon* or *Massacre,* and render, before hand, useless all attempts or enterprises, that may be made by the subjects of either monarch, on the borders of the frontiers, to the prejudice of the free course of waters of the said river, it is agreed; that from this time, the respective commandants of the two nations, shall have full and absolute power of inspection, by themselves or their commissaries, over the execution of this article ; that is to say, the French commandant, shall see that there is no infraction on the Spanish side, and the Spaniard commandant that there is none on the French side ; and if the least contravention should be discovered in this point, the commandant of the injured party, shall make his complaint to the party offending, that this latter may destroy, without delay or excuse, the work that might be raised, and place things in their former state; and if that should be refused, the commandant of the injured party shall be authorised to do himself justice at once.

What has been said in this article shall not be construed to hinder either party from raising dykes on his own side, necessary to guard his territory from floods and inundations, provided they do not interrupt the free current of the river.

Art. V.

Though in the conventions heretofore made, there have arisen some doubts and difficulties relative to the footing on which the several colonists were to remain, whose possessions had run into the territory of the other nation, this point having been settled individually by the instrument signed by the respective commissaries, on the 28th of August, 1776, the present article confirms that settlement; so that, if perchance the colonists who, agreeably to the terms of that instrument, ought to quit certain possessions, have not yet quitted them, they shall do so without the least delay.

Art. VI.

In order that the boundary-marks and pyramids remain where they are now fixed, and in the same state, the present article approves and confirms the mandate published by the common accord of the French and Spanish commandants in the said island, declaring guilty of rebellion all persons whatever, who shall have the temerity to carry away, destroy, or remove any one of the said boundary marks; that the criminal shall be tried by a council of war, and condemned to death, and that if, endeavouring to escape from either jurisdiction, he should take shelter in the other, he shall there find neither succour nor protection.

Art. VII.

Though the boundaries of the two nations are now clearly and distinctly marked along the whole extent of their frontier, it is nevertheless stipulated by the present article, that there shall be constantly an inspector, on both sides, who shall see observed and fulfilled all the points agreed on by this treaty.

Art. VIII.

Without prejudice to any thing above established with regard to the boundaries, the plenipotentiaries having the general good in view, and to render this arrangement more advantageous to the vassals of the two crowns, confirm further the agreement made by the two commandants respectively, on the 29th Feb. 1776, relative to the liberty that the French shall have to go through the places pointed out in the instrument made by the two commissaries, and not by any other way, into the Spanish possessions on all necessary occasions, not excepting the marching of troops; the

Spaniards have a right also to go, by the roads mentioned in the same instrument, signed by the respective commissaries, into the French possessions, in all cases that it may become necessary, without exception of the passage of marching troops. Observing, however, with respect to the marching of troops, that it must be preceded by a notice given mutually by the respective commandants, and according to the agreement they shall make with one another; but with respect to the transportation of merchandise, or other articles of commerce, each nation may make such regulations, and take such precautions as are most conformable to its laws, that this concession may in no wise serve as a pretext for smuggling, the passage granted by the two parties respectively, having for object to facilitate the indispensable communications that the vassals of the two powers may have with each other.

In consequence, it is provided that the French shall be permitted to repair, at their own expence, the road of communication between *St. Raphael* and the *Coupe à l'Inde*, though the land, over which the road goes, properly belongs to Spain.

Art. IX.

The present treaty shall be approved and ratified by their most christian and catholic majesties, in the space of two months, or sooner, if possible, and authentic copies of it shall be sent, without loss of time, to the respective commandants of the island of Saint-

Domingo, that they may cause it to be punctually and invariably obeyed.

In witness whereof, we the undersigned ministers plenipotentiary of their most christian and catholic majesties, have signed it, and sealed it with the seal of our arms. Done at Aranjuez, the third of June, one thousand, seven hundred and seventy-seven.

   Signed, Ossun,
       El Conde Florida Blanca.

From the copy, at the Cape, the first of December, one thousand seven hundred and seventy-seven.

     Signed, D'Argout.

Marked *ne varietur*, and filed in consequence of the resolve of this day. Done at the Cape in Council, 8th December, 1777.

     Signed, De Vaivre.

One cannot help, in looking over this map, where the line of demarcation is seen, to make this observation, that it is very extraordinary, that the extent of the French part and that of the Spanish, have followed directly the inverse of the power of each nation in the island. Indeed, when the Spaniards had yet a pretty considerable population, vast establishments, and the remarkable remnant of the ancient splendor of the Spanish island, a handful of French were settled as far as the Rebouc, to the north, and on the banks of the Neybe, to the south, without reckoning the possession of Samana; and when the French colony has been considerably strengthened, and when its state of prosperity renders still more striking the decay of the Spanish colony, the boundaries are, the Massacre, to the north, and the Anses-à-Pitre to the south; a difference that cannot be esteemed at less than five hundred square leagues.

It is in writing the history of Saint-Domingo that I enter, on this head, into particulars which by their nature even are excluded from this summary. I shall content myself at present with observing, that the loudest complaints were made against the treaty; and it is said, that its execution on the spot is not entirely conformable to the line which represents it on the paper. It is even an opinion pretty generally received, that a desire to terminate the quarrels, which lasted near an hundred and fifty years, was the reason why the French did not weigh all the concessions made to Spain, or why a previous examination was not made of all the contested places.

They mention particularly the fact of a current of water, erroneously taken for the left arm of the Massacre, as a proof of precipitation, or of a condescension equally reprehensible.

But, after all, this part of the island left to the Spaniards, now forms the colony, which they are the proprietors of, and that I have described in this work, without any notice of the revolution, which has been going on in France since 1789. It is, then, the Spanish part considered in itself, or in its relation with the French part, such as this last was in 1789, that I present to my readers.

The day will come, if my existence is preserved 'till that epoch, when the public will learn, by the history of Saint-Domingo, which I intend to lay before them, the facts relative to this revolution. These facts will then naturally follow those which present the island, such as it was, from the first establishment of the French on it, to the time, when the events in the mother country of the French part produced on the latter the inevitable influence of a powerful cause favoured by local circumstances.

DESCRIPTION

A

TOPOGRAPHICAL AND POLITICAL
DESCRIPTION

OF THE

SPANISH PART

OF THE

ISLAND OF SAINT-DOMINGO.

THE iſland of Saint-Domingo, lying in the Atlantic ocean, at the entrance of the gulf of Mexico, is one of the four great Antilles, and the moſt extenſive of them all, except the iſland of Cuba. Saint-Domingo had the honour of being the cradle of the European power in the new world, a denomination, that even the influence of this fourth quarter of the globe on the others, will never render as honourable and as ſplendid as it ought to be.

Chriſtopher Columbus diſcovered Saint-Domingo, and landed on it, the ſixth of December, 1492. The native iſlanders called it *Hayti*, which, in their language, ſignified *high* or *mountainous land*. According to Charlevoix, they called it alſo *Quiſqueya*; that is, *great country*, or *mother of countries*. Others tell us, that they called it *Bobio*, which means, *country full of habitations and villages.* Columbus gave it the name of *Hispaniola*, or little Spain; and the Spaniards, in whose name it was taken possession of, still retain it; though that of Saint-Domingo generally prevails with other nations, and is the only one ever given it by the French. This latter name comes from that of Santo-Domingo, the capital of the Spanish part, which, it is said, was thus called by Columbus, in honour of his father.

Saint-Domingo is situated between 17 degrees 55 minutes and 20 degrees, north latitude, and between 71 and 77 degrees, west longitude, from the meridian of Paris. It lies distant forty-five leagues east-north-east from Jamaica, twenty-two leagues south-east from Cuba, and twenty leagues west-north-west from Porto-Rico.

As to its extent, almost all the maps differ from each other, and most of them are said to represent the island as less extensive than it really is. According to the observations of the Count of Chastenet-Puysegur, made in 1784 and 1785, it is, not including the little dependent islands that surround it, one hundred and sixty leagues long, from east to west, and from sixty to seventy broad, from north to south.

The Spaniards, after having exterminated the natives of Saint-Domingo, and stained the European name by the most atrocious avarice and cruelty, enjoyed this important colony, without molestation, for more than a hundred and twenty year. At last, about the year 1630, a handful of English, French, and other Europeans, came and forced them to fight in its defence; and, in spite of the numbers of the first conquerors of America, and their efforts during fifty years; in spite even of their successes, which sometimes seemed to have annihilated their enemies for ever, they were, at last, compelled to divide the island with the French. These latter, being the only survivors of the first freebooters and buccaniers, or having insensibly acquired an ascendancy among them, had, so early as 1640, formed this assemblage of individuals, born under the domination of almost all the powers of Europe, into a French colony, under the direction of the general government, first established at St. Christopher's, and afterwards at Martinico.

The division of the island between the two nations has, however, always been extremely unequal, Spain possessing by far the most extensive, as well as the most fertile part.

Before I enter on the reflections and particulars relative to the real division of Saint Domingo between the French and Spaniards, it is necessary to treat of those things which are independent of its inhabitants, and the account of which forms the physical description of the island.

MOUNTAINS.

The mountains of Saint-Domingo consist generally in long chains, of which there are two principal ones, stretching the whole length of the island, their general direction being from east to west. From these principal chains, which, on each side, leave a space nearly equal between them and the coasts, but which do not always run parallel to one another, go a number of secondary chains, which running in different directions, divide the land between into valleys as various in depth as extent; and these valleys are again divided by hills and ridges of dimensions as various as are the valleys they divide: so that the secondary chains and ridges appear like so many supporters, given by nature to the principal mountains.

The secondary chains, that run from the sides of the principal ones, towards the sea, divide the intermediate space into plains of various figure and extent; and these plains are subdivided and sheltered by other ridges, which going sometimes even to the beach, serve them as a sort of boundaries or ramparts.

The two great chains of mountains rise as they advance from the east of the island; but this progressive elevation does not continue for more than forty leagues, after which the height remains the same for a considerable distance. They seem to widen as they approach the west, till, coming to the middle of the narrowest part of the island, they narrow again, still preserving their height. But, indeed, towards the western extremity of the island the mountains are, in some sort, piled one upon another.

This configuration, together with the height of the mountains, is the reason that, notwithstanding the vast extent of several plains, the island, at a distance, appears mountainous, and that its aspect is far from giving so favourable an idea of it as it deserves. But the observer who contemplates the chains of mountains, and the ridges shooting from them, as branches from a principal trunk, spreading their winding ramnifications over the plains beneath, sees in them the great cause of the fertility of the island; he looks on them as the immense reservoir of those waters, which, by innumerable rivers, are afterwards borne in every direction; he regards them as the means, destined by nature, to repel the violence of the winds, and temper the rays of a scorching sun, to vary the temperature of the air, and even to multiply the resources of human industry; in short, he beholds them as the soil chosen to bear to the end of ages, those beneficent forests, which, since the foundation of the world perhaps, have received the propitious waters the clouds lodge in their bosom, and which, from their inaccessible situation, are protected from the axe of man, whose genius does not always lead him to preserve.

These mountains contain, besides, an infinite number of mines of all sorts. Every one is acquainted with the high reputation of the mountains of Cibao, in the bowels of which, Spanish avarice has buried so many thousands of Indians, condemned to toil in search of that gold which has covered the earth with every species of crimes.

It would be almost impossible to give a description common to all the mountains of Saint-Domingo, because, their nature as well as their site vary, and a multitude of circumstances render them different from each other. While there are some, where every thing announces fertility; where most of the vegetables of the island thrive in abundance, where all invites to cultivation, and fails not to reward the labourer, there are others which offer to the view nothing but the hideous aspect of sterility, and seem to forbid all access, not only to gain, but even to the hope of procuring enough to satisfy bare necessity. Sometimes these extremities are separated by very narrow intervals, or at least, in a little space the difference is so sensible as to form a contrast truly striking. We must, then, give up the idea of a general description, which would require continual exceptions, and content ourselves with mentioning, in the detailed descriptions of the different places, whatever may be relative to the mountains.

Some persons, after an examination of the map of America, have not only agreed with the French Pliny, that the almost innumerable islands lying between the mouth of the Oronoque and the channel of Bahama (amongst which may be noticed some of the *Grenadines*, which are not always to be seen in the spring tides, or when the sea runs high), ought to be considered as the *summit of vast mountains, the bases of which are covered by the liquid element*; but they go so far as to suppose, that these islands were the tops of a chain of mountains, running across a country, the submersion of which produced the gulph of Mexico. This opinion cannot, however, be maintained, without adding to the disappearance of the immense surface of the gulph, that of another surface, which would have united the continent between Yucatan to the mouth of the Oronoque, to the islands of this Archipelago; and even that of a third surface, by the means of which the islands would have been connected to the peninsula of Florida, and to some other land which would have terminated them to the north; for it cannot reasonably be imagined that these summits of mountains would of themselves exactly terminate a continent. Besides, when we consider, that, at the two points, where we must conceive, according to this system, the two extremities of these mountains touched at Guiana and Mexico, there are no chains of mountains to support the possibility of the separation, reason rejects a system that buries a surface of many hundred thousand leagues, without producing the cause of such a submersion, and without pointing out the epoch in the annals of the world.

But, that the mountains of these islands, and of course the islands themselves, particularly of Saint-Domingo, have been covered by the sea, there is not the least reason to doubt, if we judge according to the rules laid down by the immortal Buffon. The layers are all parallel, an order contrary to the specific weight of the substances of which they are composed. Such are the proofs of the action of a fluid directed by the great causes that move the globe, and it is principally in the sides of the mountains, because the earth is there often disturbed and exposed to observation, that these proofs are found.

The mountains of the Antilles, and the Antilles themselves, if they ought to be considered as the summits of mountains, run sometimes in a direction contrary to that which Buffon considers as the most common in the continent of the new world, since, from the island of St. Christopher to that of Cuba, they stretch from east to west; but from Trinidad to Nevis they generally run from north to south. In all the Antilles the direction of the mountains supports this observation of the same author, that they divide the islands longwise, as well as the promontories and other advanced parts.

I have already shown that this direction is that of the principal chains of Saint-Domingo. The composition of these mountains is as various as their dimensions; the summits of some of them are of hard rock of sand-stone or granite, and other vitrifiable substances, offering to the view their naked tops, at once the object of melancholy and sublimity. In others, the summits are covered with a layer of mould, sometimes mixed with stones of different degrees of hardness, and more or less calcinable. In all the mountains, according to their ruggedness or steepness, the inclination of the layers differs, and particularly in the masses of rocks, which are in some sort wedged up together, this inclination is subject to numberless variations.

Here we must not pass over a remark of Mr. Adam List :* viz. that in many mountains of Saint-Domingo, there are layers of combs of polypuses, often very apparent on the sea-coast, or on the borders of the steep mountains. Sometimes these combs are filled more or less with mould, or with the polypuses themselves, in a dissolved state; and sometimes they remain hollow.

---

* A colonist of St. Domingo, an esteemed observer, and member of the Society of Arts and Sciences, at Cape-François.

The same observer was equally struck with those enormous masses of light, calcinable, and sonorous stones, which are called at Saint-Domingo, *cock-roach-stones*, and which sometimes form several layers in the same mountain, where they are found alternately with layers of other substances. These stones, which appear to Mr. Adam List to be formed of testacees and crustacees, are sometimes in extensive layers, and sometimes in little detached ones. He thinks that the crustacees, after being dissolved, have served by way of cement to the testacees, and that from the binding of this sort of mortar, come the little holes with which the *cock-roach-stones* are perforated.

Hitherto general observation has proved, that the base of the mountains of Saint-Domingo are of granite, or of *quartzum*. There are, however, several hills and flats of vegetative mould, as Mr. Adam List has also observed; but these hills, or little secondary mountains, ought to be considered as having for base, that of the soil on which they stand; for they are nothing more than the consequence of abundant rains, which, carrying the layers of vegetative mould from the superficies of the more elevated mountains, together with certain portions of gravel and sand, have at last left them in those parts where the declivity ceased, where they have formed hill after hill, and where we may find layers of stone rolled and rounded, and others sandy, vitrifiable, or calcinable. These little mountains, and the extremities of the great ones, have also beds of clay, or of marle more or less solid, which, because of its feeling like soap, is called *soapy land*, in many parts of Saint-Domingo.

Every thing speaks, then, in the mountains of this island, of their having remained a long time under water, and of the posterior agency of the rains. We may add to these proofs, those derived from the sea-shells, found in the different layers of the mountains. They are found as well in the summits of the most elevated ones, as at a great depth in those which are less so, and in number disproportioned to their distance from the sea.

There are many mountains of the island, which, by the confused mixture of the materials of which they are composed, and by the singular manner in which their layers are placed, prove that they have undergone the most violent agitations. It is very natural to impute a part of these effects to earthquakes, which it is well known Saint-Domingo is subject to: great openings in the earth, enormous masses fallen down, displaced or turned upside down, present this cause to the imagination of every one who contemplates these terrible effects. But we cannot help attributing a part of them to volcanic movements. It is true, we know of no open volcanoes in the island; for what has been said of the distant, and in some sort, unperceivable irruptions of the mountains of Cibao, wants experimental confirmation. Yet, in a great many places, particularly between the Mole and the Gonaives, a thick lava, now become a vegetative earth, by the force of all-conquering time, afford proofs of extinguished volcanoes. Here we see naked and dark-looking mountains, where the eye yet perceives the traces of the insatiable element that has endeavoured to devour them. Here a soil, which seems to have been placed upon the cavities to which it forms a vault; mineral waters, sulphureous productions, and scoria, are strong evidences of a subterraneous agent.

The mountains of Saint-Domingo are greatly elevated above the level of the sea; the elevation may even be estimated at five hundred fathoms perpendicular, in the greatest part of those of the interior parts; but those of *Cibao*, of *Selle*, and of *Hotte*, are double this height; and those which surround them, or continue their prolongation, approach to one or the other of these heights, in proportion to their distance from these principal points.

PLAINS.

The plains that surround this mountainous mass, or that fill the interval between it and the coast, form a great portion of the surface of the island. These plains descend in a slope from the mountains to the sea; but this slope is not always the same, some of the plains appearing like a long amphitheatre, while others seem reduced to an almost perfect level.

The quality of the land varies in the different plains, and even in the same plain. The soil every where participates of the nature of the neighbouring mountains, the branches of which come sometimes, as has been already observed, quite to the beach, where they present, sometimes extremities inclining towards the sea, having their sides more or less steep, and sometimes conic masses, or perpendicular heights, which are so armed with rocks and stones, that they are called *ribs of iron*.

The land in the neighbourhood of the sea, has also beds of polypuses, and the remains of crustacees and testacees. Almost every where we observe, that the plains have been formed at the expense of mountains, and of what the rains have brought down from the superficies of the latter, which was itself composed of decayed vegetation. If we find some parts gravelly, and others sandy, they are due to the waste of the stones, which the rains have washed down from the mountains.

It would, then, be an endless task, to speak distinctly of all the different sorts of soil, and the depth of the different layers, to be found in the plains of Saint-Domingo. In one place we find it a vegetative mould; in another, a mixture of this mould with pebbles or sand. Here it is a loose marle; there a pure clay. Sometimes it is a perfect marle, which the colonists improperly call *tuf*, and sometimes a vitrifiable sand, good for nothing but to torment and ruin the cultivator.

There is, besides, a pretty considerable portion of land that prolongs, in some measure, the extent of the plains, but without adding any thing to their absolute utility, I mean all that part which lies along the shore, and which, being often covered by the tide (which at Saint-Domingo does not, however, rife more than *twenty-two inches* at moft), offers but diftant refources for cultivation, if induftry fhould ever be able to turn them to account.

Even this watry portion is rendered extremely various by the proximity of a river that fpreads a fertilizing mud over one part of it, while the reft does not participate in this advantage. In fome places it is a quagmire, without any folid point, except where the roots of the flexible mangrove-tree are fo interlaced as to retain the earthy portions which are carried into the bogs, or which are produced by the diffolution of the cruftacees and fhells ; while, further on, it is already formed into a real and folid earth, raifed above the level of the fea, and bearing marine fig-trees, fearufhes, and fpots covered with falt fcum, which promife an approach toward vegetation. In fhort, we fee, from time to time, intervals where the earth is upon the point of becoming vegetative, and where fine feagrape-trees give a clear proof of a dry bottom ; in a word, a foil that might foon be rendered fit for cultivation by the means of drains capable of carrying off great quantities of water, which are hurtful at once to the labours of agriculture, and the falubrity of the air ; becaufe millions of infects and little animals, of which all quaggy places are full, there rot and exhale their putrid vapours.

It is even eafy to know, that the plains have acquired a part of their extent by the fucceffive addition of the portions that the wafte of the mountains has lodged along the coaft, fince, at the diftance of many leagues, from the shore, are to be found, at certain depths, layers of marine salt, banks of shells, and relics of sea-plants.

CLIMATE AND TEMPERATURE.

The island consisting partly in mountains and partly in plains, causes a great variety in the climate and temperature. This variety is especially produced by the situation in the region of the trade winds; as the wind coming from the east, towards which the island presents its whole length, finds in the intervals of the chains of mountains so many channels of circulation, by means of which it refreshes and tempers the mountains, an advantage that the plains, where portions of the mountains sometimes interrupt the passage of the wind, and change its direction, do not partake in. Besides, a crowd of local circumstances, such as the elevation of the land, the quantity of water that runs over it, and the scarcity or abundance of wood, have a sensible influence upon the effect of the climate.

If some powerful cause did not balance the action of the sun under the torrid zone, which darts its rays almost perpendicularly during about three months in the year at Saint-Domingo, the temperature of this island would be insupportable to man, or at least, to the man that nature had not formed on purpose for the climate. But this cause is in the wind, of which we have just spoken, the salutary effects of which soften those of the sun.

To the benign influence of the wind, may be added that of the almoſt equal length of the days and nights, and that of abundant rains, which continually fill the air with a fluidity always deſirable, and which falling in profuſion on the ſurface of the iſland, produces, with the aſſiſtance of the evaporation, cauſed by the heat, a ſort of coolneſs in the air.

Thus, by an immutable order, which charms the contemplative mind, nature maintains a ſort of equilibrium in the climate of Saint-Domingo, ſo often obliged to ſupport the curſes of intemperance, and the diſadvantageous compariſon with happier climes, which men quit, however, becauſe their avarice is not there ſo ſoon ſatisfied as under the burning ſky of the iſland I am deſcribing.

The eaſtern wind blows at Saint-Domingo, as in the reſt of the Antilles, almoſt all the day long, during the greateſt part of the year. It begins pretty regularly about nine or ten o'clock in the morning; riſing as the ſun riſes towards his meridian height, and even after he begins to deſcend towards the weſt, it continues with unabated ſtrength till two or three hours before ſun-ſet. This wind is commonly called at Saint-Domingo, the *ſea-breeze*, in oppoſition to that which I am now going to ſpeak of.

The name of *land-breeze* is given to a wind which cools the nights, and which blows from the interior mountains. It generally begins to be felt about two or three hours after ſun-ſet, and continues till ſun-riſe.

The effect of theſe two breezes form a curious contraſt. That of the ſea, coming from the circumference towards the centre, is seen advancing in that direction, agitating the leaves and other volatile bodies near the coast. The land breeze has an effect exactly opposed, and the more the situation approaches the centre of the island the sooner does it manifest itself.

It must not, however, be imagined, that the succession of these breezes is so very regular, as not to be subject to any variation. At certain times of the year, and particularly during the equinoxes and solstices, the sea-breeze becomes very strong, sometimes even impetuous, and, during several days, blows without interval, or with but short pauses; during which time the land-breeze is not felt at all. At such seasons the violence of the sea-breeze usually augments at the rising of the sun, as if encouraged by his presence.

At other times the land-breeze predominates, which happens, for instance, in the tempestous seasons. As almost all the tempests come from the interior part of the island, as soon as they begin to overspread the sky the sea-breeze dies away, leaving the empire of the horizon to that of the land, which spreads in every direction, but with unequal rapidity, thick dark clouds, loaded with thunder and lightening, and pouring down deluges of rain. After the tempest is over, the land breeze continues predominant for the night, and even till the next day, when the sea-breeze drives it back to its retreat in the mountains.

From the combined effect of the two breezes, comes an almost continual agitation in the air, which necessarily has a great deal of influence on its constituent qualities. With the sea-breeze the air acquires the quality that gives to the lungs what is necessary to resist the heat, and to cool the blood, which an abundant perspiration tends to heat and impoverish. But it is for the cheering return of the land-breeze, that the inhabitants of Saint-Domingo wait with impatience. This refreshing breeze gives to the whole body a calm sensation that the soul soon participates; it invites sleep, renders it restorative, and, in the high lands, it strengthens the fibres, and even prolongs life.

When the reciprocal combination of the breezes is inverted, one is in a sort of pain, and this is augmented when neither of them is felt. But it must be observed, that the sea-breeze seldom fails in the season of excessive heat, and that its absence generally seems to hasten the return of the land-breeze.

The four seasons that divide the year under the temperate zones, are not distinguishable at Saint-Domingo, nor in any other of the Antilles. Winter never can show his hideous aspect under a sky that keeps vegetation in continual movement. Here nature spreads a carpet of perpetual green; here she is ever decked in majestic robes. The animal creation, however decays, and perhaps with more rapidity than in other climates; but the multitudes that each moment brings forth, prevent the eye from perceiving a destruction, which is, in reality, nothing more than a change of forms, a recombination of matter.

We can distinguish but two seasons; the *rainy*, called *winter*; and the dry, called *summer*. But it must not be concluded that these seasons have the same epochs in every part of the island.

The two seasons are more sensibly distinguished in the mountains than in the plains; and, in general, the changes of the atmosphere are more frequent in the former. There the temperature is milder; the inhabitants hardly ever experience a sultry heat, or those breezes, which, when violent, rather desiccate the air than refresh and change it.

It is on every account much more pleasant to live in the mountains than in the plains. The country life seems there to assume a character more simple, and more independent of the restraints which politeness have imposed on the towns, and the plains in their vicinity.

In the mountains it is rare for the thermometer to rise to above seventy-two or seventy-seven degrees, while in the plains it keeps nearly as high as in the towns, and, consequently, is sometimes at ninety-nine degrees. The nights are sometimes cold enough to render a blanket not unwelcome; and there are mountains where even a fire is a very agreeable companion in some evenings. It is not that the cold is ever considerable, since the thermometer keeps up from fifty-nine to sixty-four degrees; but the contrast of this temperature with that of the day, produces a sensation to which the terms, heat and cold, are not to be applied in the same manner as in cold countries.

For the same reason, on the tops of some of the mountains, such as Cibao, Selle, and Hotte, in the season improperly called cold, a still more lively senfation is felt: the water has sometimes a thin pellicle on its surface; no trees will grow but those of the fir kind, and even these are stunted. Before sun-rise, the action of the feet upon the ground, produces a noise something like that produced by walking upon the snow. So true is it that we ought to attribute this sensibility to the contrast abovementioned, that those persons who, during the excessive heat, quit the plains, and particularly those on the sea-side, and arrive during the day on the top of one of the high mountains, are hardly able to support the cool, even of the evening.

It may with truth, then, be affirmed, that at Saint-Domingo, the temperature changes almost with every position of the mountains, while it is nearly uniform in the plains. Here, however, it varies in proportion as the plains are distant from the mountains.

The rains under the torrid zone are ever abundant, and at Saint-Domingo they fall with a profusion which has the double effect of tempering the heat, and distributing among the numerous rivers an enormous volume of water. These cataracts do not fall in every part of the island at the same epoch: it sometimes happens that the dry season in one part is the rainy one in another. However, the dry months are commonly those of the first and third quarters of the year; and the rainy ones, the two first of both the second and fourth quarter; that is, the two that succeed the passage of the sun across the equator.

These rains which are one of the great causes of the fertility of the island, are at the same time hurtful to the mountains, and to all that part of the island where the land lies much upon the slope, because they carry the vegetative mould from the surface of the earth. The French colonists, who have aided these depredations by the cultivation of coffee, and by a system which counts the time to come as nothing, have cut down even the trees that covered the summits of the mountains, and attracted the rains, insomuch that a diminution of the rains is now perceivable in the French part, were they were formerly very considerable and regular.

In almost every part of the island the rains come with the tempests, brought by the south and south-west winds. The northern coast only is subject to the reception of rains from the north-west, which are called *norths*. The north-west wind reigns generally from the end of October to the end of March. Some years, however, it begins sooner, or does not continue so long; and some years it is not felt at all. It is almost always accompanied with gentle but constant rains, which adds to the cold felt at these times, and which is remarkable in that the Europeans newly arrived, or even seasoned to the country, are more affected by it than the Creoles. In 1751, this rain continued for fifty-two days without ceasing, and in 1787, at the Cape, it continued for an hundred and two days successively. In general, during the *norths*, the roads are impassable. They are felt, in the interior of the island as far as ten leagues from the north coast. Thus, then, they are felt from Cape *Del Enganno* to the point of the peninsula of St. Nicholas Mole, and from the Baradaires to Irois: however, the coast from

Leogane to the Caymites, though facing the north, is preserved from them; but this is, without doubt, because this part of the coast is sheltered by the peninsula of the Mole, and by the little island of Gonaïve.

The rains that come with the tempests are, on the contrary, common to all the island, excepting, however, with respect to the epochs, as I have already said. One must have seen these rains fall to form an idea of the prodigious volume of water they pour down. Sometimes during a whole month, and at nearly the same time every day, a terrible tempest fills the air for several hours together. Drops of water, each of which seems to contain fifty of those of Europe, form, by their union, a shower; the noise of which indicates its weight. In an instant the gutters are overflowed, and the streets impassable; a minute after and the streets become rivers; in a few hours the smallest brooks are changed into torrents, and the rivers into floods. In the mean time the air is darkened, the leaves on the trees point perpendicular to the earth; every flat becomes a sheet of water; the firmament seems on fire; the thunders, for there are sometimes five or six distinguishable at a time, seem to dispute the dissolution of the world, and their simultaneous claps produce one of those meteorological scenes the best calculated to give an idea of the destruction of the universe.

But accidents from thunder, though common enough, are nothing in comparison, to the mischiefs occasioned by the floods. The waters, overflowing the banks that contain them at other times, rush forth with the rapidity of an arrow, and a force that nothing can refift, bearing afar deftruction and death.

The clouds that contain the tempefts are fometimes high enough to receive a degree of cold fufficient to produce hail; but this is a rare phænomenon, and which never lafts but a few minutes.

This contraft of violent heat and heavy rains, necef-farily renders Saint-Domingo humid; and this humidity is augmented by the evaporation from the furrounding fea. Hence the mift, the influence of which is fo much the more dangerous when it follows a hot day, becaufe it is then fufficient to fupprefs tranfpiration; hence the caufe of iron and all other ferruginous fubftances being fo foon covered with ruft; hence, too, the diffolution of the falts, and the tarnifhed appearance of almoft all metals, however brilliant the polifh they may originally have had.

The humidity of the air is particularly obfervable near the fea-fhore, and this is one reafon why the coaft is more unhealthy than the interior parts of the ifland. But, everywhere this humidity is more or lefs the caufe of ficknefs, and inconveniencies. However, thefe ficknefles are of a lefs alarming nature in the rainy feafons; becaufe then there is lefs tendency to putridity; becaufe the inflammatory difpofition of the blood is then allayed, and becaufe the falt particles, with which the air is loaded more or lefs in the different parts of the ifland, are then almoft faturated. Thefe particles thus lofe the mifchievous faculty of filling the blood with the acrid principle, one of the great inconveniencies of which is, the aptitude that it produces to contract diforders on the fkin, and all fuch as are caufed by the thickening of the lymph.

RIVERS.

I have already had occafion to obferve more than once, that Saint Domingo, is, in general, very well watered by rivers, ftreams, and brooks without number. There are, however, certain fpaces deprived of this advantage, which nothing can make up for in hot countries, and I fhall fpeak of thefe exceptions as the order of the defcription prefents them.

After what has been faid of the formation of the ifland, it will be readily conceived that the rivers cannot have a very extenfive courfe; particularly if we calculate the interval between their fources and their mouths. But the formation of the ifland, at the fame time that it renders this abfolute interval of little extent, requires that the water fhould run in a ferpentine direction to find a paffage from among the mountains. In thefe mountains they run almoft everywhere upon a bed that the rapidity of the current has rendered pretty deep. Sometimes this bed is of earth, or fand of different forts; at others, the water comes tumbling over ftones or rocks, or ftealing along between them. Here it glides flowly along; there it flies fwift as the wind, and fometimes rolls in cafcades, or even forms a fort of cataracts or falls.

When the rivers arrive in the plains, the nature of their bed frequently varies; but they never fail to lose a part of their velocity.

It is generally impossible to conceive, from the tranquil aspect that these rivers usually wear, what they become when they overflow their banks. A river that but now hardly covered the pebbles on its bed, or wet the foot of the traveller, is changed by one tempestuous shower into a flood, menacing all that it approaches; and should its banks give way, it spreads its watry devastation over the plains.

To give a better idea of the distance that these floods sometimes extend to, I should observe, that the plains of Saint-Domingo, all of which were formed, perhaps by the deposit of the waters, when, having no regular course, they alternately filled and opened their beds, have all, at present, a slope from the banks of the rivers by which they are watered. From this singular circumstance it follows, that the beds of the rivers are in the most elevated parts of the plains; so that, when they overflow their banks, they find a declination that carries them to a great distance, and the water, once beyond its natural boundary, can never enter it again. Evaporation, and the hollows made by the water itself, are the only means of removing it from the surface, which it covers, for a shorter or longer space of time, after having rotted every plant that its current has not torn up.

It is not rare to see, at Saint-Domingo, a river that has a different soil on each side of it; one, for instance, a clay, and the other a fort of marle. In the mountains there are rivers that run between rocks which are nearly or quite perpendicular. When the rocks on the two fides rife in the fame direction, which is not always the cafe, and a road along a dell croffes the river, the traveller is naturally feized with an awful gloom, when, wading acrofs, he cafts his eye on the rocks above, and confiders his own nothingnefs in this kind of tomb, where he is, as it were, buried alive. In fome parts the fcene is ftill more picturefque, becaufe there the rocks are arched in fuch a manner that the light can hardly enter. Paffing in fuch a part, during one of the tempefts I have fpoken of, is truly difmal; and if thofe who have affirmed that there is no echo at Saint-Domingo, had ever been in fuch a fituation, they would have avoided this error, and been convinced that found is reverberated in that ifland as well as in other places; and that, if it commonly produces only a confufed noife, it is rather to the multiplicity than to the abfence of the echos, that this caufe ought to be attributed.

The waters, confidered as a drink, are not equally good in every part of Saint-Domingo. The variety of the foil on which they run, the extraneous fubftances that they wafh in their paffage, the rapidity or flownefs of their currents, all have an influence on their quality. In general, they are more limpid, as well as more wholefome, in the mountains than in the plains; but we may add here, that the inhabitants of Saint-Domingo do not pay attention enough to the choice of this fluid, the influence of which on health, and consequently, on the duration of life, is, however, become well known, since the discoveries in chemistry have revealed to us so many secrets.

GALES AND HURRICANES.

After having spoken of the benefits derived from the wind and rains, when they are moderate; after having spoken of the mischiefs they cause, when they go beyond the bounds that we believe, improperly without doubt, to be those of their utility, it is painful to recall the disasters that are experienced from them in the Antilles, at those calamitous epochs, when the two ruinous elements seem to conspire in order to desolate these fertile countries. The very name of hurricane awakens in the mind of the colonist the most distressing ideas; and if Saint-Domingo does not often feel this scourge in its utmost fury, yet, it feels it sometimes enough to render an omission of the description of a hurricane inexcusable in this place.

From the middle of July to the full moon in October is, exclusively, the hurricane season in the Antilles. After a close day, when the atmosphere is in a perfect calm, always between sun-set and sun-rise, the wind rises all at once; strong at first, it augments in strength every moment of its duration. Soon the rain comes pouring down; the flashes of lightening succeed almost without interval, till all the element seems to the dazzled view of the spectator, to be in a blaze. The violence of the wind now threatens destruction; every door must be barred; every passage, every aperture closed, or the edifice, however strong, is levelled with the ground. The negro, not daring to trust to his feeble hut, flies for safety to the house of his master, or to some other building, now become the common asylum. Fear seizes on every heart; every cheek turns pale. The men, the most robust, run to seek the women, and to take the affrighted children in their arms. In these moments of awful terror, one calls to another, and if any one fails to answer, the cries of those to whom he is dear are the presages of his fate.

Still the fury of the wind encreases, and if it sometimes seems to shift from certain positions, in an instant it veers to another point; or else, rivals in destruction, two winds, from points diametrically opposite, meet in dreadful conflict, irritated by mutual opposition. Universal fury succeeds; every wind is unchained; all join in the work of devastation. In a little time the manufactures on the habitations are so completely destroyed as to leave only a vestige behind. The stoutest tree, he that seemed to defy the power of time, is obliged to yield to that of the wind: his sheltering foliage, his extended branches, and his mighty trunk, became so many levers to tear up his roots, and hurl him to the ground. Another tree resists the wind, but the thunder strips down his bark, and dries up his pores for ever. The shrub, the humblest plant even, cannot escape the all-destroying fury; and if the bending reed is not broken, his head, bowed down to the earth, submissively acknowledges the power of the elements.

The earthquakes, which almost always bear a part in these great catastrophes, complete what the wind could not accomplish alone. Thus it is that the buildings in masonry are damaged, and sometimes destroyed. It often happens, too, that the fall of a house adds a conflagration to the scene; because the wind soon blows every spark into a flame. Sometimes the lightening also sets this devouring element in motion.

One would imagine that the scene of devastation was now incapable of addition; but there is yet a scourge: the waters, rising to a prodigious height, and having no longer a settled course, rush down in every direction, washing away men, animals, utensils, the produce of the earth, mannufactures, trees, plants, and even portions of the land itself.

Thus, at these terrible seasons, all the elements seem to threaten confusion and chaos. We must, however, add to this tremendous spectacle that of the sea; the very aspect of which, seen from the shore only, is enough to appal the boldest heart. It roars like distant thunder; every wave seems alternately to menace the sky and to dive down into a bottomless abyss. Man, who often braves the ocean with success, can do nothing in this war of winds and waves, and, in his trepidation, fears even the land which he regrets to have quitted, where perhaps his preservation would be still more uncertain.

These hurricanes generally last, with a violence nearly equal, for five or six hours, every one of which is an age, especially if the hurricane begins in the night, because, in such a case, darkness itself is a cause of alarm. At last, a sort of calm, if compared to what has preceded, but which is in reality a tempest, permits affrighted man to lift up his head, and behold the surrounding ruins. From that moment he begins to know his misfortunes, and to count his losses.

The southern part of Saint-Domingo is pretty much subject to hurricanes; but they are called, in those parts, *southern gales*; because they are not attended with such dreadful consequences as the hurricanes in the windward islands. The part lying between Cape *Del Enganno* and Irois is most afflicted with hurricanes; but, it ought to be observed, that sometimes the fury of the wind reaches beyond the mountains, facing at once to the south and north, and then they devastate that part of the island also lying between Irois and Port-au-Prince.

He who judges of every thing as it relates to self, and who is exposed to the numberless mischiefs of hurricanes, can with difficulty be persuaded of their utility; but the philosopher, whom observation has convinced of the admirable order with which the universe is governed, will ever suppose this utility, though imperceptible; and rather than blaspheme against a cause so disastrous, he will believe that such extraordinary movements of nature, are necessary changes combined with the principles of the preservation of the globe; and that, without them, perhaps the Antilles would have been uninhabitable; from the incredible number of insects which, in those countries, cover the earth, and fill the air.

The days that follow a hurricane are very fine and pleasant. The sky is serene, and the temperature of the air mild. This contrast is so much the more striking, as all the vestiges of devastation are still in view. Every one is employed in reparation, and re-establishment; all are busy; mutual aid; beneficence every where exercises its healing and affectionate empire. The time at last arrives when the hurricane and its effects exist no more, except in memory, till another comes to renew the disastrous scene; but hope, the first, the last, the supreme good of man, fills up the happy interval.

SKETCH OF THE ANIMALS, MINERALS, AND VEGETABLES.

The climate of Saint-Domingo is extremely propitious to the propagation and unfolding of the productions of nature, and of this we have continual proofs in the three classes of beings,

The animal class, as far as relates to quadrupeds, is almost entirely composed of animals brought from Europe, and it is well known that, at the time of the discovery of the island by Columbus, there were but four kinds of quadrupeds, all extremely small, and that these have almost undergone the fate of the original inhabitants of the island.

The island abounds in birds proper to its climate, as well as such as are common to the countries of Europe; and among the fish that swim round its coast, there are several kinds that belong equally to the two worlds.

In the mineral clafs alfo there is a good deal of analogy; there are mines of iron, copper, and lead; but there are befides, mines of gold, filver, and precious ftones, and even of mercury, and here the ifland has a real fuperiority.

With refpect to the vegetable clafs, it would be difficult to exprefs or paint all its majefty. Nature fpreads its beauties over Saint-Domingo with an unceafing activity, and a profufion which may ferve to give an idea of its inexhauftible fecundity. Trees, fome of which embellifh the countries of Europe alfo, yet cover the uncultivated parts of the mountains, and even certain portions of the level part of the ifland. Their utility is proved by continual experience, though their diftance from the places where they might be advantageoufly employed, is often the caufe of their remaining in tranquillity. The beauty of their wood, its hardnefs, and its incorruptibility, render them extremely fit for buildings as well as furniture, and artifts daily prove that fome of them may be applied to a thoufand ufes.

There are alfo a multiplicity of fhrubs, and many of them are precious in their production. They, as well as many of the trees, bear moft excellent fruits, and efpecially of thofe forts in which nature has depofited the acids, calculated to combat the difpofition towards putridity that the exceffive heat gives to different fubftances.

Vegetation is ftill richer in plants. What additional treafure botany might acquire in the new world, and even in the ifland of Saint-Domingo alone, where a great number of European plants have been naturalized, where there are numbers, too, that are to be met with in other parts of the globe, and where we may remark this singular circumstance, that many of those plants which are the riches of the island, are not natives of the soil, but have been imported from other countries!

Some fruit trees of Europe have also succeeded pretty well, while others, either from want of analogy between the climates, for want of care, or from some other unknown causes, remain simply objects of curiosity; and, in this respect, they are as well calculated to give an idea of trees of the same sort in France, as the plantain-tree and sugar-cane, shown in the botanical garden at Paris, are to give an idea of these plants, such as they are at Saint-Domingo.

In the mountainous parts of the island the fruits are of a superior quality. There also garden vegetables are, in beauty and taste, equal to those of the same sorts in France.

What a pity that, in a country where nature has done so much for man, he should, in general, do so little for her! This reflection is more particularly applicable to the Spanish part of the island.

In order to interest the reader the more in what I have to say of this last, and to associate in some measure the fate of the too-unfortunate Indians with the ideas inspired by an account of the land from which they have been extirpated, it appears necessary to give a rapid sketch of the division of the island at the time when Columbus brought the arts, the sciences, and the vices of the old world in exchange for the riches of the new.

DIVISION OF THE ISLAND UNDER THE CACIQUES.

In 1492, the year in which Saint-Domingo was discovered, it formed five kingdoms, each of which had its sovereign, and these sovereigns were called Caciques.

The kingdom of *Magua*, a word which, in the Indian language, signified *kingdom of the plain*, was the first. It was governed by the cacique *Guarionex*, whose capital was situated where the Spaniards had since built the town of the Conception de la Vega. This kingdom was bounded by the sea on the north and on the east, from Cape-Raphaël to Isabelique; on the south, by the chain of mountains which runs from Cape-Raphaël to the group of Cibao; and on the west, by a line running from this group to Isabelique. The whole of this kingdom now belongs to the Spaniards.

Marien was the second kingdom. It was bounded on the north and on the west by the sea; on the east, by the kingdom of Magua; and on the south, nearly equally by the kingdom of Maguana, and that of Xaragua. Thus the kingdom of Marien extended from Isabelique to the mouth of the river Artibonite, which river served it as a boundary as far as its source, in the mountains of Cibao. The major part of this kingdom is, of course, in the French territory, which possesses also the place of its capital, being situated in the neighbourhood of Cape-François. *Guacanaric* was the sovereign of this kingdom.

The third kingdom was called *Higuey*. It was bounded to the east and to the south by the sea, from

Cape-Raphaël to the mouth of the Jayna. In the north, it joined to the kingdom of Magua, and in the west, to that of Maguana. *Cayacoa* was its cacique. The Spaniards possess the whole of this kingdom, in which is situated Santo-Domingo, the capital of the Spanish part of the island.

Maguana was the fourth kingdom. It was bounded to the south, by the sea; to the north, by chains of mountains, that separated it from the kingdoms of Magua and Marien; to the east, by the river Jayna, as far as Cibao; and to the west, by the chain of mountains running from Bahoruco, through Mirebalais, to the heights of the river Artibonite. The sovereign of this kingdom was *Caonabo*, a Carib, who had become cacique of it by dint of valour and address. This kingdom also belongs exclusively to the Spaniards, and their town of St. Juan de la Maguana, now stands were formerly stood the capital of this Indian kingdom.

The fifth kingdom was called *Xaragua*, and comprehended the long strip of land which runs from east to west, and which is now called the *southern strip*, of the French part. To the east, it extended as far as the kingdom of Marien, comprehending the ponds, the plain of the Cul-de-Sac, and St. Mark, and that part of the plain of Artibonite, which is situated on the southern side of the river of that name. The cacique *Behechio* governed this kingdom, the capital of which was also called *Xaragua*, and was situated on the spot where we have since seen the town of the Cul-de-Sac. These particulars show, that there is but a very diminutive part of this kingdom that is not now comprehended in the French poffeffions.

I now come to what is properly called the Spanifh part of the ifland.

In defcribing this colony I have followed the order adopted by the licentiate Don Antonio Sanchez Valverde, a creole of Saint-Domingo, and prebend of the cathedral of Santo-Domingo, in the interefting work he publifhed at Madrid, in 1785, entitled, *An idea of the value of the Spanifh ifland, and of the profit the mother country might derive from it:* That is to fay, I begin at the weftern point on the fouthern coaft of the Spanifh part, and turning round the eaftern part, I continue on to the wefternmoft point of the north part; and then, following the boundary line, return to the point from whence I fet out, defcribing fucceffively whatever falls in my way.

I fhall frequently profit from the information of Don Antonio Valverde, who appears, befides the above work, to have had the intention of writing the hiftory of the Spanifh part of Saint-Domingo, eight years before I undertook that of the French part. Aided by materials that his father had been twenty years in collecting, and being himfelf an inhabitant of long ftanding, and great experience in the Spanifh part, his native country, his hiftory cannot but excite the impatience of the curious. And, this impatience is increafed when we confider, that every thing concerning this colony remains as yet in the moft profound obfcurity, and that the depredations of the infects, on books and papers, leave but little hope of verifying facts anterior to 1717 or 1720. I allude here to the state of the archives of the royal court, those of the cathedral, and of the Dominicans, at Santo-Domingo, in 1785.

EXTENT OF THE SPANISH PART.

The Spanish part of Saint-Domingo, which is the easternmost part of the island, is, as near as can be determined by a simple approximation, and without geometrical exactness, about ninety leagues in its greatest length from east to west, and sixty leagues in its greatest width. This may be reduced to a mean length of eighty leagues, and a mean width of forty. It has, then, a surface of 3,200 square leagues, which comes very near the calculation of Don Antonio Valverde, who found it to contain, according to the map recently published by Don Thomas Lopez, 3,175 square leagues. About 400 square leagues of this surface is in mountains, which have this advantage of the mountains in the French part, that they are generally more capable of cultivation, and have sometimes a soil that disputes the preference with that of the valleys. There remains, therefore, a fine fertile surface of more than 2,700 square leagues, divided into valleys and plains of different lengths and widths.

We may assert, with Charlevoix, that no other island of the Antilles offers to the Spaniards so solid means of establishing themselves in those seas, as Saint-Domingo; and with Valverde, we may assert, that this island is for them a key to the gulf of Mexico, a convenient place for all their vessels to touch at, an excellent rendezvous for their squadrons and fleets, and in short, a most important hold for naval operations of all sorts. It was from this cradle of the Europeans in the new world, that all the expeditions were sent, which brought about its submission. Here it was that the Spaniards prepared for the conquest of Peru and Mexico; and here it was that they laid the first foundations of their power in America.

So many circumstances have conspired to render the Spaniards proud of the possession of Saint-Domingo, that they will probably never pardon the French for having extorted a part of that possession.

Round about the island of Saint-Domingo, and situated at a very little distance, there are several little islands, some of which belong to the Spaniards: as, Altavele, Beate, Saone, Saint-Catherine, Mone, Monique, of all which I shall speak after having treated of Saint-Domingo itself.

What has been said of the mountains of the island in general, is applicable to those of the Spanish part. If we may judge of them by the stoutness of the trees, and the thickness of their foliage, they must be extremely fertile. Some of them, however, have a rugged and sterile appearance; but this is almost always the effect of some mine, of which there are many in these mountains, of various sorts, and various fecundity. The mountains of the Spanish part are high enough to attract the rains, which are remarkably regular, and the salutary effects of which seem to be longer preserved in the soil by the thick and lofty forests with which these mountains are covered. It is these rains that furnish the waters with which the Spanish part is more amply supplied than the French; it is they that preserve that perpetual verdure, that coolness so delightful in a hot climate, and the enlivening beauty of all the vegetable creation.

Two lines, one drawn in a direction from east to west, from Cape-Raphaël to Saint-Mark, and the other, in a direction from north to south, from Port-de-Plate to the river Nisao, would intersect each other nearly at the centre of a considerable group of mountains, called *Cibao*. This is the highest spot of the whole island, and here the principal rivers have their source. From this group, as from a common centre, run different chains of mountains of various heights, between which are the rivers. These mountains are subdivided in their prolongation, and thus form little valleys and dells, through which the streams and rills find a passage to the plains. One might also say, that this mountainous mass is but one system of mountains, bounded to the north by the plain of La Vega-Réal; to the east, by the bay of Samana; to the south-east, by the plain of Santo-Domingo; to the south, by a part of the same plain, and by those of Bani and Azua; to the south-west, by the plain of Neybe; to the west, by the plains of St. John, of Banique, of Gohave, and Hinche, as far as Dondon, which itself is one of the branches of Cibao; and to the north-west, by the plain of Cape-François.

The highest and most extensive chain of the group of Cibao, is that which stretches towards Dondon, and from thence to Port-de-Paix. I shall call this *the first chain*, to render my description more easy to follow.

Another high and steep chain, starting from the same group, runs towards the east, and ends at Cape-Raphaël, or the Round Mountain; this is the chain of Sevico, or the *second* chain.

These two chains, considered as a prolongation of each other, form the longest chain of mountains in the island, and serve to divide the Spanish part of the island into a northern and southern part.

The plains in the Spanish part are far more extensive than those in the French part. This will clearly appear from what follows; beginning again at the westernmost point of the coast.

The first Spanish plain lies at the foot of the mountains of Bahoruco, and on the west side of them, towards the point of the island of Beate. This plain is about ten leagues long from north to south, and eight wide, from east to west.

There is a second plain on the east side of these same mountains of Bahoruco, stretching down towards the bay of Neybe, the length of which, from north to south, is supposed to be fifteen leagues, by a width which varies from two to six leagues, through the interposition of the mountainous parts. This second plain runs up the river Neybe, and on that side joins on to the plain of Neybe.

The plain of Neybe, the length and width of which often varies, is bounded on the east by the river from which it takes its name; on the weft, by the pond of Henriquille, and by mountains running towards Mirebalais. It is, from the river Neybe to the fources of the Pedernales, about twelve leagues eaft and weft, by nine leagues north and fouth; though, in fome places, the width is not more than three leagues. This plain, after dwindling to a narrow valley, ftretches towards the river Seybe, and unites itfelf to the plains of Acajoux, Banique, Farfan; and then, following the river Neybe, joins the plains of St. Thomas and St. John.

The river Neybe feparates the plain of Neybe from the plain of Azua, to the north of which lies a chain of mountains. The plain of Azua is reckoned to be about twelve leagues from weft to eaft, from the mouth of the river Neybe to the Anfe de la Chaudiere, by a width about equal. At the Anfe de la Chaudiere begins the plain of Vani or Bani, which, to the mouth of the Nifao, where it ends, is twelve leagues long, by from four to nine leagues wide.

From Nifao to the fouth-eaft point of the ifland, called *Punta-Efpada*; that is to fay, for the fpace of about fixty-five leagues, following the turnings of the coaft, there is no interruption to the plain; except that of the little arable hills lying between the river Roman and that of Soco, and which, extending eight leagues from north to fouth, and five from eaft to weft, narrow, in that place, the plain which is commonly from eleven to thirteen leagues broad.—So much for the plains on the weftern coaft.

On the eaftern fide the level country ftill continues on, from the *Punta-Efpada* to the Cape of the Round

Mountain, or Cape-Raphaël, sixteen leagues, by a width nearly equal.

At the western extremity of this plain begins another, which is reckoned thirty-eight leagues from east to west, reaching to the point corresponding with the mines of Cibao, and from ten to fifteen leagues wide.

From the mines of Cibao to St. Yague, the plain grows narrower by two or three leagues, then widening all at once to five, and sometimes even eight leagues, it continues on to the river Dahabon, or the river of the Massacre, stretching a length of thirty leagues more, or thereabouts.

But what I have hitherto said of the plains, does not comprehend all those of the Spanish part of the island. There are a great number in the interior parts, of inconsiderable dimensions it is true, but which make an increase of level land, where cultivation is more easy.

In the interior also are the two great plains of St. John, and Acajoux, of which I have already spoken.

The first of these plains, united to that of St. Thome, is from ten to eleven leagues in length, from the foot of the mountains from whence come the great and little Yaqui (which mountains bound the plain to the east), to the mountains to the west, towards which flows the river Seybe, and nearly equal in breadth from north to south. The second plain (Acajoux) is on the other side the river Seybe, and extends fourteen leagues westward, being from five to nine leagues wide, for the most part.

There are, besides, in the interior parts, the plains

of Banique, Hinche, Guaba, and St. Raphaël; besides some others, of which I shall speak hereafter.

Finally, on the whole of the northern coast, from the bay of Mancenille and Monte-Christ to Samana, the land is every where level, and occupies an extent of more than sixty leagues long, and from two to three leagues wide.

Over the whole of this country, mountains and places, containing as I have already observed, about 3,200 square leagues, are spread 125,000 inhabitants, of which 110,000 are free, and 15,000 slaves; which does not amount to quite forty individuals to each square league. If we recollect what Las-Casas has advanced, that Saint-Domingo contained three millions of inhabitants, at the time of its discovery, a number believed to be exaggerated, and which I reduce even to a third, we see that the Spanish part, which makes more than three-fifths of the island, should contain about 700,000 souls, more than six times its present population.

CHARACTER AND MANNERS OF THE SPANISH CREOLES.

The Spaniards possess, as we have seen, the most extensive and most fertile part of the island, and their character wants no comparison with that of the French, when we know that this possession is of no sort of use to them, while the French portion of the island furnishes three-fifths of the produce of all the

French West-India colonies put together: a produce amounting annually to 250,000,0000 of French livres.*

The Spanish creoles, now become infensible of all the treasures which surround them, pass their lives without wishing to better their lot. A capital, which of itself indicates decay, little insignificant towns here and there, a few colonial settlements, for which the name of manufactories, would be too great an honour, immense possessions, called *Hattes*, where beasts and cattle are raised with little care, are all that present themselves to the view, where nature spreads so many allurements to a people who are blind to all her charms.

Such negligence implies few wants, and the Spanish creoles know only such as are easily satisfied. A shirt, a sleeved-waistcoat, and a pair of ticking breeches; such is the common dress of the men, who very often go bare-foot. At Santo-Domingo, however, and in some of the principal places, many of them wear a sort of loose coats, of camlet or silk; but most commonly they go out in great coats, which they call *cloaks*.

The women wear a petticoat, commonly black, a sort of bed-gown, and a shift which does not always descend much below the waist. Their fine long hair, without powder, is sometimes braided, and sometimes tied up with a ribon coming round the forehead. To wear a cap, made of a sort of net-work called

---

* More than forty-five millions of dollars, or than ten millions sterling.

refcille, or to wear in the hair great white pins, ornamented with paltry stones of various colours, is a luxury known to the towns only. Sometimes, indeed, you see their heads decorated with field-flowers, but you see at the same time, that taste has had no hand in the decoration. They wear ear-rings also, which they change frequently. It is from Cape-François that they get these trinkets, which they admire with a sort of coquetry.

The Spanish creoles are generally sedentary. It is rare for them to quit their island, which their government, besides, renders very difficult, and one would be tempted to believe that they were afraid of the sea, were it not known that in time of war they fit out privateers, in order to seize on those riches, which are always a temptation to people who are poor.

The general character of these people is a heterogeneous mass of meanness and pride. Crawling, servile to the last degree when occasion requires it, they affect haughtiness, the same moment. They borrow, for instance, under the pretext, sometimes absolutely absurd, that what they borrow is for a sick person, things that they are too proud to ask for, and that their idleness will never permit them to repay. They are timid with their superiors, and with their inferiors insolently disdainful. Superlatively malicious, they carry their revenge to the very grave, not knowing that it is laudable to be great and generous, even to an enemy.

In the country places, the women do the cookery, and carve at table; sometimes they do not sit at table at all, but dine on one side, seated on the floor. However, this humiliating distinction wears away in proportion as their communication with the French becomes more frequent, and on the frontiers it is almost entirely done away. Fashion begins, through the means of the French, to have some little influence on the Spanish women; and to give them a relish for the variegated charms of that capricious divinity. Accordingly, we see many of them on the frontiers wearing jaunty short-gowns after the French fashion, and otherwise imitating the dress of their more amiable neighbours.

The general occupation of the women is sewing. When they sew, they hold on their knees a little cushion, filled with the down of a plant called *Spanish-Beard*, to which they fix their work. They are not secluded from all society, as in Spain: nor do they wear a veil or hood, except when they go to church. While at church, they are on one side, and the men on the other, according to a law made for the Spanish colonies, the 18th of October, 1569; and neither men nor women are permitted to sit down. In the country churches, the women have a little piece of calf-leather to kneel upon; in those of the towns, they have a little carpet. There was a time when these people were so miserable, that mass was said before day-light, that the sight of their shabbiness might not dishonour the service; and even now, there are certain places where many of the women stay from church for want of veils. These veils, which cover half the face, and the ends of which are held in the hand, descend as low as the waift. They are of black ftuff among the common people, and of filk of the fame colour among thofe who are called *people of fafhion*.

The graces muft neceffarily be fcarce among a people who know not their value; accordingly, the charms to be found among the Spanifh creoles, are due to nature alone; and, indeed, nature feems here to have been rather fparing, as if fhe feared to lavifh her favours in vain. All the pleafures derived from the company of agreeable women, are unknown to the creoles of Saint-Domingo. Love alone keeps up an intercourfe between the fexes, but it is not that delicate and voluptuous love that characterifes another people.

The Spanifh creole women, though ignorant of the art of pleafing, are extremely amourous, and equally jealous; and, it feems that, in this refpect, we may apply to them all that I have elfewhere faid of the French creoles. Thofe lively affections which prove the amorous complexion of the perfons who are fubject to them, naturally produce an inclination towards gallantry; and perhaps the lover fucceeds with more eafe, when his prayers are feconded by the effects of the climate. One would think that the fpirit of fuperftition which reigns among thefe people, muft be an obftacle to fuch immoral practices; but obfervation will convince us of the contrary: fo true it is that morals can have no other guardian than morals themfelves.

From what I have juft faid, the reader will eafily conceive, that this part of Spanifh America is not without its share of that shameful superstition which characterises the mother country, and which has brought every Spaniard under the monastic yoke. In places little frequented, these creoles are sometimes extremely happy to be permitted to kiss the hand of a haughty monk, who, with holy affectation, presents his hand, and receives, as an homage that does honour to him who renders it, a proof of that abject submission which the humility of his calling forbids him to accept.

Here, as in all the rest of the Spanish dominions, the priests are excessively jealous of their authority, and they never fail to find pretexts for declaring the cause of religion to be interested in every thing, that their temporal interests suggest as a mean of manifesting their power.

Excommunication is a weapon of such frequent use with them, that we are at a loss which to be most astonished at, the abuse itself, or the tameness with which it is suffered. If a prohibition is issued, however foreign to religious matters, for instance, to slaughter cows and heifers, the penalty, in case of disobedience, is excommunication. But it is principally with respect to the paschal duties, that this penalty is dreaded. When the term in which those duties ought to be performed is expired, the names of the delinquents are publickly called over in the church, three Sundays running; a bell is tolled, as an advertisement to them, and after these formalities, the ecclesiastical thunders are hurled on their devoted heads.

This superstitious character explains at once, why the number of churches, chapels, and convents, is much greater in Saint-Domingo, than the population seems to require.

The Spaniards have hardly any but religious books, and are very fond of the images of saints. Were we to form a judgment of them from their behaviour in public, from the affected devotion with which they tell their beads, or stop to recite the *Angelus*, we should certainly conclude, that they despised the things of this world, and that their thoughts were totally engrossed by those of the world to come; but this veil is not close enough to hide hypocrisy, and it can deceive those only who allow this sort of profanation to assume the name of virtue.

Marriages are very common at Saint-Domingo, because an illicit commerce between the sexes, absolutely public, would not be permitted; but Hymen has not here, any more than elsewhere, the power of chaining down the passions, or of giving them a constant direction to the same object.

The women are generally pretty lusty, especially those who live in the interior of the island; elegance of shape is an advantage as much unknown to them as the graces of the toilet. They do not permit the men to salute them in the French fashion, which they look upon as indelicate; but those who are familiar with them, they permit to embrace them in the following manner: the man puts his right arm round the lady's neck, his left round her waist, and thus he presses her to his bosom. It is for those who have had an opportunity of comparing the two manners, to say which is preferable, and direct our judgment on so important a point

The Spaniards of Saint-Domingo live very frugally. In the country places particularly, they live upon beef and pork, to which they give different names according to the manner of cooking; and this manner proves that they are no connoisseurs in this sometimes dangerous art.

A side of beef corned, sprinkled with lemon-juice, and dried in the sun, they call *sesinne*, when cooked with pimenta; and when this same meat is minced up, it is called *tassau*. They add to these dishes the smoked flesh of the wild pig, called *tossine*, after having stuck it here and there with leaves of allspice. With these dishes they eat conserves made of the cocoa-nut, or others, very celebrated, called *pâtes de guava*. As they are generally in want of sugar, which they manufacture very badly, they use, in their conserves, the syrup that is made from the juice of the cane, or honey, which is very plenty with them. The fruit of the plantain-tree, Indian corn, and cassavium, serve them in place of bread.

But the Spanish women know nothing of the caribbee dish, so celebrated under the name of *calalou*, in some colonies, and under the name of *gombau*, in others, and that the women of all the French Antilles esteem beyond every thing. They have even the misfortune not to know, that a *calalou* may become the pretext of festivals, where all ceremony is laid aside, or of pleasures that a propitious mystery renders more delicious and enchanting.

Subsistence of another sort comes from the water. There are an abundance of fish and tortoises round the coast, nor are they less abundant in the rivers. And here we must commend the care of the Spanish fishermen in burning the manceneel-trees growing along the banks, lest the fruit of this poisonous tree, by being the food of the fish, should be the death of those who eat of them. The temperance of these islanders is again remarkable in their drink, which is generally water, and of that even they often drink no more than a single tumbler at the end of their repast. They are fond enough of *taffia*;* but, as they have none, except what is smuggled to them, it is at once very scarce and dear, selling so high as thirty French sous a pint.

The Spaniards eat no sallad, and blame those who do; because, they say, it is a custom resembling the grazing of brutes; but they make up for this self-denial, in their use of chocolate. This is the usual supper of a Spaniard, and what seems to please his appetite the most of any thing. They begin, however, latterly, to use coffee, and even to cultivate the coffee-tree on some of their mountains. The use of tobacco is as general as that of chocolate. Every company is invested with a cloud of its smoke. It is extremely lucky that nature has fortified the heads of the women in such manner as to render them incapable of enduring a fumigation, the very idea of which would frighten the women of other climates. But we shall not be so surprised that they endure without repining these volumes of smoke, when we know, that

---

* A sort of spiritous liquor, made out of the sugar-cane.

they themselves are in the habit of a sort of chewing of the leaf. They pretend that this is an effectual preservative against the scurvy. It may be so, but one must be long accustomed to the effect of this substance upon the teeth, not to regret the white, so justly boasted of as one of the greatest ornaments of beauty.

The Spanish creole women have, in general, very fortunate and easy times of delivery. Their fibres not being much extended, and their little domestic fatigues, contribute, without doubt, to this happy effect; and, besides, their minds being tranquil and unfatigued with imaginary wants and cares, is most assuredly an additional cause.

Nevertheless, the population of the Spanish part of the island is not proportioned to its extent, though children are commonly raised with no great deal of difficulty; but, in a country where there is no industry, where life resembles vegetation, there must ever be vast spaces uninhabited, and men must be thinly sown.

The Spaniards of Saint-Domingo, take after dinner, a little nap, which they call a *sieste*. This favourite custom, among a people always indolent, convert, the most populous place of the island into a desert, during the hours that its inhabitants are, in some sort, tired of their existence.

This tranquil life commonly prolongs the life of the Spanish creoles, and leads them on gently to old age. This would be an advantage worthy of envy, if life were to be measured by the number of our days, and not by the manner in which they are employed.

Sickness is not very common in the Spanish part of the island, where there are scarce any physicians or surgeons, except in the town of Santo-Domingo, where some refugee French follow these two professions. Their sobriety is undoubtedly one of the reasons of their health. The disorders the most common among them, are pleurisies and malignant fevers.

They do not make use of inoculation, and consequently the small-pox exercises all its ravages amongst them. They have a practice of rubbing the pox with hog's-lard, to hasten their maturity, and to wash them with urine after they begin to dry up.

There is another disorder, perhaps still more fatal to the human race, because it poisons the fountain of life, and which is said to be a native of America. Of this most dreadful disorder the Spanish creoles make a subject of pleasantry, and this is sufficient to prove that it is not rare among them. They apply remedies extracted from plants and simples, particularly those of the sudorific class.

It is, perhaps, to this kind of indifference that the leprosy, with which the colony is frequently afflicted, owes its birth. They have even been obliged to establish a lazaretto at St. Yague, and another at Santo-Domingo. The lepers are married to one another, when they wish it, and the men, women, and children remain shut up; unless it may be such children as have not received the least infection from their parents; these alone are suffered to quit the lazaretto.

The dwelling houses in the Spanish part are far from being either sumptuous or even commodious.

In the country they are nothing but frames made of flight wood, clofed up with boards, or fometimes with piles, and covered with the leaves of palm-trees, or thofe of the *latanier*. Thefe habitations are lighted with pieces of pine-wood, torches, or candle-wood, in a country where tallow is common, and where the bees would prepare the wax, that indolence will not mould into candles. Sometimes the feats are nothing more than lengths of the trunk of a tree fawed crofs-wife. There are ufually feveral mahogany tables, one of which generally remains in the middle of the principal chamber. The corners of the rooms are filled with cupboards, which are often formed by a curtain that ferves to hide what is intended to be kept out of fight.

The beds are commonly an ox or horfe's fkin. A mattrafs is a very great luxury. The bedftead is often made of four forked ftakes with palm-tree boards tied on them crofswife by a fort of wild fupple-jacks. Here the Spaniards, ftretched on their horfe's fkin, tafte the fweets of fleep, which certainly no other people could do, in fpite of the ftings and bites of tormenting infects. Near the fea-fide, innumerable multitudes of fand-flies and mufquitoes, force whoever would fleep, to hide himfelf under a fort of pavillion, formed by faftening a piece of linen to the ceiling, and lengthening it in fuch manner as to hide the bed. Befides this, it is generally neceffary, as a previous ftep, to drive out the fwarms, by filling the room with a thick fmoke. Among the infects which are the moft troublefome by day, may be reckoned the *macarabon*, a fort of large fly that has the points of its wings blaker than the rest of its body, and that is inconceivably troublesome from ten o'clock in the morning to four o'clock in the afternoon.

In the towns, and other frequented places, the inhabitants procure conveniences unknown to those in the country; but, how far are they from being equal to those enjoyed in the like places in the French colonies.

The Spanish creoles have few particular attachments or inclinations, which indicate lively passions, or which give a striking and distinctive feature to their character. The men are rather curious in their arms; they have little portative pattereros, called *trabauds*, which they carry before them on horseback.

The singing of these islanders is extremely monotone, and agrees well with that sort of melancholy, which would appear downright sadness among the French. They dance, but like morris dancers, in the sound of a hoarse guitar, which all the time complains most grievously of the awkwardness of the fingers that squeeze it; or else to the sound of a calabash only, on which they freely exercise their unharmonious hands. Hearing such singing, or beholding such a dance, gives us an idea of any thing sooner than of the children of pleasure.

There are some places where things go infinitely worse; and where a custom prevails that offends against all the rules of decency. I mean that of a little ballette, *fandinguette*, where a young girl, mostly pretty, dances amid a circle of spectators, who successively toss her their hats. These she puts on her head, or under her arm; or else forms a pile with them on the ground. When the dance is ended she carries the hats to the owners, from each of whom she receives a trifling reward, the amount of which is fixed by custom, and which cannot be refused with civility, or surpassed without insult.

The Spaniards take but little delight in the cultivation of their gardens. Each has a very small one, in the middle of which he places a cross. Its produce consists in a few pimenta plants, thyme, here and there a pomegranate, but very rarely any kind of vegetables of solid utility. There are no flowers, except now and then a pot of pinks. I have said that the women love to deck their heads with flowers, and, among some nations, this taste alone would be sufficient to make the cultivation of them common; but the Spaniards, notwithstanding their celebrity as lovers, care but little about pleasing the beloved object.

The population of the Spanish part is composed of three classes, the whites, of which I have just spoken, the freed-people, and the slaves.

The freed-people are few in number, if compared with the whites, but their number is considerable, if compared with that of the slaves. By a principle of religion, adopted by the Spaniards of Saint-Domingo, they look on the legacy of liberty, that a master leaves to his slaves, as an act of piety; and as the father-confessors inculcate this opinion, we ought not to be surprised that it is common to see many slaves at a time rendered free by the last will of their masters. Another sentiment produces the same effect: an illicit affection often gives liberty to her that has inspired it, as well as to those who are its fruit. Besides, as soon as a female slave can pay down to her master, two hundred and fifty dollars (fifty-six pounds five shillings sterling,) she is sure of her liberty, and the child she bears becomes free by the addition of twelve dollars and a half, or of double that sum, if he be already born. A law of their colonial code, says, that when a proprietor wishes to sell the children of a slave, the father, if he be a Spaniard, shall be preferred before every other purchaser.

If we believe Don Antonio de Valverde, the facility of freeing slaves (for the ratification of which the government requires no compensation) has in general a tendency to fill the country with vagabonds, and women, who, ever recollecting how they became free, and having no honest means of subsistence, give themselves up to a shameful commerce, the bane of morality.

That prejudice with respect to colour, so powerful with other nations, among whom it fixes a bar between the whites, and the freed-people, and their descendants, is almost unknown in the Spanish part of Saint-Domingo. Their colonial laws respecting freed-people subject them to a particular tax, incapacitate them to serve as registers, or notaries, forbid them to have Indians to wait on them, or to carry arms, on pain of perpetual banishment. Other of these laws subjects them to the penalty of returning to slavery, if they take part in, or favour the revolt, the pillage, or robbery of slaves. Some of them go so far as to forbid this class to wear any thing in gold, pearls, silk, or even a cloak to come lower down than the waist, on pain of forfeiting these ornaments. But, all these laws are absolutely disregarded in the Spanish part. It must, however, be allowed, that many of the Spanish creoles of this island, would turn with disgust from an alliance with the descendants of their slaves; and, to be thorougly convinced of this, we have only to observe the indignation of Don Antonio de Valverde, a creole, against Mr. Veuves, who, in his work, has ventured to assert the contrary. This class is, in fact, excluded from almost all employments, civil as well as military, as long as the colour of the skin betrays its origin; but the political constitution of the colony admits of no distinction between the civil rights of a white inhabitant and those of a freed person. It is true, and even strictly so, that the major part of the Spanish colonists are a mixed race: this an African feature, and sometimes more than one, often betrays; but, at the same time, its frequency has silenced a prejudice that would otherwise be a troublesome remembrancer. With respect to the priesthood, people of colour are admitted into it without difficulty, according to the principles of equality, which from the basis of the Christian religion, and which are here suffered to operate in favour of all, except the negroes: the Spaniards have not yet brought themselves to make negro priests and bishops, like the Portuguese.

From the removal of this prejudice with regard to colour, necessarily arises a lenity to the slaves.

They are usually fed as well as their masters, and treated with a mildness unknown in the colonies of other nations. Besides, every slave having it in his power to become free, by purchasing his liberty of his master, who cannot refuse to accept the offer, if it amounts to the sum specified by the law, it is natural to believe, that, seeing him ever upon the point of becoming as free as himself, he will forbear to treat him with that superiority which masters enjoy over their slaves. Thus the fate of the slave is softened by the hope of freedom, and the authority of the master by the habit of being confounded, in some sort, with those who were the other day in slavery.

A recent declaration of the king of Spain, the object of which is to favour the cultivation of Saint-Domingo, and of which I shall hereafter speak more at large, seems, however, intended to produce a change in this respect, since it establishes for principle, that slaves are not to be precarious property.

But, as long as the negroes remain so few in number, and are spread over such an immense surface of country, there can never be but a handful here and there; and it being impossible in such a state, to subject them to an exact discipline, which is useful in great manufactures and habitations only, their treatment will ever be analogous to the situation of their masters, to whom they will be rather companions than slaves.

The Spanish colonial laws subject the maroon negroes to the punishment of whipping, and being ironed: the negro cannot absent himself without a written permission from his master: one who dares to strike a white person is liable to be put to death, and they are all forbidden to carry arms. But, as I have already observed, these laws are, as to these points, null at Saint-Domingo; yet, where they require that the royal court should listen, and do justice to slaves who demand their liberty, or complain of ill-treatment, they are punctually obeyed.

If we adopt the opinion of some individuals of the Spanish part, we should add to the three classes already mentioned, a fourth, which would be extremely interesting, on account of the long succession of misfortunes that it would recall to our minds. I mean certain creoles, very few in number, whose hair resembles that of the Indians; that is, it is long, straight, and black. These creoles pretend that they are the remaining descendants of the aborigines of the island. They are amazingly proud of this descent, notwithstanding it is rendered incredible by historical authority, which every where assures us, that this race of men were entirely exterminated. All that can possibly be granted them, is, that they descend from a mixture of the aborigines and the Spaniards; and here we may affirm, that, in 1744, there remained at Banique several Indians, who proved their descent from the subjects of the too-unfortunate Cacique Henri; and it will be seen, when I come to speak of *Boya*, that at that place there are yet some of the same cast.

The creoles of the Spanish part have hardly ever any education to signify, because there is no place of public inftruction (though there is an univerfity at Santo-Domingo), or becaufe they are not near enough to thofe where the firft rudiments are taught. Accordingly, the inhabitants of the country places fcarcely know how to write or read. Hence the want of focial intercourfe; for ignorance ever tends to keeping men afunder, as it furnifhes them with nothing to communicate to each other.

Another caufe concurs in the feparation of the Spanifh creoles, and that is the badnefs of their roads. A poor colony, among whom the power that poffeffes the mines of Peru and Mexico was obliged to iffue a paper currency, with an exchange of forty-five per centum, can undertake nothing of confequence. This paper, the laft of which was called in, in 1788, has been replaced by that of the Bank of St. Charles. We have need of no other proof of there being no public inftitutions, than this, that the prifons are maintained by the charity of well-difpofed perfons. The roads are nothing but paths, where travelling is extremely difficult, and confequently flow. They are paffable a horfe-back and a foot only, and the traveller muft take care to provide every neceffary for nourifhment and lodging. Eight leagues a day is very great work, and in this fpace he often does not meet with a fingle habitation. Thefe roads, bad as they always are, are at particular times, and in particular places, rendered worfe by rivers fubject to overflow, which the animals fwim acrofs, and which the men pafs in canoes or hides. I fhall fpeak of all this more at length by and by.

After having thus described the roads, it is hardly necessary to say, that this colony has scarcely any commerce: commerce requires roads and canals, the means of circulating the productions of nature and art, which are its nourishment and life. The Spanish part has no relation to signify with the mother country; which had submitted it to the exclusive privilege of the Company of Catalonia. This company, like all others, sent but very insufficient supplies of necessary things. The bank of St. Charles has lately supplanted the company; that is to say, the cause of privation has changed its name.

The resources of the colonists are, of course, extremely confined. They have, however, some establishments, but all rather below mediocrity. Let us take a view of the different sorts successively.

They reckon in the whole colony, but twenty-two sugar manufactories of any consequence, the rest not being worth mentioning; and even these twenty-two have, all together, but about six hundred negroes. These six produce syrup, and some sugar, but the others, which are called *trapiches*, where animals are employed to turn the mills and press the canes, without shelter, in the open air, make nothing but syrup. All the productions of these manufactures are consumed in the island, and in favourable years the proprietors are obliged to abandon a part of their crop for want of a market, and because the price is so low, that the sales do not defray the expences of the labour. For the same reason there are very few of them who clay their sugar, except, perhaps, a few hundreds for conserves, or other purposes in that way; but now and then, when an occasion has offered to sell, or send to Porto-Rico, or Old Spain, which has sometimes been done in very small quantities, the goodness of the sugar has proved that of the soil, but nothing in favour of the manufacturer.

There is no more coffee cultivated than what serves for the trifling consumption of some few inhabitants of a country, where chocolate is preferred to it; and besides, those who live near the frontiers, purchase what they want of the French. The few grains of coffee that the Spaniards have planted, they got from Dondon. The coffee-tree flourishes well in every part of the island, and produces in abundance, particularly in certain elevated parts of the mountains. It varies, however, in quality, as well as in size, according as the land lies more or less high, and with other local circumstances; but the coffee is every where good, and there are some lands which produce as good as even that of Moka. Each coffee-tree in a state of bearing is reckoned to produce a pound weight.

From the indifference shown for the cultivation of the cotton plant, it would be impossible to conceive that cotton is of value enough to excite industry, that it grows naturally at Saint-Domingo, and that it is of an excellent quality, even when it comes without the least care. It flourishes in stony land, in that which is the most barren, and in the very crevices of the rocks.

For sometime after the discovery of the island, the Spaniards cultivated a little indigo, and, at the end of the fixteenth century, they fent confiderable quantities of it to the mother country; but this fhrub has fhared the fate of depopulation: it has been abandoned, and the Spanifh colonifts know nothing of it at prefent but that, from its natural luxuriance, and numerous roots, it is an obftacle to their feeble labours, in the fields where it grows fpontaneoufly.

Tobacco is a native of the ifland, and is to be met with every where. Valverde obferves, that its leaf exceeds in largenefs that of the tobacco of every other part of America; that its quality, which is good in almoft every part of the ifland, fometimes equals that of Cuba, or the Havanna; that it is as much efteemed as this latter in the manufactures of Seville, and that it is even preferable to it in fegars. This tobacco is even bettered by being made into fnuff, and that which is in rolls or carots, is fought for by the French, becaufe, when mixed with other tobacco, it communicates ftrength to it by the nature of its juice. Notwithftanding thefe favourable circumftances, the Spaniards contented themfelves with planting a very little at St. Yague, and la Vega, and this only for the confumption of the colony, and for the purpofe of fmuggling with the neighbouring iflands. But, fince the king of Spain has encouraged the cultivation of this plant, by taking a part of its produce, a good number of perfons are employed in it in the two quarters we have juft named, and in that of Cotuy, and it is poffible that it may become more general.

Cocoa is an object of the firft confequence in the Spanifh part. It is alfo a native, and is found in a great number of places. According to Valverde (from whom I borrow this article), at the time of the discovery of the island, the cocoa was, after the mines and the sugar, the most abundant source of the riches of the colonists. In the sixteenth century there was no other cocoa than that of Saint-Domingo, and this island then provided all Spain with that article. There was even too much, which led the colonists to solicit the court of Madrid to permit them to transport it into foreign countries. The kernel of the cocoa-nut of Saint-Domingo is more acidulated than that of the cocoa-nut of the province of Venezuela and Caraca, to which it is not inferior; and in the Indies, constant experience proves, that the chocolate made with an equal mixture of the two cocoas, has a more delicate flavour than that which is made of the cocoa of Caraca alone. But this cultivation, as well as all others, has greatly diminished. It must be confessed, that the hurricanes, which are often felt in the southern and eastern parts of the island, are a dreadful enemy to the cocoa-trees; but there are so many other places where they thrive in a manner that calls to mind the epoch when they were of such utility! There is hardly cocoa enough produced for the consumption of the colony, because, since 1764, when the cultivation was so far re-established as to export a little to Cadiz, the winds have destroyed a great part of the trees which produce these nuts, the use of which is at once wholesome and agreeable. We yet see in the plain de la Vega-Real, and in other places of the northern part of the colony, a sufficient testimony of the former utility of this shrub; that is, innumerable wild cocoa-trees growing in the middle of the woods.

With respect to the achiotte, which was very productive in the sixteenth century, when there were great plantations of it, we see only the vestiges of its cultivation.

The same may be said of the ginger, whole cargoes of which were formerly shipped to Spain. The cassia has shared the same fate.

There are yet some little settlements in the Spanish part called *Conacos**, a name equivalent to *provision-farm* in the French part. These are generally the lot of colonists rather in low circumstances, or most commonly of people of colour, or freed-people.

If the rapid sketch that I have here given of the different objects, capable of exciting the industry of the Spaniards, comprehended them all, it would be very difficult to conceive how they are able to procure themselves subsistence, and the means of satisfying their wants; but it remains for me to speak of another sort of settlement, at once the most common, the most useful, and the most analogous to the manners and character of the colonists: I mean the *Hattes*.

A *hatte* is a sort of grazing farm, or breeding farm; they are distinguished in the Spanish part by the adjunction of the name of the animals which are the principal object of the *hatte*. Thus, they call some *horse-hattes*, others *cattle-hattes*, and others, used only in the breeding of pigs, are called *corails*, a word signifying *enclosure* or *pen*.

---

* A piece of land enclosed for cultivation.

The Spanish part of Saint-Domingo abounds in horses, asses, oxen, sheep, goats, and hogs, which have been propagated in a manner that drew a sort of admiration from the first Spaniards who wrote on America. Oviedo said, in 1535, which was forty-three years after the discovery of the island, that the cows, the first of which were brought from Spain, were, at so early a period, in such great numbers, that many ships returned to Europe loaded with their hides; and that sometimes five hundred of them were killed at a time, with lances, only for the sake of these hides. For a half-penny one might buy four pounds of meat; a cow with a calf, for a dollar and three quarters (seven shillings and ten-pence half-penny, sterling), and a wether, for the eighth of a dollar (six-pence three-farthings, sterling). Oviedo, who says, that he sold those of his habitation still cheaper, adds, that many flocks of sheep and goats, and several droves of hogs, were become wild in the woods.

If, then, there was such a superior abundance in the time of Oviedo, when the colony was fuller than at any time since, of natives as well as Europeans; and a continual depopulation having decreased the number of consumers for a long time past, the flocks and herds which were already become so numerous, and the animals which were become wild, ought, one would think, to be so multiplied, as in some sort, to over-run the whole island.

The fact, however, is far from answering to this calculation. The hattes continue; they are, as I have said, the most numerous sort of the Spanish settlements.

They vary in extent, and in the number of animals raised on them: but, in general, they cover a space disproportioned to their utility; which is another proof of the little account that is made of territorial possessions, almost useless to the Spaniards. There are, at this time, some hattes covering a space of many square leagues, and which do not contain above four or five hundred head of cattle, great and small, and, sometimes less. The lands belonging to these hattes are immense savanas, or natural meadows, in which there is here and there a piece of woodland; and this woodland, called *venerie*, frequently forms the boundaries between the hattes, and is common to those on both sides of it. The woodland, besides, being useful to shelter the cattle from the heat of the sun, serves to attract the wild animals, and to render the chase, from which the colonists derive part of their living, less laborious.

Over these extensive tracts, the cattle separate into little flocks and herds, called *hattas*, and feed at a distance from each other; every *hatta* is under a sort of command of a male, a stallion, a bull, or a ram; this male is ever at the head, like a stag in a herd of deer, or a bell-wether in a flock of sheep; any he does not suffer the leader of another flock or herd, to encroach on his rights. But, notwithstanding this kind of aggregation, ten or twelve animals are frequently dispersed over a quarter of a league, or half a league square.

This wandering, which produces a sensible difference in the nature of the cattle, has, according to Valverde, made the graziers divide them into four classes: the *domestic*, the *gentle*, the *shy*, and the *wild*.

The *domestic animals* are the least numerous class. They are brought up to graze round about the house, and to be at any time brought into the pens where the cows are usually milked.

The *gentle animals* are those which stray but a little distance from the house, form themselves into *hattas*, and readily come into the pens, when called or driven home.

The *shy animals* stray to a very great distance from home, and quit one another entirely.

The *wild animals*, which are also called *mountaineers*, remain always in the most retired parts of the mountains.

In the direction and care of a hatte, besides the proprietor (who does not, however, always reside on it), there is employed a sort of overseer, called a majoral; sometimes an under-majoral, and several pioneers and lancers. The majoral and under-majoral see that the cattle are brought together when necessary, caught, sold, &c. in a word, they give directions in every thing belonging to the hatte, and the pioneers and lancers are employed in taking care of the animals.

But, in the greatest part of the hattes in the Spanish part, the proprietor himself is the majoral, and his children are the pioneers and lancers, unless these employments are performed, in whole or in part, by negro slaves. That the reader may have a better idea of the situation of one of these graziers, or rather herdsmen, I shall here transcribe Valverde, who will tell us how he is fed, how he lodges, and what are the toils of his life.

The dwelling that shelters him and his family, is a miserable hut, the sides of which are of piles or planks, badly joined, and the roof of straw. There is commonly a room of from twelve to eighteen feet square, in which is a table, two or three stools, and a hamac. The bed-chamber is another room, not so large as the former, containing several truckle-beds, such as I have described them further on. If it rains, the gutters formed by the openings, let the water into the inside, and the floor, which is not paved, and which differs from the neigbouring meadow only in that the continual treading has worn off the grass, is in a moment ancle deep in mud.

The breakfast consists of a dish of chocolate, of coffee, or of ginger-water, with a roasted plantain. For dinner and supper the whole family eat rice, roots, and fruit of the country produce, such as sweet potatoes, yams, cassavium, plantains, with some meat, often fresh, but oftener salted or dried; as to eggs and poultry, these are delicacies seldom seen on the table of a grazier.

He rises with the aurora to go and visit the half-cultivated lands from whence his subsistence is to come; or to catch the horse which is to carry him in search of his cattle. He walks barefoot on the grass yet loaded with dew; or, if it has rained, he splashes through the mud. The burning sun soon darts his rays upon him, and thus he is scorching in some parts of his body, while others are soaking in water. He is obliged to support the inconvenience of the rains in the woods, the mountains, and the meadows; he goes sometimes a foot-pace, and sometimes a gallop, in quest of his scattered herds, to turn them, to keep them together as much as possible; and to drive to the pens such as are hurt, or attacked with any distemper.

This exercise, which cannot be one day neglected, without running the risk of losses, is yet nothing, since this sort of rounds are no more than home employment, and extend no further than to the care of the animals called *domestic:* the other classes of animals require other fatigues. The animals called **gentle**, though they keep pretty much together, are not driven to the pens without great difficulty. If they are numerous, it requires several days to bring them home; during which, the master, with his people and his pioneers, continue riding in every direction, to drive them together, and shut them up.

When the *shy animals* are to be caught many persons must be called together to assist, and these must be aided by a number of dogs. On such occasions the drovers are obliged to climb the sides of the mountains, and direct the animals, when found, towards a common centre, where the number and address of those who surround them on horse-back, may be capable of keeping them together. For this purpose, each man has either a strong lance, or a staff in imitation of one, made of polished wood, with an iron spike at the end of it, about nine inches long, of a demi-circular form, and made to cut inwards.

When the animals fly so as to leave no hopes of bringing them to the intended spot, the drivers have recourse to other means. One of them is, the man who pursues the animal on horse-back, watches a favourable moment to seize him by the tail, when he has lost the equilibrium, and thus throws him down. At the same instant, and with an agility almost incredible, he dismounts and throws himself upon the animal, before he has time to rise. If it be an ox, his neck is twisted, and his horns are stuck into the ground till he can be coupled to another, (this is called *macorning*), and then both are led by cords. When this cannot be effected, they kill the animal with the lance, or cut his ham-strings with the instrument above described, and which is contrived for this purpose*.

This laborious task is hardly ever performed in the hattes, except at the times when the tribute is called for. The tribute is the contribution which each proprietor of a hatte is obliged to furnish in live stock, for the consumption of Santo-Domingo, the capital; and which is settled in each canton, at the beginning of the year, by the alderman, who, the preceding year, has had the inspection of the weights and measures. It consists of eighty head of male animals, of more than three years old. If the hatte is extensive, it furnishes the tribute all at once, and at different epochs, if otherwise.

---

* *Dampier* describes this instrument in his voyage. V. 2. p. 350.

After all the labour we have defcribed, it muft not be imagined that the *fhy animals* are to be conducted to the pens; they are far too wild for that. Yet we muft look upon them as gentle, if compared to the *mountaineers*. Thefe are an abundant fource of fatigue for the poor graziers, whofe fubfiftence, in a great meafure, is derived from this troublefome clafs of animals.

When one of thefe herdfmen fets off in queft of his cattle; he is generally on foot, and even barefooted, his weapon is a lance, and his companions his dogs. If he goes on horfe-back, he is obliged to difmount at the entrance of every wood, and at the bottom of every mountain that comes athwart his route, for they are inacceffible to a man on horfe-back. He cannot enter a foreft without twifting his body into a thoufand poftures. He fends out his dogs, which have been taught their bufinefs rather by hunger than inftinct. One of the *fhy animals* hardly perceives a man, whether on foot or on horfe-back, when he begins to fly to the woods, fo that he can be caught by the dogs only. Here they attack him, and he defends himfelf and attacks them in his turn, till the herdfman arrives; who, following the noife of the dogs, runs with his lance in his hand, breaking the brufh-wood before him, trampling on thorns, and ftumbling over ftumps, on which he often leaves morfels of cloaths, and fomtimes of his flefh. The moment he appears, the furious animal rufhes towards him; the herdfman with his lance waits the attack without flinching. If he miffes his mark, he flies for fhelter to a flender tree, round the trunk of which he continues to dodge the animal, till he has so harrassed him as to be able to kill him with his *machette**.

The benefit arising from his victory is very small, and costs him yet a great deal of labour. In a climate where meat can rarely be kept longer than the day in which the animal has been killed, and where it is almost the only resource of the hattes, the grazier can with difficulty remain more than eight days without renewing his fatigues, his battles, and consequently his dangers.

When he has killed a beast, he has to strip it, and after that he must cut it in pieces, in order to carry it home on his shoulders; or else he hides it in a place of safety till he can bring his people to aid him in carrying it away. It often happens, that the place of his triumph is so situated that some of the pieces cannot be brought home, without throwing them down the steeps that he finds in his way, where it would be impossible for him to pass with a load, without risking his neck.

Such is the life of a wretched herdsman, which, indeed, bears but too near a resemblance to that of the greatest part of the Spanish colonists. In his laborious rounds he slakes his thirst with the juice of certain fruits, and particularly with that of the oranges, which are sometimes sweet and sometimes sour. His feet acquire, by the habit of going without shoes (says Valverde), a sole, or sort of horn, of the thick-

---

* A sort of cutlass.

ness of one's finger, and that the numberless thorns he treads on never pierce to the quick. To see him cut with a razor this coat from the bottom of his foot, the beholder would imagine, that he was cutting some substance different from himself, so insensible does it seem.

What, then, would be the situation of these unfortunate colonists, if they had not, in their laborious calling as herdsmen, the least precarious source of subsistence? The breeding and fattening of cattle is almost the only object of their commerce; because the French part consumes a great number of animals which it receives, almost entirely, from the Spanish part.

Through an inexcusable negligence, and which is now become almost irreparable, there never has been but a few trifling hattes in the French part, and for more than a century past, it has been in an absolute dependence on its neighbours, with respect to fresh provisions, which are supplied by the Spaniards, whose views are generally turned towards this traffic, to them very lucrative.

Each proprietor gives in, by computation, the number of his stock, not including the *mountaineers*, which pay no tribute at all. This number is divided into three classes; one of which is looked upon as kept apart for propagation, a second for home consumption, and the third is regarded as an article of exportation to the French part. This exportation pays a duty, which has sometimes been carried to five dollars (twenty-two shillings and six-pence sterling), per macorne, or pair of horned cattle; but as it requires a written permit from the Spanish president, this permit alone amounts to an arbitrary imposition. The graziers near the frontiers, sometimes agree with those who live at a distance from them, to furnish their tribute to the Spanish slaughter houses, in order to keep their own cattle for the French market; but the profit they derive from this is not forgotten in the tax on their exportations.

The consumption in the French part of the island, is, then, one of the causes of the decrease of cattle in the Spanish part. The *epizootie* has also made great ravages among them, though it has never been so fatal there as in the French part. The extent of the hattes, and the freedom with which the animals roam about, have alone contributed to put a stop to a distemper, that was never otherwise opposed in the Spanish part.

We must add to these causes of decrease, a disorder of an ancient date. As there were, during the last century, and in the beginning of this, great quantities of hides smuggled from this colony to the Dutch, and other nations, the herdsmen raised dogs of a large breed to pursue the animals; these dogs soon multiplied considerably, and did a great deal of mischief, because they generally fell on the youngest of the cattle. It was when this immense quantity of flesh was left to putrify, that appeared for the first time, a sort of green gilded flies resembling cantharides. As soon as a horse, a horned-beast, or a hog, has a bit of its skin rubbed off, or a sore of any kind, the fly lays an egg in it, which foon changes into a maggot, by which the animal is gnawed to death. The Spanifh colonifts have, indeed, applied with fuccefs, the fmoked ends of tobacco ftalks, or cigarres, as well as hellebore-root; but as thefe remedies can be applied to thofe ulcers only which appear on the fkin, which is not always the cafe, and as they are impracticable with regard to the cattle that run wild, this diforder carries off great numbers. Befides, through the extreme negligence of the herdfmen, the fly attacks the navel of the younglings, which perifh by this means.

The drought, which is frequently experienced, deftroys alfo many of the cattle, or is, at leaft, a bar to their propagation. Generally fpeaking, the proprietors are not able to take the neceffary care of their ftock, and even the extent of their hattes is an almoft infurmountable obftacle. It is now become very difficult for the grazier to get together his cattle, in order to fettle his tribute; but when he does, he takes care to count them, and to mark with his ftamp all thofe that are eighteen months old. In the month of April, when the rainy feafon is coming on, the favanas muft be burnt to renew the grafs, and thofe forts of it, which, like the plume-grafs* (very common at the foot of the mountains), and the wire-grafs, overrun the favanas, and ftifle the feeds of the ufeful kinds. At this time the cattle retire to the woodlands, where they feed on the juicy bines, and are fhaded from the fcorching rays of the fun. This burning of the

---

* A fort of Andropogon, which Bomare calls *Barbon*.

favanas brings quite into the French part, lying lower than the Spanish territory in a direction favourable to the almost constant easterly wind, and at a considerable distance from the frontiers, a sort of fog, produced by the smoke.

The reader has seen, from the detail in which I have entered here, and a part of which I have purposely taken from the work of a Spanish creole of Saint-Domingo, to what a state of mediocrity and decay the Spanish colony is reduced; and that it would, strictly speaking, be null, were it not for the commerce in cattle with the French part of the island, which Don Antonio de Valverde goes so far as to call its only support. This commerce is an enormous loss to the French; but it is lessened by the necessity to which the Spaniards are reduced, through the unskillfulness of their government, which exposes them to every want, of seeking other provisions in the French part. Formerly they traded with the French part openly; but I shall hereafter on explain how they have been obliged to reduce this commerce, which was so advantageous at once to the mother country and the colony, by heightening the value of the merchandises of the former, and by re-imbursing a part of the money annually paid for cattle by the latter.

After having thus endeavoured to describe, under every point of view, the inhabitant of the Spanish part, it is natural to continue the description of the country he inhabits, as, besides, the relative and local circumstances will often inevitably lead us back to domestic scenes.

The limits of the two colonies were at last settled by the definitive treaty of the third of June, 1777, which brings the French part into narrower bounds than those before acknowledged. I think I have fully demonstrated this by the historical detail, an abridgment of which I looked upon it as indispensably necessary to place at the head of this volume, to the end that the reader might be the better convinced, in reading the treaty, that it is not founded on the principles of strict justice.

BAHORUCO AND ITS VICINITY.

The westernmost point of the Spanish frontiers, on the southern coast or narrow, is the mouth of the river *des Pedernales* (Flint river), called by the French *rivière des Anses-à-Pitre*. To the east of this river, which often disappears towards its source, lie the elevated mountains of Bahoruco or Maniel. These do not belong to Cibao, since they run in a direction nearly north and south, towards the Salt-pond and Brackish-pond, where they join the prolongations of chains which run from Cibao towards Mirebalais. The mountains of Bahoruco are extremely fertile; they form, by their prolongation to the sea on the south side, a point, which, if continued on, would come out very near the easternmost point of the little island of Beate.

Valverde tells us, on the subject of these mountains, the temperature of which he highly extols, that when

Don Manuel d'Azlor, prefident of Saint-Domingo (fince viceroy of Navarre), was one time in them, on the purfuit of the fugitive negroes, he had tents erected for his encampments during the night, and covered them with the leaves of the cabbages cultivated by the negroes.

This fituation, where every thing feems to befpeak mines of gold, and where gold-fand is feen in the water, has, for eighty years paft, been the place of refuge of the fugitive Spanifh and French negroes, who have, fometimes in their incurfions, committed depredations on the French part lying in their neighbourhood. In fpite of repeated attacks, in which they been routed and difperfed, in fpite of a warrant of the king of Spain of the 21ft of October, 1764, authorifing the Spanifh prefident to propofe to the fugitive negroes of that nation, to affemble at appointed places, and form themfelves into hamlets, where they fhould be confidered as freed-people, they have ever preferred this wandering life; and the nature of the mountains where they form their holds, together with the fcanty population of the Spanifh part, have as yet enabled them to defy their purfuers.

I fhall fpeak of thefe brigands, in my defcription of the French parifhes, which have been the theatre of their horrid devaftations, and fhall content myfelf at prefent with obferving, that, ever fince the year 1785, they have ceafed their incurfions, and that they have adhered to the promife they made at that time to Mr. de Bellecombe, the governor-general, not to interrupt in future, the peace of the French territory. It is, however, very certain, that no inhabitants care to settle in their neighbourhood, and, consequently, that the frontier, in this part, is uninhabited. Bahoruco, properly so called, has no other inhabitants than these fugitives.

Along the coast, lying to the west of these mountains, are several points and coves. The word *Anses-à-Pitre*, is the name common to all that part of the coast, from *Pointe-des-Pieges*, which is situated at a league west of the mouth of the river Pedernales, and is consequently on the French territory, to False-Cape, forming an extent of about twelve leagues.

Ships of the greatest burden may anchor at half a league distance, opposite the mouth of the river of the *Anses-à-Pitre*, and others still nearer. This river, the water of which is some of the best in the island, is pretty deep and broad, but not navigable. It rises in the northern part of the mountains of Bahoruco. In war time the English ships of the line and privateers are stationed for a long time together opposite this part of the island. Sometimes they erect barracks on the level part on the east side of the river, where they remain for months at a time. The oxen, the wild hogs, and the game, furnish them with wholesome food in abundance. In this situation they are sheltered by the False-Cape, and the Beate; and as they plant sentinels in positions that command a view at a great distance, they carry on their warfare very commodiously, having plenty of subsistence, wood and water, and an excellent point of observation.

In going from the mouth of this river towards the Spanish part, we meet with the river and cove of Trou-Jacob, and then the point of the same name. This point, like those which precede it in the Anses-a-Pitre, is surrounded by a deep ragged rock of about four hundred fathoms wide. But, at the point, or cliff of Trou-Jacob, begins a bold rocky beach, which continues on to Cape-Rouge. Between this and point *Voutes-d'en-bas*, or the Needles, is Rousselle cove.

After the point called the Needles, or *Voutes-d'en-bas*, there is a delightful cove, called *l'Anse-des-Aigles*, (Eagle-cove), or simply *Anse-sans-Fond*, (Bottomless-cove), where it is said that ships may approach near enough to be fastened on shore. There is, besides, another anchoring place, called *l'Anse-Thomas*, after Point-Chimahe, which shelters *l'Anse-des-Aigles* or *Sans-Fond*, towards the south. After l'Anse-Thomas follows False-Cape, which some maps erroneously confound with Point-des-Aiguilles.

From False-Cape, where the coast begins to bear towards the east, to point Bahoruco, one may pass in the channel between Beate and the main island, with a bottom of from six to nine fathoms, leaving the little islands of Beate to the south; but this depth is reduced to less than three fathoms, on the shallow, running from Beate towards the north.

From False-Cape to Cape-Bahoruco, the coast is of ragged rock, and very bold and high; from ninety-five to an hundred and eighty feet above the surface of the sea. It has some coves, however; as l'Anse-à-Burgaux, the Trou-du-guet, l'Anse-des-Truyes,

Vol. I.   L

where the coast runs towards the south; and besides, l'Anse-des-Vases, preceding Point-Bahoruco, called also Point or Cape Beate, and Cape-à-Foux. This last is the southernmost point of Saint-Domingo, and that which ends the rocky coast beginning at Trou-Jacob.

That the reader may not misconceive me when I speak of a bold rocky beach, and these anses or coves, I must observe, by way of explanation, that the coves are formed by portions of sand and mould, lying between the sea mark and the rocky beach, and that the latter forms a kind of barrier to them.

In speaking of the plains of the Spanish part, I have said, that, at the foot of the mountains of Bahoruco, beginning at Point Beate, there are two plains, one to the west, of about eighty leagues square, and the other to the east, of about sixty leagues square. The eighty leagues of the first of these plains, which is bounded to the west by the French parish of the Cayes of Jacmel, are fit for any kind of cultivation, without mentioning the neighbouring mountainous parts, where coffee would succeed very well. Upon a moderate computation, this valuable tract would be sufficient for a hundred and fifty sugar manufactures, allowing to each better than three hundred *quarreaux**, capable of employing thirty thousand negroes; and in this number of manufactures, which cannot be thought exaggerated, nearly half would not be more than four or five

---

* A French measure of St. Domingo, containing one hundred paces, of three feet and a half square, or 122,500 superficial feet.

leagues from the sea. It is easy to conceive how favourable this plain would be to the cultivation of the other colonial productions, as indigo, cotton, and tobacco.

According to this calculation, there might be in the other plain, lying to the east, more than a hundred sugar manufactures, which would employ twenty thousand negroes. The settling of these two plains would change the fugitive slaves, of whom I have before spoken, into civilized people.

On the east of the mountains of Bahoruco, runs the river Nayauco; and beyond it Cape Mongon, 3,000 fathoms from Point-Bahoruco. From Cape Mongon, following the coast, which runs almost north, we come to the little port, called by the Spaniards *Petit-Trou*, a term evidently French, as are many of those I have already had occasion to mention, in describing the part from the river Pedernales; and this alone is sufficient to prove that the French have been settled in that quarter.

The *Petit-Trou* is not deep, and is, besides, very shelvy; but as this canton abounds in wild fowl, it frequently attracts the hunters who call themselves *mountaineers*, from the name of a sort of wild oxen that they hunt, or *oreillards*, because these oxen have not their ears cut, like the *domestic* and *gentle* ones. Little barks come to this place from Santo-Domingo, to fetch the meat and lard derived from the chace. The French also hunt at Petit-Trou, as, from its unoccupied state, they meet with success without being looked upon as intruders. This part might be made use of for the purposes of conveying out the wood and other productions that might be cultivated in its vicinity.

NEYBE.

On the north of the Petit-Trou, towards the mouth of the river Neybe, we find the bay of Neybe, situated between the mountains of Bahoruco and those of Martin Gracia. This bay is also called, Bay of Julienne. Large boats may anchor here; but if the different mouths of this river, the greatest part of which vary annually, were formed into one or two (which would not be very difficult), it would be navigable for many leagues up the country, for vessels which are now obliged to remain in the bay. And there would be another advantage arising from this; barges, or flat-bottomed boats might get much higher than they now do. The river *Neybe*, or *Neiva*, a word which, in Spanish, signifies *white*, rises in the interior mountains of the island, near those of Cibao. It runs in a westerly direction for several leagues; but, when become large it turns towards the south, and, passing through the valley that takes its name, after having received many other rivers, large and small, in its course, falls into the sea at seven different places.

The valley, or plain of Neybe, contains about eighty square leagues. The river of its name, and some mountainous parts separate it on the east, from the plains of Azua, and Vani or Bani; and to the west, it is bounded by the river of Dames, and the Spanish-

Pond, called also *Pond of Xaragua*, and *Pond of Henriquille*, designated in the French maps by the word *Riquille*. We may observe here, that this name *Henriquille* or *Little Henri*, comes from the Cacique Henri, who found an asylum on the little island situated in the middle of it, during what the Spaniards call his rebellion. We even see at some distance from here, and at the extremity of the French part, leading towards the sea, the remains of an ancient intrenchment in the form of a half-moon, joining on to a mountain at each end, and fortified within with two rows of little pits, which touch each other, and which served, without doubt, to protect the intrenchment. The neighbouring caverns are filled with heaps of human bones.

The plain of Neybe is extremely fertile, and well adapted to commerce, on account of the largeness of its river. The chace also is there both useful and agreeable. The birds multiply amazingly fast. This seems to be the chosen spot of the flamingos and pheasants, which keep in flocks, and are found in every part of the plain, particularly in the watry places. Here it is also that are found the royal or crowned peacocks (a mixture of the white and coloured peacock), which are highly esteemed, because they have a more delicate flavour than the common peacocks, and because the beauty of their brilliant plumage surpasses that of the peacocks in Europe.

This plain would be a commodious and eligible situation for more than a hundred and fifty sugar manufactures, or plantations, an opening to which would be rendered easy by the means of this great river, that has long been the boundary of the French possessions, and that they have ever desired to see adopted as one of their limits, which would, in some measure, open to their industry a second French colony to found, and a field of rich productions. But in this wish they have, as yet, been disappointed, and this soil, so rich, where nature can discover its fertility only by the leaves and the size of the trees, is little better than a desart.

There is, however, at about nine leagues from the river Neybe, a little town, which is also called Neybe, containing near about two hundred houses, and capable of turning out three hundred men fit to bear arms. The land between this town and the river is a salt-marsh. It is reckoned fifteen leagues from hence to the town of Azua, and the road between, which crosses the Neybe, is partly in the barren mountains, which stretch along to within two leagues of Azua.

From the little town of Neybe, to the point where the line of demarcation cuts Brackish-pond, it is about sixteen leagues. This space is travelled in keeping along on either side of Henriquille, one end of which is but a little way from the town of Neybe. The path on the south-west side of the Henriquille runs along the foot of a mountain at a very little distance from the edge of the pond. After having passed by the Henriquille some distance, the traveller comes to the Spanish guard, at a place called the Bottom *(el Fundo)*, and near which is the house of the commandant of this frontier. Here also is the Brackish-pond, which cuts asunder the boundary line. The path is again on either side of this pond, called by some *Lagune d'Azuey*, but on the right side it is impassable on horseback, while on the other side it is tolerably good. The latter is the longest.

This road, by the ponds, and through the town of Neybe, Azua, Bani, &c. is the line of communication between Port-au-Prince and the town of Santo-Domingo. From one of these towns to the other, by the road here described, it is ninety-six leagues; for they reckon it fourteen from the guard at *el Fundo* to Port-au-Prince. To shorten this way a little, and particularly to render it less disagreeable, one may cross the Brackish-pond in a canoe.

It is necessary to observe, that the Spaniards did not begin much before the year 1730, to form settlements to the west of the Neybe, at which time the French had some little settlements even in that part of the island.

In the territory of Neybe, there is a sort of plaister, and of talc also, which latter is found in some other places. There is, too, a little mount of sea-salt in fossil, much prized by the Spaniards for domestic uses. The natural reproduction of this fossil is so rapid, that a pretty large hollow is absolutely filled up again in the course of a year.

AZUA.

Having crossed the river Neybe, we come to the territory of Azua, which is bounded to the north-west by the territory of St. John of Maguana, to the west by that of Neybe, to the south by the sea, to the east by Bani, and to the north by mountainous lands, which stretch in their prolongation behind the territory of Bani.

These mountains belong to the third chain, which, beginning at Cibao, runs in a south-west direction along the left bank of the Little Yaqui, and on its eastern side slopes down from the mouth of the Nisao to Neybe. From this chain, one of the most extensive as well as most elevated, run a great number of other chains, stretching towards the south, and leaving between them and the sea the plains of Azua and Bani, with intervals of various width. The secondary chains, the principal of which are, first, the two which form the valley of Azua in this part, and which ends near the town; second, those which run along the right bank of the Ocoa, and end at the little *Anse-d'Ocoa*; third, those which are terminated in the flat of la Croix; and fourth, those which end at the Cerre (little hill) of the beacon of Bani, separate the rivers Tavora, Bia, Sipicepy, Ocoa, Bani, and Pailla (mention of each of which is made in the order here followed), in their direction from west to east, with a great number of intermediate brooks, and other water courses.

There is a road running across the territory of Azua, which begins at the end of the territory of St. John of Maguana, at the crossing-place of the river Little Yaqui, which takes its rise at Cibao, near that of Grand Yaqui. On the left bank of this river runs the chain of mountains juſt mentioned, and cuts the road in the manner I am now going to deſcribe.

The road croſſes the Little Yaqui (which is always pretty deep) very near where it falls into the Neybe, and then continues on, on the level, a quarter of a league to the hatte of *Bitta al Pendo.* A league further on it comes to the hatte of the Salt river (Rio-Salao), and at a good quarter of a league thence it croſſes this little river *Salao,* which falls into the Neybe at a very little diſtance from the ſame place. From here to Biahama, where there is always water, it is reckoned more than a league. Between the rivers Salao and Biahama, but neareſt the latter, the road croſſes a ravin, or hollow made by the partial current of the water, which runs on one ſide of a *cerre* that is bounded on the other by the river Biahama. Here the road aſcends the *cerre,* and afterwards deſcends it towards the Biahama; but a little before it arrives at this river, it paſſes the hatte of the ſame name. The Biahama is then croſſed near its confluence with the Neybe. So that the road here deſcribed runs along the Neybe from the croſſing place of the Little Yaqui.

After croſſing the river Biahama, the road aſcends, and afterwards deſcends towards the ravin called the Mole which lies at full three quarters of a league from the Biahama. Here the road turns off from the Neybe, which in its courſe often divides itſelf into many branches. From the ravin of the Mole the road aſcends again half a league to the ſummit of the Paſſage *(el Puerto),* a prolongation of the chain running from

Cibao along the left bank of the Little Yaqui. The Paſſage is ſcarcely a league and a half from the river Biahama. Here the road goes down the mountain, and, after advancing about eighteen hundred fathoms, comes to the river *Sangoſto*. This river the traveller is obliged to paſs and repaſs ſeveral times in the diſtance of half a league, ſometimes advancing on one bank and ſometimes on the other, till he arrives at the confluence of the *Sangoſto* and the *Tavora*. After this, the road turns a little towards the right, and follows the courſe of the Tavora for nearly two leagues, till it comes to the hatte bearing its name, which is three long leagues from the ſummit of the mountain of the Paſſage.

The torrent of Tavora, which is pretty confiderable, and extraordinarily rapid, runs directly towards the ſea. Its bed is ſeventy-two fathoms wide in many places, and its banks are from twelve to fifteen feet almoſt perpendicular. There is never any water ſeen here, except in rainy or ſtormy weather; but there are ſeveral little ſprings above the hatte of Tavora, which, uniting at different points lower down, form watering-places for the cattle. The road croſſes ſeveral branches of the torrent which are dry and covered with ſtones. The hatte of Tavora is on the right bank of the torrent, and at the point where the great road, we are now following, meets the road leading to Port-au-Prince. From the Biahama to the Tavora, the road is called *caſcaal*, a name given by the Spaniards to all roads that are, like this, ſtony and difficult to paſs.

A league and a quarter from the hatte of Tavora, the road quits the bed of the torrent, and nearly another league and a quarter comes to the road which goes to the bay of Neybe. After advancing another half league it meets with the river Houra, a bed without water, from whence to the town of Azua it is but a good half league. I shall return to this town by and by.

Directly after having passed through Azua, the road comes to the little river Bya or Via, and two leagues further on, it crosses a road of communication between certain hattes. About half way between these cross-roads and the river Bya, there is on the right of the road a pretty high *cerre*, which extends to the sea. A league from this, after passing two ravins, it arrives at the river Sipicepy, at half a league from which begins the savana of the same name. This savana may be about a quarter of a league long, and three hundred fathoms wide, of nearly an oval figure. At the end of the savana, the road enters into woods of palm-trees, called the *palm-trees of Ocoa*, which continue for the space of three leagues, to the river of the same name.

A short half league from the savana of Sipicepy, the road comes to the sea-side, and follows the beach (which is of sand and a sort of slate-stone) for full a league and a half, when it crosses the little savana of Ocoa, which joins up nearly to the sea. All the interval where the road runs along the beach is a steep ridge of fifteen or twenty feet high, which has between it and the sea only a narrow passage of about eight or ten feet wide; and, as the road here is covered with large slate-stones, it is excessively incommodious for travelling. From the top of the steep begins a gentle slope, which is the side of a secondary chain of the mountains of Cibao.

At a quarter of a league from the little savana of Ocoa, is the fork formed by the great road and a cross road leading to the anchoring-place of the Spanish vessels in the bay of Ocoa, which is nine hundred fathoms from the road. A little further on, near the road-side, are the ruins of the old sugar plantation, Zuazo, of which I shall speak hereafter. Half a league from this is the crossing-place of the river Ocoa, to arrive at which the road turns off from the side of the bay, and winds round the mountain at the foot of which this river runs. This mountain ends the secondary chain coming from Cibao, just before mentioned.

Here ends the territory of Azua, concerning which I have many particulars to treat of, before I conduct the reader to that of Bani.

After doubling the eastern point of the bay of Neybe, we come to the decayed port of the old town of Azua, founded in 1504, by the Adelantado, Don Diego Columbus. He had given it the sur-name of Compostella, in honour of Gallego, commander of the order of St. Jago de Compostella, who had a habitation in the neighbourhood; but this name has worn away with time, and has been succeeded by that of Azua, the same that it bore when in possession of the Indians.

This old port which is exactly of the same nature with the bay of Neybe, was formerly of use in transporting the excellent sugars of the plain of Azua, where the canes produce six years running, without wanting to be renewed. These sugars, as we are assured by the historians of that time, and by Oviedo and Herrera in particular, were shipped on board of vessels anchored at Ocoa and Santo-Domingo.

The plain of Azua begins in the west at the river Neybe, and continues on eastward to the Anse-de-la Chandière, It contains about one hundred and fifty square leagues. The canton of Azua is also called Via. This canton boasts of having had among its inhabitants Cortez, the conqueror of Mexico, who was town-clerk to the municipality of Azua. Besides the river from which it takes its name, this territory contains several others; that of the Muses, of Tavora, of Mijo; and besides, that of Yaqui, which separates it from the territory of St. John of Maguana, and which must not be confounded with the river called the Grand-Yaqui, as this latter runs in the northern part of the island, and falls into the sea at Monte-Christo.

All these rivers were at once so many causes of fertility, and so many means of transporting, either to the port of Azua or the bay of Ocoa, according to the situation of the habitations, immense quantities of sugar, cassia of the best quality, and the most valuable wood.

Every production of the canton of Azua, excels by its quality and exquisite taste. Formerly there were sugar-canes here nineteen feet high. Some persons pretend, however, that the land in the northern and eastern parts of it, is far from being equal to that in the south and south-west. This fertile canton furnishes, the whole year round, great abundance of the finest oranges, and so sweet and luscious, as not to leave the least tartness upon the palate.

Azua contains also several gold mines, which were formerly worked, but which are now absolutely abandoned. Since the tremendous earthquake of the 18th of October, 1751, which began at three o'clock in the afternoon, there have been discovered, in the mountains of *Viajama*, mineral waters bubbling up in many places; and the nature of these waters leads to the supposition, that the mountain from whence they spring contains great quantities of sulphurous matter. Azua abounds in talc also.

The mountains of this canton are covered with fustick-wood, which makes a dye of a fine yellow. It is easy to work also, and takes an excellent polish.

This territory enjoys an advantage which is truly invaluable; that of preserving a breed of horses, which has not degenerated worth a speaking of, from the much esteemed breed of Spain. At the discovery of America, it was found that this hemisphere had no horses, and it is easy to conceive what an impression the sight of a man on horse-back must produce on the minds of the affrighted islanders. But this noble animal soon became familiar in the new world, and as useful to its inhabitants as to those of the old. Degeneration is a sentence that nature has passed on almost every thing transplanted to distant climates, and, in general, horses have loft much of their height in the West-Indies; perhaps, too, their conftitution may be enfeebled; but, with refpect to their qualities they have fuffered no degeneration, and thofe of Azua have preferved even all their corporeal advantages. It is remarked only, that their coat is not of fuch various colours as in Spain; and this is attributed to the little care that is taken in mixing the breed to mix the colours at the fame time,

We muft obferve here, that there are three kinds of Spanifh horfes at Saint-Domingo. The firft kind are full of fire, very flender and delicately made, and fit only for the faddle; thefe are kept for riding, or for ftallions. The fecond kind are not fo handfome, are of a middling ftoutnefs, but full of fpirit, and go well, and with eafe; thefe are very fit for carriages, or for thofe who are not the beft of horfemen, they make good and fafe faddle-horfes. The third kind are poor weakly animals; they are generally of a yellow-dun, or cream colour: their fight is very tender, and they are of fo little fervice, that their cheapnefs alone can induce any one to purchafe them. They cannot be put in a carriage of any kind, except it be for a trifling diftance, and even then, care muft be taken not to fatigue them. There is, befides, in the Spanifh part, a race of Friezland horfes brought from New-York and Philadelphia.

The Spanifh horfes are rather of an ungentle nature, very often ftartifh, and are almoft always alarmed at the approach of a man. It would be imprudent to go behind them without great care, or come near them without having been firſt ſeen at ſome little diſtance, for they are given to kick with uncommon ſpite; and this diſpoſition is perceivable even in thoſe which are a mixture of the Spaniſh and French breed. The manner in which theſe horſes are bred up, and which differs but little from the breeding of wild animals, muſt neceſſarily contribute a good deal to their viciouſneſs. The horſes of Caraca being yet more eſteemed than thoſe of Spaniſh St. Domingo, particularly as ſtallions, the latter colony ſometimes fetch them from the former, as alſo from St. Martha and Rio-de-la-Hache, in order to mend the breed.

Azua, which was pillaged by the French privateers, before the year 1543, had continued to fall ſo faſt from the flouriſhing ſtate at which I have obſerved it was arrived, that, in 1737, its population hardly amounted to five hundred ſouls. But the fatal ſtroke to it was the earthquake of 1751. It hurled down the houſes, and drove the ſea over the ſpot where the town ſtood; ſo that they were obliged to rebuild it on the oppoſite bank of the little river Bya, at a league and a quarter from the ſea, and a ſhort half league from two chains of mountains, which come from Cibao, and which form the valley along which runs the river Bya.

Azua is agreeably ſituated in an open plain, the poſition of which is extremely wholeſome. The town ſeems, ſince 1780, to be riſing from its wretchedneſs, without, however, being arrived at a ſtate that renders it worthy of much attention. In the centre of it is a large ſquare: the church is but lately finished. The inhabitants, who, in a great part, are descended from the colonists, which came from the Canaries, are industrious, tall, and well made.

The town of Azua lies twenty-four leagues west of the capital, it contains about three hundred houses, and more than three thousand inhabitants in the whole extent of the territory bearing its name. This territory might certainly have four hundred sugar plantations, and furnish employment for eighty thousand negroes. It finds five hundred men bearing arms, including a company of cavalry.

Azua had a coat of arms granted to it on the 6th of December, 1580, consisting of an escutcheon, azure, a star in chief, argent, waved, argent, and pointed, azure.

Between the port of the old town of Azua to the west, and the Pointe-des-Salines to the east, is the celebrated bay of Ocoa. In the eastern part of its entrance lies the port de la Chaudière, large, open, and deep enough to admit vessels of any burden.

The bay of Ocoa is eighteen leagues from the capital. Here it is that the river of the same name, of which I have already had occasion to speak, falls into the sea, at seven leagues from Nisao, and nine from the town of Azua. This river has an abundance of water, and its navigation is safe and easy. The shape of the bay of Ocoa, which many persons describe as being in the form of a horse-shoe, is actually that of an *omega*. The two capes, or points, that form the entrance of it, are about three quarters of a league from each other, widening as they approach the interior of the bay, till they form a circumference of three or four leagues. This bay is capable of containing the largest squadrons, and even the most numerous fleets; and the landing is so good, that the stoutest ships may approach near enough to fasten their bowsprits on the shore. The elevation of the coast on each side shelters the bay from the wind, renders the sea always calm, and makes it a most excellent anchoring-place. On the side where the river Ocoa falls into the bay, are the woods of palm-trees, mentioned above. This happy site, and particularly where we yet behold the ruins of a mill, orginally belonging to the licentiate Zuazo, seem to invite inhabitants. The sugar formerly made on this plantation, was both excellent and in great quantity. Two cart-loads of it paid, on the 15th of April, 1592, the ransom of the town of Azua, to Christopher Newport, an Englishman.

The bay of Ocoa was thought by the Spaniards to merit the name of Fine-Port *(Porto-Hermoso)*. The Spanish ships anchor in it. The beach of this bay is of sand; its environs are in a manner abandoned; there are some place, even, where there is nothing to be seen but dildoe-trees, and plants of that description. It is said that the air is not very wholesome in the neighbourhood of the bay.

BANI, OR VANI.

At the river Ocoa, which is crossed at the place I have already mentioned, begins the territory of Bani.

This canton is bounded to the weſt by that of Azua, to the eaſt by the Niſao, by the ſea to the ſouth, and by the mountains to the north.

What I have ſaid concerning the river Ocoa, relates only to its principal branch, which is always full of water. About a league from this branch, is the paſſage over the ſecond, or little branch. Between the two there are a great number of ſtill leſs branches, very ſtony, and full of dildoe-trees and other bruſh-wood. This interval is called the Savana of the *Boye*, and near the middle of it, about ſix hundred fathoms on the left of the high road, are the hattes of the ſame name. Between this ſavana and the ſea, not far from the mouth of the river Ocoa, is the *Cerre de More*.

After croſſing the little branch of the Ocoa, the road runs up the ſide of a pretty ſteep hill to a large flat, where there is a delightful ſavana, called *Savana-de-la Croix*. From this flat, which is very extenſive from north to ſouth, and which may be fourteen hundred fathoms from weſt to eaſt, the traveller has a proſpect of the fine bay of Ocoa, and the charming palm-tree wood, which ſeem intended as an ornament to each other, and which cannot fail of awakening ideas of grandeur and power; this ſcene receives an addition, too, from the wild and deſerted tracts in its neighbourhood, which ſerve it by way of foil, and the whole forms a contraſt that conveys a profitable leſſon to the reflecting mind.

The hattes of la Croix (or the Croſs), are on the left of the road, near the middle of the flat. Near the ſummit there is a wooden croſs on the right ſide of the road. It is evident that this religious symbol has given its name to the canton.

From the flat, the road comes down to a large and deep ravin, which is a league and a half from the little branch of the Ocoa. Directly afterwards it comes to the hattes of Deep-Stream *(Arrayo Hondo)*, and then to another very wide and deep ravin. After this begins the savana of *Mantenne*, and about a quarter of a league on, the hattes of the same name. From these hattes the road lies across a little wood, in the middle of which is a ravin. At half a quarter of a league beyond the wood, on the left hand side of the road, are the hattes of Don Pedro Martin, which are only a league and a quarter from those of Deep-Stream, and two leagues and a quarter from Bani. The road reaches this last place, after having crossed seven ravins, and turned to the left round the little mountain, called the Cerre-de-la-Vigie. This cerre, or little hill, situated in a direction west-quarter-south-west from the town, is the extremity of a great chain of mountains running from Cibao, and ending at a league and a half from the sea.

The town of Bani is about three hundred fathoms from the right bank of the river of the same name, three thousand and four hundred fathoms from the sea, and fourteen leagues from Santo-Domingo, the capital. Is site is a large and fine savana, which was formerly a hatte. This little town, which is not of very long standing, was formed by an assemblage of herdsmen in its neighbourhood. It has not more than eighty scattering houses. The whole parish is reckoned to contain eighteen hundred souls, great part of whom are *Ileignes* (come from the Canaries), or freed-people. The town of Bani is nearly in the middle of the plain, in its length from east to west. This plain may be reckoned at about eighty square leagues, and it is from it that the town takes its name.

At half a quarter of a league from the town of Bani or Vani, the road comes to the river of Bani. There is mostly water in this river; it has, however, been seen dry. After having crossed the river, the road passes through a wood of three quarers of a league, at the end of which it arrives at the river Pailla, which may be crossed dry-shod. The road now passes through a wood, then across the savana of Pailla, and along by some hattes; after this savana it goes through another wood, and from thence over another little savana. Here there is a road leading away to the right, to the habitation called the Habitation of Water *(de la Agua)*. Continuing on, the road comes to the savana of Catharine. This savana is something larger than that of Pailla, of a circular form, and more than seven hundred fathoms in diameter; it has also several hattes. At the end of this savana is a ravin, three quarters of a league distant from the Nisao, at which last river the road arrives, after having crossed three other little savanas, the two last of which have some hattes. Here ends the territory of Bani.

In examining the coast of this territory, we see that, from the Point, called the Pointe-des-Sabines, or the Point of Ocoa (and which ought to be called the *Pointe-la-Chaudiere*, according to a plan made by

Don Joseph de Solano, in 1776), the southern coast runs from east to west, as far as the river and point of Nisao. Between these latter little barks or launches may come to anchor, and particularly at the mouths of the Nisao, and further east, in the cove of Catharine, where the river Bani falls into the sea. It was by the means of this convenience that the Jesuits got an opening for the produce of their habitations and sugar manufactures, as does at present Don Nicholas Guridi, who holds part of the former possessions of those fathers.

The river Nisao rises in the mountains in the centre of the island, and falls into the sea on the western side of the point of the same name. The point itself is on the west of that of *Palonque (provision farm)*.

Oviedo speaks very advantageously of the river Nisao, on account of the rich produce of its banks, and the fine flocks and herds in its neighbourhood.

The territory of Bani abounds in excellent pasture for cattle of all kinds, the flesh of which acquires here a relish extraordinarily delicate, and produces a great quantity of tallow. The milk is rich and abundant. The horned cattle are accustomed to graze here, particularly in the long droughts caused by the almost continual impetuosity of the breezes, which do not give the clouds time to dissolve into rain. This is, indeed, the cause of great losses of cattle sometimes; but such is the happy nature of this situation, that, with a little rain, these losses are soon repaired. Some persons have, by the digging of wells, found a remedy for this evil; but every proprietor has not the means of applying so expensive a remedy.

The canton of Bani enjoys, with that of Azua, the advantage of a fine breed of Spanish horses.

There might be established in the plain of Bani more than a hundred and twenty sugar manufactures, furnishing employment for twenty-four thousand negroes.

CITY OF SANTO-DOMINGO, AND TERRITORY DEPENDENT THEREON.

At the Nisao, a river running from the mountains of Cibao, begins the plain and canton, or territory, of Santo-Domingo. It is bounded to the west by that of Bani, to the south by the sea, to the east by the river Ozama, and several others and to the north by the mountains. To make my description more intelligible, I must begin by speaking of the mountains.

One chain of them, which runs along the left side of the Nisao, in a direction nearly south, inclines on one side towards that river and on the other towards the Jayna, and, by the aid of little ridges that run from it crosswise, separates the rivers Nahayo, Senaqua, Nigua, and Itavo. This is the fourth chain of Cibao.

Another chain, coming also from Cibao, divides the river Jayna from that of Isabella, and leaves a very wide interval of plain between its extremity and the sea. This I shall call the fifth chain.

In the space between the Isabella and the Ozama, the land is pretty level, and this is one of the extremities of the plain of Santo-Domingo. But this land rises as it advances to the north, towards Cibao; for which reason it may be considered as a sixth chain of little extent, or rather as a cross ridge of the mountains of Cibao. The slopes of this ridge end towards the savanas of Monga, Cansamanseu, Prietta, and Souire, where they divide the rivers Isabella, Gribeplatta, Guiacuara, Icaco, Ozama, Cavoa, and Lymon.

There is yet another chain, called the Pardave, and which I call the seventh chain. It is very high, and runs in an eastern direction, dividing the river Iasse from that of Bermejo. Both these rivers fall into the Ozama on the left side, and thus bring a very considerable augmentation to that river.

Let us now follow the road of communication between Bani and Santo-Domingo.

At the end of the canton of Bani we cross the great branch of the Nisao, which is always pretty full of water. Between this branch and the little branch, an interval of half a league, we cross several inferior branches, which, like the little branch, are always dry, except in the time of the rains. All this space is rocky, and the road over it, of course, very bad.

After crossing the little branch of the Nisao the road leads through five little savanas; the first of them, which is the only one of any extent, contains some hattes, called *hattes of Niagua*. At a league from the little branch there is a ravin, from the side of which the road runs up a hill of considerable height, at the top of which we are agreeably surprised to find a beautiful savana, called the *great savana*.

This favana contains feveral hattes, fituated on the left hand fide of the road, and under the fhelter of a wood. When the road comes to the end of the flat it defcends the hill to another ravin, which runs down to Nahayo cove. From this ravin to the other it is rather better than a league. The road now winds round the cove of Nahayo, and, after croffing a ravin at about midway, comes to the river Nahayo, which falls into the fea at the north-eaft angle of the cove. This cove is about half a league wide at its opening, and is of nearly the fame depth.

The river Nahayo is never dry. After croffing it, the road turns round a little rocky cape, which feparates the cove of Nahayo from that of Senaqua, and then leads away to the right quite to the beach, which is here level and fandy. It follows the beach for about half a league before it comes to the river Senaqua, which is croffed, like the Nahayo, very near its mouth. The diftance between thefe two croffing places is no more than a league and a half.

From the Senaqua the road has an eafy afcent up the fide of a hill, which divides the Senaqua from the Nigua. On the top of this hill there is a flat, where, on the left hand fide of the road, at half a quarter of a league diftance from the Senaqua, is the hatte of the Mouth of the Nigua *(Boca de Nigua)*. After defcending from the hill, the road arrives at the river Nigua, which is divided in two branches at this place, neither of them ever dry. Between this river and the Senaqua the diftance is a little above three quarters of a league.

Vol. I.   O

Oviedo praises the Nigua, the utility of which he had been a witness of, on account of the great manufactures situated on the banks of it, and particularly those of sugar. Following the bed of this river it is nine or ten leagues in length. Its source is on a very high rock, which, says Valverde, seems to be the boundary of my habitation of Villegas. The water descends, adds he, in two branches, upon a great flat of sand, which entirely absorbs it, without leaving a trace of the manner of its disappearance. But, as the water, which runs from the sides of several mountains, and that of many streams and little rivers meet at this place, they form all together a pretty considerable body of water, which is, however, very much reduced in the dry season, when it receives only the stream of Galan, and some others of little consequence.

At about a league below the rock above described, there is a little island lying between the habitations of Boruga and Pedregal to the east, and that of Villegas to the west. Opposite to this island there is a rock from about the middle of which fall three spouts of water, separated from one another by a space of eight feet, or thereabouts. These spouts never cease, and each pours a volume of water of at least eight inches diameter.

It was on the land below this rock, that the first water mills for the making of sugar at Saint-Domingo were erected. Profiting from this rich present of nature, the Spaniards collected the water flowing from the three spouts into a spacious bason, which, in spite of time and neglect is yet entire, and goes by the name of *the reservoir*. The aqueducts, which led to two or three great mills, being now choaked up, the water takes its natural course through the reservoir called the *Reservoir of Nigua*, and falls into the sea, after having received the tribute of the streams of Villegas, Marceline, John-the-Cavalier, Velasquez, Yaman, and many others.

This description certainly relates to the same places that are mentioned by Charlevoix; vol. I. page 19, where he says, that the commander Ovando sent Pedro de Lumbreros, and Pedro de Mescia, to examine a lake on the top of a high mountain, from the foot of which comes the river Nisao.

Better than twenty years ago a little town, or parochial establishment, was formed between the Nisao and the Nigua. This settlement was called the town of the *Water-Mills*, on account of the circumstances just mentioned. It has neither church nor tithes; the cure being supported by the offerings, and a capitation on the negroes in its dependence. The population consists of about 2,500 persons; partly free people of colour.

This parish, which is, properly speaking, no more than an annex to Santo-Domingo, has what is called a chapel of ease, but which is, in reality, a sort of hermitage, where the priest alternately performs mass, giving notice every Sunday or holy-day, at which of the two places he intends to celebrate divine service the Sunday or holy-day following,

Fifty more sugar plantations might be established in this parish, and an equal number for the cultivation of indigo and cotton.

The mouth of the Nigua is about seven leagues from that of the Nisao. The space between them is generally flat, and was formerly all under cultivation. The land is so fertile here, that the immense forest of Mount Najayo, the whole of which has grown up since the land has remained uncultivated, continually furnishes the timber necessary for building in the capital and its environs, without suffering any perceptible diminution. According to the testimony of Valverde, the impenetrableness of this forest was the principal defence of the Spaniards, against the English invaders Penn and Venables, who found it prudent to abandon this expedition, and direct their attack against the island of Jamaica, where they were more successful*. All this portion of the island is absolutely uncultivated at this moment.

The river Nigua being crossed, the road ascends to the habitation called also *Nigua*. This habitation is placed on a commanding eminence at four leagues and a half from Santo-Domingo. Down the opposite side of this eminence the road runs pretty steep, and soon after crosses the little river Itavo, which is dry, except in the rainy seasons. On the left bank of the

---

* It is worth while to observe here, that Valverde has fallen into a gross error respecting *Venables*, who, he says, was killed in the attack on St. Domingo; when it is well known that Venables returned to England after the conquest of Jamaica, from whence he sailed on the 25th of June 1655; that both he and his associate in the expedition, were confined in the Tower, by the Lord Protector Cromwell, and that they were not released till deprived of their employments.

Itavo there is a hatte on each side of the road. After this the road comes to a ravin, on the left side of which is another hatte. From this ravin the road follows the beach of the cove of Jayna for near three quarters of a league, at the end of which it comes to the river Jayna. This river might be rendered navigable an advantage that might also be communicated to the rivers Nisao and Nigua.

The rivers Nigua and Jayna are not very far distant from each other; but as they advance from their springs they get further and further asunder, the former running westward from the latter. Between them lies an extensive and fertile plain, which was originally a most abundant source of riches to the colonists. The quantity of pure gold that was dug from its cavities, its sugar, cocoa, indigo, and other plantations, paid duties to a greater amount than those now paid by all the Spanish part of the island put together. The habitation on the banks of the Jayna, which is now of no kind of value, was formerly known by the name of Whale, instead of that of Cagnabola, it at present goes by. The former name had been given it on account of the cargo that the proprietor of it annually sent to Seville, being the surplus that he could not sell at the capital, and which was shipped in a vessel called the Whale. In the neighbourhood of Jayna, there is indigo become wild, which is at once a proof, that this useful plant formerly flourished in the canton, and that it might yet become the means of considerable profit.

The river Jayna is not fordable; it is crossed in canoes and skins, at two hundred and fifty fathoms from its mouth, and the animals are obliged to swim across it.

Towards the source of this river were the celebrated gold mines of St. Christopher, discovered by Francisco de Garaz and Miguel Diaz, in the neigbourhood of which Columbus erected the fort, called the fort St. Christopher. Not far from these mines, we find the parish of St. Rose, or of Jayna, which has in its dependancy the ancient rich population of Bonnaventure, now reduced to a handful of individuals, whose employment is the breeding of cattle, or the washing of gold-sand. The establishments in the plain of St. Rose, and those on the banks of the Jayna ought to be looked upon as depending on the city of St. Domingo. They are reckoned to contain, at least, two thousand persons, for the most part people of colour, free and slaves.

On the banks of the Jayna, in the habitation of Gamboa and Guayabal, there is a very rich silver mine, which they had begun to work, but which was given up in consequence of eighteen negroes having been killed by a falling in of the earth. There is another mine of the same metal between the hattes of la Croix and those of St. Michael.

After crossing the Jayna, the road goes by the battery of the flat, formed by a tongue of land of which I am going to speak, and which is at three leagues distance from Santo-Domingo. A league further on, we come to some settlements under cultivation; from hence the road follows the water side as far as fort St. Jerome, which is but little more than a quarter of a league from Santo-Domingo. The road now winds a little to the left, and, after having crossed the road which leads to Cotuy without going through the city, enters the capital on the north-west side.

The coast corresponding to the country along which this road runs, forms an extent of about twelve leagues from Nisao to Santo-Domingo. From the point of Nisao, which advances about four leagues southward, the shore turns all at once to the north-east, and continues in that direction as far as the mouth of the Jayna. It was here that Penn and Venables landed in 1655. This disembarkation, made under sail, proves at once the accessibility of the coast, and its defenceless state, though so near to the capital of the colony.

About half way between the Nisao and Santo-Domingo, is the little settlement of Jayna, if we may give that name to two or three new habitations. This settlement is situated at the eastern extremity of a cove, on the left hand side of the river Jayna, the name of which it takes, and not far from its mouth. The Jayna, if we set out from its mouth, goes northward for about three hundred and fifty fathoms, then east-quarter-north-east for six hundred fathoms, and after that takes again its direction to the north. This sort of elbow, formed at three hundred and fifty fathoms from the mouth, leaves, between itself and the sea, an eminence that commands all the cove of Jayna. This cove is of sand, and is more than eighteen hundred fathoms in width.

As no difembarkation can be effected on the coaft between Fort St. Jerome and the river Jayna, the pofition of this eminence, on which there is a flat, is extremely advantageous, and accordingly it is fortified with the battery above fpoken of. The land here is abundantly fertile, and the fite delightful and wholefome. There is great plenty of water in its neighbourhood; for at about forty fathoms from the mouth of the Jayna, the banks begin to be pretty high, and the height encreafes even to fixty feet. The Jayna is not every where fordable, and I again obferve, that the bank on the right fide of it is covered with an impenetrable wood.

The coaft lying between Jayna and Santo-Domingo is of rock almoft perpendicular, in general from fix to fifteen feet high. Oppofite this coaft there are a great number of fhoals, each of about forty fathoms wide.

The Fort of St. Jerome, is on the fea-fide, and near the road. It is, properly fpeaking, no more than a fquare redoubt in mafonry: but it is conftructed with art. It is a fortified fquare, the fide of which is, twenty-five fathoms, and its rampart has an elevation of nearly twenty feet, with a foffe in proportion. It is capable of containing a hundred and fifty men, with all neceffary provifions and warlike ftores; fo that it could not be taken without a regular attack, and a breach being firft effected; and an intelligent and brave commandant might, in any cafe, make an honourable refiftance.

We are now arrived at the port of the capital. This port is formed by the confluence of the rivers Ifabella and Ozama, which by their junction form a Y. Each of thefe rivers receives in its courfe the tribute of many others of lefs confequence, and of a very great number of ftreams and ravins, brooks and fprings. Both of them take their rife in the mountains lying to the north-weft of the city, and meet at a league above it. They form before the city an anchoring place for veffels of any burden, even thofe of the line. The Ozama is, before Santo-Domingo, as wide as the Charante, at Rochford, and its banks are twenty feet perpendicular; this height is, however, reduced to four feet to the north of the city. This river, during a league, runs twenty-four feet deep, upon a bottom of mud, or of foft fand.

The port of Santo-Domingo is magnificent in every refpect; a real natural bafon, with a great number of careenings for the veffels that can get at them; for at the mouth, which takes the name of the Ozama alone, there is a rock, which prevents the entrance of veffels drawing more than eighteen or twenty feet of water. Oviedo fays, he faw the fhip the Imperial, of more than four hundred tons, pafs this rock, which, it is afferted, might be removed without great difficulty. I fhould add, that this bar does not rife, as it was founded in 1681, by Mr. de Maintenon, commander of a French frigate, who then found on it no more than feventeen feet of water.

One may judge of the enormous volume of water that thefe two rivers bear to the fea, by the red caft that they give it in the time of the floods, and which is perceiveable as far as the eye can diftinguifh. Nor do they at thefe times overflow their banks; except in very extraordinary inundations, fuch as that of the month of May, 1751. The Ozama is navigable for nine or ten leagues from north to fouth. Upon its banks are feveral fugar-manufactures, tile-kilns, and provifion farms, of all which I fhall hereafter fpeak.

The road before the mouth of the Ozama is very indifferent, and lies expofed from weft-fouth-weft to eaft. It is impoffible to anchor in it in the time of the fouths; and the norths drive the veffels from their moorings out into the fea, which here runs extremely high.

The city of Santo-Domingo was originally founded on the left bank of the Ozama, in 1494, by *Bartholomew Columbus*, who gave it the name of *New Ifabella*, and when, or how this name was changed for that of Santo-Domingo, is totally unknown; unlefs we admit what I have already given as the affertion of fome authors, that Chriftopher Columbus gave it the name of his father. The inhabitants of the town of Ifabella, (founded by Chriftopher Columbus, in 1493, on the north coaft of Saint-Domingo, in honour of the queen of Spain), removed to New Ifabella, in 1496. It is affirmed that they were attracted there by an Indian, who was princefs of the country lying on the weftern fide of the Ozama, and who was fallen in love with a Spanifh deferter of St. Iago-de-la-Vega, named Miguel Diaz, who, after having committed a murder, fled into the country yet under her command. It is even pretended that she married him, and that she was baptized under the name of *Catharine*.

Don Diego Columbus, son of Christopher, afterwards built on the west of the river, a house for his own accommodation. Its walls are very stout, according to the fashion of that time, and it was surrounded with an enclosure to defend it from the enterprizes of the Indians. This circumstance, so trifling in itself, was one of those, whence the enemies of Diego took occasion to impute to him the design of making himself the sovereign of the island.

The capital continued on the east side, till the month of July, 1502, when a hurricane destroyed almost all its buildings, which were generally of wood, and covered with thatch. This event induced the governor, Don Nicholas Ovando, a grand commander of the order of Alcantara, to change this situation, in 1504, for that of the western bank of the Ozama; though the former enjoys a pure air, and an abundant spring of wholesome water, while the latter is destitute of both these advantages; the air being very indifferent, and there being a want of water, because that of the Ozama is brackish at many leagues from its mouth. To remedy this last inconvenience, Ovando undertook to conduct the river Jayna to a great reservoir in the principal square of the city, which reservoir is yet to be seen; but he had not time to accomplish his object. At this time there was a ferry for the inhabitants to fetch their water from the spring of the old town; but this laborious means of obtaining so necessary an article, led them to the construction of cisterns, a practice that has ever since continued in use, though by no means favourable to health. We yet see the traces of the fortifications of the old town. At the time it was abandoned the inhabitants were very much tormented by the ants.

The new city was soon built, and that, too, with a grandeur of design not unworthy of the first metropolis of the new world. Ovando constructed the fort which is on the south-west angle, and which is called the *Chateau*, or the *Force*; and at the same time he built a magnificent house for himself. Many individuals built whole streets upon speculation. The plan of the city is a trapezium of about five hundred and forty fathoms on the east side, along the Ozama, near five hundred fathoms on the south side bordering on the sea, and of about eighteen hundred fathoms in circuit.

To the west, and to the north of the city, the land is rough and rocky for about half a league, but after that it becomes good, and the country delightful. Towards the sea the site of the city lies very high, which forms an insurmountable dyke against the fury of the waves; and, to defend it against enemies of another sort, it is surrounded with a rampart, begun during the presidency of Don Alonzo de Fuenmayor, archbishop of the island. This rampart is eight feet in diameter, and about ten feet high. The revetement is of hewed stone, and the scarp is cut in the rock; but without any terrass. There are yet some marks of a ditch, but none of a covert way, or of glacis. The bastions are flat, and very small, according to the fyftem of fortification in ufe in the beginning of the fixteenth century. Thofe of the four angles are larger, and are retrenched in the gorge. As to outworks, there are now to be feen only two ravelins, intended to cover the gates leading towards the country, and fome few cavaliers of an irregular figure, on the fide towards the fea.

There is a great deal of ordinance at Santo-Domingo, particularly of caft ordinance. The height of the Ileignes, which runs parellel to the rampart on the north-weft of the city, commands it entirely; and its crown is not more than two hundred and fifty fathoms from the ditch. This circumftance alone is fufficient to prove, that the place is not calculated for a long defence. Befides, a rampart with baftions fo fmall, that a fingle bomb might difmount the whole of its cannon, and at the fame time fo ill-contrived, that the line of defence cuts the face inftead of the flank, and is hardly worthy the name of fortification.

The ftreets of the city are fpacious, and ftraight as a line, which gives it a pleafing appearance. Ten of thefe ftreets run from north to fouth, and ten others from eaft to weft. The buildings are in the tafte of the ancient towns of Spain and Italy. The greateft part of the houfes firft built, are of a fort of marble found in the neighbourhood, and thofe of a more recent conftruction are of *tapia*, a fort of *pife*. This kind of building is ufually performed thus: a cafe is made of planks, between pillars in mafonry: this cafe is filled by degrees with a reddifh clay, which is rammed down as it is thrown in, till fuch time as it forms a solid, or sort of wall, between the pillars. The clay, thus pressed together, acquires an amazing hardness, and the walls are sometimes so solid and strong, that the pillars of masonry are useless.

The houses of Santo-Domingo are tolerably handsome, in a simple stile, and nearly uniform. A considerable part of these, built within these fifteen years, are of wood, covered with the leaves, or *taches*, of palm-trees. The roofs are generally plat-formed; being calculated so as to conduct the rain-water to the cisterns. The apartments are sometimes hung with tapestry, or stuff, but this goes no higher than about half-way to the ceiling; an imitation, it is said, of the tapestry in Spain.

The climate of the capital is, happily, very temperate. The nights of those months which answer to the winter in Europe, are even found to be cold.

This city was formerly justly celebrated. The conquerors of the rest of Spanish America, here formed their projects, and found the means of putting them in execution; and Gonzalo Fernandez Oviedo, in speaking of it to the emperor Charles V. told him, that there was not a town in Spain worthy of being preferred to it, either for the land in its neighbourhood, the pleasantness of its situation, the beauty of its streets and squares, or the amenity of its environs; and that his imperial majesty often resided in palaces less spacious, commodious, and rich, than many of the edifices of Santo-Domingo. But, we shall see in the sequel, it has fallen prodigiously from this splendor.

Santo-Domingo is the place of residence of the president, who is the chief of the colony, as well in civil as military affairs; and who takes his title of president from the place he fills in the royal court, which was established in this city in 1511, and the first president of which was Louis de Figueroa, an hieronite monk. This title has not, therefore, always been that of the chiefs of the Spanish part: before the epoch above mentioned, they were called governors general; and since, they have very often joined to the quality of president, that of governor, and captain-general. This plurality of titles has been borne by two bishops of the colony, and by one of its arch-bishops.

The royal court is, with the Spaniards, a superior tribunal, from which their lies no appeal. Its members, in ordinary, are a regent, or dean, and six oydors (auditors or counsellors), who, when on the bench, wear a robe and band, and have their hair in drop curls; which is also the dress of the barristers and attorneys. The attorney-general, is callen the Fiscal. The jurisdiction of the royal court of Santo-Domingo, comprehends the colony of Saint-Domingo, the island of Cuba, that of Porto-Rico, and that of Marguerite and Trinidad. The provinces of Maracaïbo, Cumana, and Spanish Guyana, were withdrawn from it in July, 1787. The suits in this court are extremely tedious and expensive. The dean receives annually six thousand dollars; and each counsellor, three thousand three hundred, as salaries. The royal court never gives costs of suit, unless judgment has been pronounced with unanimous consent. If there be one voice only for the losing party, the costs are compounded; because, it is supposed, that a party, who must be looked upon as less learned than a judge, may easily be deceived on a question of law, when there is a judge of his opinion. According to the rules of the Spanish jurisprudence, three judges are sufficient to pronounce sentence, even in criminal matters.

Notwithstanding the number of judges, superior and inferior, and notwithstanding the veneration that the people have for them, crimes are very common, and often go unpunished in the Spanish part of this island. The criminal code, is not, however, so severe as that of the French colonies. The most common punishments are the *preside* (hard labour in chains) and the *sep* (stocks). When there is no hangman for a public execution (for he is always a convict whose punishment has been remitted on condition of his performing this office), the criminal is shot by negroes, and these even are offenders who are already condemned to hard labour.

The royal court co-operates besides, with the president, in the administration of the affairs of the colony. Every president, as I have elsewhere observed, must chose an auditor (a counsellor of the court) to advise with on disputable matters, left to the judgment of the president, as governor and public administrator. He may, notwithstanding, neglect to follow the advice of this assistant; but then the responsibility falls on himself.

When the president dies, or when he is absent from the colony, the regent, or dean of the royal court, supplies his place in civil concerns. The members of this court, who are all lawyers from Spain, enjoy their places during pleasure only; and they are changed, sometimes, and sent to the different Spanish provinces in America. They enjoy the highest degree of respect and consideration at Santo-Domingo. The peoples' attention to them is so great that they stop to salute them, or their wives, when they pass along the street. They dispute precedence with the colonels, and acknowledge no one above them but the governor, as their president. They have *clients*, who call them their god-fathers, and who, on their account, enjoy the public favour. In the year 1781, there was a member of the council of Port-au-Prince, whom the consequences of a shipwreck had brought to Santo-Domingo, and who received the greatest attention from the members of the royal court, and every mark of esteem and honour.

The governor of this colony, though president of the royal court, has no voice in the decisions of suits; and accordingly, he never assists at deliberations touching causes between individuals. But of this I shall speak hereafter.

Santo-Domingo is also the principal see of an archbishoprick, founded in 1547, by pope Paul III. Pope Julius II. erected the kingdom of Xaragua into an archbishoprick, in 1511, having for suffragans a bishoprick at Larez-de-Guahaba; and another at the Conception-de-la-Vega; but this plan not being car-

Vol. I.   Q

ried into effect, he, in 1517, created a bishoprick at Santo-Domingo, and another at the Conception-de-la-Vega, both suffragans of the archbishoprick of Seville, and both which were united, in 1527, into one, that of Santo-Domingo. Garcia-de-Padilla, a Franciscan, and confessor of queen Leonora, wife of Don Manuel, king of Portugal, had been appointed bishop of Santo-Domingo, in 1512; but dying before his consecration, Alexander Gerardino, an Italian, grand almoner of the emperor Charles V. was the first who, as bishop of Santo-Domingo, performed the episcopal functions in that city. Alonzo de Fuenmayor, the fifth bishop, was promoted to the archbishoprick at the time of its creation, by Paul III. as already mentioned; and Santo-Domingo now rekons thirty-five archbishops, who have filled its see. The suffragans of this see at present are, the bishops of Cuba and Porto-Rico, and the abbey of Jamaica; which last title has been preserved by the convent of Dominicans in the capital. The archbishop of Santo-Domingo takes the title of *Primate of the Indies*: he enjoys a revenue of eight or ten thousand dollars a year, together with the highest honours and veneration. The people in general fall on their knees to receive his benediction, while those of a certain order pay him no more than the honour of a respectful inclination as he passes. It is also customary to kiss his ring; and the president himself does not always neglect this superstitious duty.

At the time of the erection of the bishops at Santo-Domingo, in 1511, the pope granted them tithes, and first fruits of *every thing*, except gold, silver, other metals, pearls, and precious stones, in which they were to have no share whatever. He gave them, besides, spiritual authority and jurisdiction, and all the rights and pre-eminences of the bishops of Castille, and which still belong to them, from law as well as custom.

There was, too, at the same epoch, a concordate between the king and these bishops. He gave them the tithes, on condition that they should pray for the kings of Spain, and *for all those who should lose their lives in making discoveries*. They were also to distribute the tithes to the clergy, to the church wardens, and the poor-houses. All the beneficies and dignities were declared to be in the gift of the king, with the proviso, that they should be bestowed on the Castillians, and not on Indians; that the persons promoted should be the offspring of a legitimate union, and that their appointment, if made in the island, in the name of the king, should be subject to a delay of eighteen months, in order to receive his ratification. The concordate expresses, besides, that none but capable persons, learned in the Latin tongue, should be nominated; that the ecclesiastics should have the tonsure, wear their hair round, a cassock, open or close, but descending to the heels, and neither red nor green, *nor of any other unseemly colour*; that two sons of the same father should not be ordained; that there should be no more holy-days kept, than those ordered by the church; and, finally, that the tithes should be taken in kind, and not in money.

The collegiate chapter created at Santo-Domingo, in 1512, had, at first, twenty-five members, divided into dignitaries, prebendaries, and under-prebendaries. The poverty of the island, afterwards, was the cause of the three dignitaries being suppressed; and, sometime after, two prebendaries, which were followed by the suppression of the three under-prebendaries; thus was the chapter reduced to seventeen persons. Finally, in lieu of cannonships, worth four or five thousand dollars, or more, the tithes and parochial duties did not amount to a decent subsistence; so that they were given up to the public treasury, from which the chapter is allowed a competent salary, and this salary has been augmented since about fifty years. Each prebendary receives eight hundred dollars, and each dignitary a thousand. Three hundred dollars of this is regarded as fixed revenue, and the remainder as aids. I have just said that the fixed revenue is paid by the king, who accepts, in lieu thereof, the tithes and first fruits, or novales, of the chapter. The tithes are collected after the rate of one-tenth on ordinary crops, and of one-seventh on fruits. With respect to productions which require manufacturing, such as sugar, indigo, &c. the ecclesiastical dues extend no further than a twentieth. About 1785, his majesty exempted the lands newly cleared, from all tithes whatever.

Santo-Domingo has a seminary also.

Among a number of public edifices that merit attention in this city, we may reckon the ruins of the house that Diego, son of Christopher Columbus, had begun, entirely of hewed stone. It was in the northern part of the city, on the side of the rampart running along oppofite the Ozama. The walls are yet remaining, and fome of the fculpture round the windows. The roof and ceilings are fallen in, the lower floor is become a pen for cattle; and a Latin infcription remaining over the portal, is now hidden by the hut of the herdfman.

The cathedral, built of the fame fort of ftone as the houfe of Diego Columbus, lies in the fouth-eaft. Oppofite its entrance is a fine fpacious oblong fquare, at the fouth-weft end of which is the town-houfe. The cathedral has a nave and two wings. It is in the Gothic ftile, but abundantly noble and magnificent; and merits admiration on account of the boldnefs of its vault, which, notwithftanding the earthquakes, the ravages of which are but too well known in its neighbourhood, has never, till within thefe fifteen or twenty years had a fingle flaw. This edifice, which was begun in 1512, and finifhed in 1540, and which was conftructed after the model of a church at Rome, has the honour to poffefs the remains of a man, whofe genius has had an influence over the whole globe; thofe of Chriftopher Columbus. This great man, this father of the art of modern navigation, defired to have his afhes conveyed to the ifland, that may be confidered as the foundation of his fame. He even ordered, that irons, intended to recall to his mind thofe with which calumny had loaded him, fhould be buried in the tomb with himfelf; but the Spaniards undoubtedly refufed to accomplifh his will, in a point which would have ferved to perpetuate the memory of a fcandalous and cruel perfecution.

There is no one, certainly, who does not expect to hear of a mausoleum of Columbus, in the metropolitan church of Santo-Domingo; but, so far, alas! from any such thing existing, the certitude of his mortal remains being deposited here, is, in some sort, supported only by tradition. As to written evidence, the incursion of the English, in 1586, under Francis Drake, may account for a want of it; for the town being given up to pillage, and the archives of the cathedral being burnt, or otherwise destroyed, none of its records, anterior to that date are, of course, to be found. The most ancient go no further back than 1630, except one old register containing the minutes of the chapter, from 1569 to 1593; and this is half destroyed by the worms, and by the hand of time.

Columbus died at Valladolid, on the 20th of May, 1506. His body was carried to Seville, and there deposited; and not in the convent of the Carthusians, on the other side of the Guadalquivir, as some authors, and especially Oviedo and Zuniga, have asserted. It was placed before the choir, in the cathedral, under a stone, on which were engraven these miserable verses in Castillian, and which are still legible:

A Castilla y Arragon,
Otro Mondo diò Colon.

The historians tell us, that from this place it was conveyed to Santo-Domingo, and there lodged in the cathedral; but they do not mention the date of the removal. The proceedings of a synod, held in 1683, of which there are still some copies existing, in speaking of the cathedral church of Santo-Domingo, remark, that, on the outside of the steps of the great altar, repose, in two leaden coffins, one on the right hand side, and the other on the left, the remains of Christopher Columbus, and his brother, Don Louis; but nothing is here said to direct us as to which is placed on the right, or which on the left.

As whatever relates to Columbus, must necessarily be in the highest degree interesting, and especially to those who write on the island of Saint-Domingo, I was extremely anxious to procure certain information concerning his sepulchre in this cathedral; and, for this purpose I applied to Don Joseph Solano, admiral in the Spanish service, and commanding the fleet then lying at Cape-François. The obliging disposition of the admiral, the particular proofs I had before received of his inclination to serve me, his having lately been president of the Spanish part, and his intimate connections with Don Isidore Peralta, who had succeeded him in the presidency, all seemed to promise me an efficacious and successful recommendation. In consequence of my application, Don Joseph Solano wrote in the most pressing manner, and I shall here transcribe the answer of the president, Don Isidore Peralta.

"*Santo-Domingo*, 29th *March*, 1783.

"My Dearest Friend and Patron,

"I received your lordship's kind letter of the 13th "instant, the answer to which I have kept back till "now, in order to have time to get the desired infor-

" mation relative to the sepulchre of Christopher
" Columbus, and to enjoy the pleasing satisfaction of
" serving your lordship to the best of my power, and
" to enable you to experience on your part, that of
" obliging the friend who has requested you to collect
" this information.

" With respect to Christopher Columbus, though
" the insects destroy the paper in such a manner that the
" archives are full of holes, I hope that I now send your
" lordship sufficient proof that the remains of Chris-
" topher Columbus are enclosed in a leaden coffin,
" surrounded with a case of stone, which is buried on
" the gospel side of the sanctuary; and that those of
" Don *Bartholomew*, his brother, are interred in the
" same manner, on the epistle side of the sanctuary.
" Those of Christopher Columbus were brought
" hither from Seville, where they had been deposited
" in the family vault of the dukes of Alcala, after
" being conveyed from Valladolid, and where they
" remained till removed to the cathedral where they
" now are.

" About two months ago, as some repairs were
" making in the church, a piece of thick wall was
" taken down, and built up again immediately after.
" This accidental event was the occasion of finding the
" stone case above mentioned; and which, though with-
" out inscription, was known, from uninterrupted and
" invariable tradition, to contain the remains of Co-
" lumbus. Besides this, I caused a search to be made,
" to see if there was not, in the ecclesiastical archives,
" or in those of the government, some document

"capable of throwing light on the subject; and, in
"consequence, the canons have, upon examination,
"found that the bones were, in great part, reduced to
"ashes; but that the principal bones of the arms had
"been distinguished.

"I send your lordship also, the list of all the bishops
"that have ever belonged to this island, which is
"a more valuable curiosity than that of the presidents;
"for, as I am well assured, the former is complete,
"while in the latter there are several chasms, produced
"by the insects already mentioned, which are more
"destructive to some papers than to others.

"As to the edifices, the churches, the beauty of
"the streets, the motives that led to the removal of
"the capital to the western bank of the river that
"forms its port, I also send you some interesting
"particulars; but with respect to *the plan asked for in
"the note,* there is an insurmountable difficulty;
"which is, that as governor I am forbidden to com-
"municate it. The superior understanding of your
"lordship will at once perceive the reason."

The following certificates sent by Don Isidore Peralta are now in my possession, perfect in all their forms.

"I, Don Joseph Nunez, de Caseres, doctor of di-
"vinity in the pontifical and royal university of the
"Angelic St. Thomas Aquinus, dean dignitary of
"this holy church metropolitan and primatial of the
"Indies; do certify, that the sanctuary of this holy
"cathedral church, being taken down on the 30th of

" January laſt, in order to be rebuilt, there was found,
" on the ſide of the choir where the goſpel is ſung,
" and near the door which opens on the ſtairs, leading
" to the capitular chamber, a ſtone caſe, hollow, of a
" cubic form, and about a vare* in depth, encloſing a
" leaden urn a little damaged, which contained ſeveral
" human bones. I alſo certify, that ſome years ago,
" on a like occaſion, there was found, on the epiſtle
" ſide, another ſtone caſe, reſembling the one above-
" deſcribed ; and that, according to the tradition
" handed down and communicated by the old men of
" the country, and by a chapter of the ſynod of this
" holy cathedral church, the caſe found on the goſpel
" ſide is reputed to contain the remains of admiral
" Chriſtopher Columbus, and that found on the epiſtle
" ſide, thoſe of his brother ; not being able to verify,
" however, whether the latter be really the remains of
" his brother Don Bartholomew, or of Don Diego,
" ſon of the admiral. In witneſs whereof I have here-
" unto ſet my hand. Done at Santo-Domingo, this
" 20th day of April, 1783.

  Signed, " D. JOSEPH NUNEZ DE CASERES."

" I, Don Manuel Sanchez, Canon, Dignitary, and
" Chanter of this holy cathedral church; do certify,
" &c. *(word for word as in the preceding certificate)*
" Done at Santo-Domingo, this 26th day of April,
" 1783.

  Signed,   " MANUEL SANCHEZ."

---

* About two feet eight inches, Engliſh meaſure.

"I, Don Pedro de Galvez, Preceptor, Canon, "Dignitary of this cathedral church, Primate of the "Indies; do certify, that the sanctuary being taken "down, in order to be rebuilt, there was found, on the "side of the choir where the gospel is sung, a stone "case, with a leaden urn in the inside of it, a little da- "maged, which contained several human bones; also, "that it is remembered, that there is another of the "same description on the epistle side; also, that ac- "cording to a tradition handed down through the old "people of the country, and a chapter of the synod "of this holy cathedral church, the case found on the "gospel side, contain the remains of admiral Christo- "pher Columbus, and that found on the epistle side, "those of his brother Bartholomew. In witness "whereof I have hereunto set my hand, this 26th day "of April, 1783.

Signed, "DON PEDRO DE GALVEZ."

Such are the only proofs of the inestimable deposit contained in the primatial church of Santo-Domingo, and even they are immerged in a sort of obscurity; since it cannot be positively affirmed, which of the two cases holds the ashes of Christopher Columbus; unless, by following tradition, we determine from the difference in the dimensions of the cases; because, that in which it is said the remains of Columbus are lodged, is thirty-two inches deep, while the other is only two-thirds as deep.

Since 1783, other endeavours have been made to come at some facts, from the records of the Spanish part, relative to Columbus; but still without effect. I acknowledge myself extremely obliged, on this account, to the complaisant zeal of the Chevalier de Boubée, then commander of the frigate, the Belette. This gentleman, in a voyage which he made to Santo-Domingo in 1787, took the trouble, as well for the sake of my work, as to satisfy his own curiosity, to examine the archives of the chapter, which the Dean and Recorder very complaisantly permitted him to do.

What a subject of reflection for the philosopher! Scarcely are three hundred years past since the discovery of the new world, and already we hardly know what are become of the precious remains of the sagacious, enterprising, and intrepid discoverer! We see him expressing an anxious solicitude, that his ashes may repose in the capital of the immense island, which first established the truth of his opinions with respect to the existence of a western hemisphere; they are transported hither posterior to the construction of the principal edifice, the cathedral; and yet, oh! supine indifference for all that is truly noble! not a mausoleum, not a monument, not even an inscription, to tell where they lie!

I must, however, observe here, that Don Antonio d'Alcedo assures us, in his entertaining and useful dictionary, under the word *America*, that the following epitaph was placed in some part of the cathedral:

Hic locus abscondit præclari membra Columbi
 Cujus nomen ad astra volat.
Non satis unus erat sibi mundus notus, at orbem
 Ignotum priscis omnibus ipse dedit;

Divitias summas terras dispersit in omnes ;
　Atque animas cœlo tradidit innumeras ;
　Invenit campos divinis legibus aptos ,
　　Regibus et nostris prospera regna. dedit.

But this epitaph does not now exist, and it is even forgotten in the colony.

A synod, held an hundred and forty-three years after the perfection of the metropolitan church, makes mention, indeed, of the remains of Christopher Columbus being deposited in that edifice; but without entering on any explanation, although it ought to have been recollected, that the pillage of Drake, forty-seven years before, had caused the destruction of the archives, and that the insects alone might have annihilated many important pieces. And this synod, besides the neglect just mentioned, commits an unpardonable error in giving a brother to Columbus, of the name of *Don Louis*, though he never had a brother of that name, his two brothers being *Don Barthlomew* and *Don Fernando*.

But what must excite our astonishment more than all the rest is, that even the family of Columbus has fallen into the general supineness, to give it no harder name. This family, by his means alone, became very considerable; since, at his return from his fifth and last voyage, he was made duke of Veragua, a province of Mexico, erected into a duchy for him, and at the same time duke of Vega, a town in Jamaica, and marquis of that island. Yet, this family, from whom gratitude demanded so much, has not, even for its own glory, erected a monument to Columbus, either at Valladolid, where he died, or at Santo-Domingo, where his remains are deposited! This reproach still applies to the duke of Liria, possessor, by alliance, of the immense riches of the family of Columbus; but it is trifling in comparison with that which falls on the whole Spanish nation, for the contemptuous neglect, which it has shown towards a man, to whom it is indebted for the greatest part of its renown. Columbus has not received even the tardy justice that is rendered to great men, when Death has disarmed Envy of her stings. It was not enough that, during his life-time, he should see the name of another given to the discovery, by which he had, in a manner, augmented the Universe; every thing must unite to reward his labours by the most shameful, and most unheard-of ingratitude. Shall I add, that in 1787, scarcely four years after Don Isidore Peralta had ascertained the finding of the coffin of Columbus, the original of the instrument, intended to perpetuate the fact, was no longer to be found at Santo-Domingo, where Mr. Boubee sought it in vain, after the death of Don Isidore Peralta. Thus, had it not been for the inclination, and motives that incited me to procure some particulars concerning this illustrious man, the authentic act, which I have above recorded, would, perhaps, have no longer existed. But the genius of Columbus has stretched its wings over the globe entire; he will ever be the glory of his age, and future times will avenge him on all those who enjoy the inestimable fruits of his labours, and even of his persecution, without expressing towards him a single sentiment of gratitude.

But, I must endeavour to subdue my indignation, which is undoubtedly participated by the reader, to pursue my account of the edifice, which contains the ashes of this wonderful and ill-treated man.

In this cathedral is preserved, as a most precious relick, a cross, said to be the very same that was planted by Columbus on a height near la Vega. The Indians attempted in vain to remove it, to cut it down, and to burn it. Struck with terror, they perceived the Virgin sitting on one of the arms of the cross, and the arrows they shot at her, returned to pierce their own bosoms. The emperor, Charles V. had it transported at his own expence. It is covered with silver in filigrean work, and kept under three keys, deposited with the dean of the chapter, the elder canon, and the elder prebendary. There are indulgencies for those who invoke it, and it is said to have produced a multitude of miracles.

Admiral Don Ignatio Caro was interred in the cathedral, in 1707; the Castilian Don Pedro Niela, chief of the colony in 1714; and Colonel Don Isidore Peralta, near the remains of Columbus, in 1786.

We may, besides, remark at Santo-Domingo, the dwelling house of the president, which is called the palace, because the royal court assembles there. This house is a little to the north of the cathedral, in a little square, and faces, on one side, towards the Ozama. This square serves as a market-place; that is to say, it brings together forty or fifty negroes, to sell country produce. The printing-office, the prisons, and many ancient private houses, are in the neighbourhood of the palace.

There are three parochial churches at Santo-Domingo: that of St. Barbe, which lies towards the northeaſt of the city; that of St. Michael, which ſtands on the ſpot where ſtood a chapel, that was deſtroyed by the earthquake in 1751, and where Michael de Paſſamonte had founded an hoſpital under the protection of his patron; and that of St. Andro. But the two latter are but little more than chapels of eaſe to the firſt, being in ſome ſort, out of the limits of the city. There are, beſides, the church of St. Lazarus and the chapel of St. Antonio, near the church of St. Barbe.

The city contains three convents for men, which have increaſed in importance ſince 1782. That of the Dominicans, founded by the emperor Charles V. with a univerſity, dedicated to St. Thomas Aquinus, is in the ſouth. That of the Cordeliers, is towards the north; it was built at the expence of Ovando, in 1503, on a little hill, containing a mine of mercury; and preſident Don John Joſeph Colombo is interred in its church. The third convent is of the order of Mercy; it is to the weſt. The conſecration of its church took place in 1730, and it contains the aſhes of the preſident, brigadier Don Fernando Conflans, Ramirez de St. Yague, who died in 1723.

There are alſo two nunneries; that of the Clariſſans, nuns of the ſecond order of St. Francis; thus named after St. Clariſſa, their patroneſs. This monaſtry is ſituated a little to the north of the convent of Cordeliers. The other nunnery is of Dominicans, or the Ladies of St. Catharine, and is ſituated to the weſt of the convent of male Dominicans. All the churches of the capital are beautiful, rich in ornaments, in vafes of gold and filver fet with precious ftones, in pictures, in ftatues of metal and of marble, but the cathedral furpaffes the others in every refpect.

Santo-Domingo has three hofpitals, one of which was eftablifhed by Ovando, in 1503, and dedicated to St. Nicholas, his patron. Another is for incurables only, and it bears that name which muft awaken diftreffing ideas in every feeling mind.

The Jefuits had founded a college, which was begun about 1735, and finifhed nearly twenty years after.

In this city refide all the principal agents of the general adminiftration, and the major part of the garrifon. This latter confifts of a regiment of trained militia, which, at the beginning of the prefent century replaced three companies of regulars, the firft that were fent from Spain into this colony, where they arrived towards the latter end of the laft century. This regiment is compofed of twelve companies of fixty-two men each. There is, befides, a company of artillery and two engineers. In time of war the militia of the colony are embodied, and their officers receive half pay in time of peace.

All the ftaff at Santo-Domingo, is a governor, a town-major, and deputy town-major. The officers of the troops command in the places where they are detached to; and where there are no regular troops, the officer of the militia commands.

The population of the city of Santo-Domingo is not very confiderable, and yet it is extraordinarily augmented fince about 1780. The cenfufes lately taken in this capital do not amount to more than twenty thousand souls of every age and sex; but to be convinced that this is below the exact number, we have only to know how these censuses are taken, which themselves bear a trait of the Spanish character.

They are made out, says Valverde, by persons appointed by the Spanish priests or vicars, and who go from house to house, to verify who do not perform their paschal duties. This method has this inconvenience attending it, that it does not comprehend children under seven years of age, and it excludes the heads of families absent from their homes, or from the city. But the principal cause of inexactness, is, one half of the parochial territory of the city is on the outside of the walls.

This territory comprehends the part called *the Plains*, a great part of the Monte-de-Plate, and again as well to the east as to the west of the city, a very considerable number of country seats, and provision habitations, where there are a great many families of blacks, of people of colour, and white cultivators. So that, as these never appear in town but in the interval between Lent and St. John's day, to fulfil the ordinance of the church, and as they remain there only a day or two at the house of some relation or friend, or with the factor who sells their produce for them, there are always five or six thousand individuals not included in the census. Thus, then, the population of the city and its dependencies, ought to be reckoned at twenty-five thousand souls.

What a prodigious decrease, if we compare this population with that of the first years after the discovery of America! When the capital contained a considerable number of those unfortunate Indians; when the Spaniards, insatiable for gold, crowded thither from every part of the mother country; when preparations were making for conquering Porto-Rico, Cuba, St. Marguerite, Trinidad, and many other places; for the discovery of the continent, and the conquest of Mexico; when colonists quitted it to go and people many other places, whether in the island itself, or elsewhere, as the town of Coro in the province of Venezuela; when its port was continually filled with ships coming to take in hides (of which the colony sent to Spain more than thirty-five thousand in the year 1587), caffia, tallow, and even live stock for the other parts of America; when, in the beginning of the sixteenth century, the rich mines of the colony, and in particular the silver mine found near the capital, induced the emperor to establish a mint at Santo-Domingo, where money was struck off with the same standard as in Spain; when, in short, every sort of prosperity was known in the island, and more particularly in the capital, which served as a point of union for all.

Nevertheless, even the present situation of Santo-Domingo is flourishing, compared to what it was from 1550 to the beginning of this century. All the riches and all the splendor of the colony were, to make use of the expression of Valverde, like the delicate beauty of a flower, which hardly gives us time to admire its colours and breathe its sweets. In a word, the ruin of the island was as rapid as the progress of its prosperity. It would be equally difficult and tedious to enumerate all the causes of it, but the principal ones may easily be pointed out.

The first, which has something disgusting and horrible in itself, was the cruel persecution of Christopher Columbus, which produced the commission given to the commander Bovadilla, and whence came, contrary to the injunction of Ferdinand and Isabella, the slavery of the Indians, and the division of them among the whites, to work the mines, where the greatest part of them lost their lives. Ovando, the successor of Bodavilla, having done nothing but imitate, and even surpass his crimes, the colony was soon divided into factions, and became a prey to civil discord and war, which the four monks, sent out by cardinal Ximenes, were not able to put an end to.

The Indians, now become the victims of the most attrocious avarice, fled to the continent, or to some propitious island; other died of the small-pox, a distemper unknown among them before the discovery, and which destroyed more than three hundred thousand in a very little time. Accustomed to an easy, free, and independent life, and being all at once reduced to servitude, and that of the most rigorous and laborious sort, many other disorders, equally destructive, began to make their appearance among them, and completed the extirpation of this race of men, whose only crime was, possessing a land, the bowels of which contained treasures, that they alone had had the happiness to despise. With the extinction of the

Indians came that of the products of the mines; the fifths of which had yielded to the public treasure as much as six millions annually.

Other new conquests and settlements also contributed to the depopulation of Saint-Domingo. Marcello de Villabos, one of the auditors, took hence the colonists, who went to settle St. Marguerite. The same year, Rodrigue de Bastidas, sailed from it with a squadron, in order to people the coast of St. Martha, of which he was appointed governor. Mexico and Peru also exhausted the island. Francisco de Montejo drew hence the settlers for Yucatan; Lucas Balquez de Ayllon and Pamphila de Narvaez, those they wanted for the two Floridas; and Heridia for Carthagena. The richest of the inhabitants were those who quitted the colony the first on account of the civil dissentions. In vain did an ordinance of the council of the Indies, of the sixteenth of December, 1526, prohibit emigrations, as it excepted the case of conquests and new settlements, on condition of replacing the colonists that should be taken away. The emigrations continued, and the substitutes were never found.

Saint-Domingo struggled, however, in some sort, against its decay, for a considerable length of time, since, at the end of the sixteenth century, there were yet some resources, though trifling, in the culture and numerous flocks and herds of the island, for which it was indebted, in great part, to the labour of negro slaves; but its trade with Spain was no more. It was only once in two or three years, at most, that a few regifter fhips were to be feen its ports. Its only external relation was with Mexico; and had it not been for foreigners, and the Dutch in particular, the colony would have funk under the mifery which it had fo long groaned under.

The court of Spain, entirely unmoved at this afflicting picture, was induced, in confequence of the contraband trade, which gave an appearance of living to the poor remains of the colony, to demolifh, in 1606, the maritime places which ferved as an outlet to it; and obliged the inhabitants of many of the northern parts to retire into the interior of the ifland, becaufe they were confidered as the agents of the prohibited commerce.

Finally, the fmall-pox, the *farampion*, a fort of meafles, the dyfentery, efpecially in 1666, called the unfortunate year of the fixes, fo depopulated and reduced the colony, that at the beginning of the prefent century it was a fort of wildernefs. The capital, which more than any other part, had felt the deplorable effects of fo many deftructive caufes, had, befides, fuffered hardfhips particular to itfelf. It was, indeed, only menaced by the attack of the Englifh, in 1551, under Guliermo Gaufon, with a ftrong fquadron, and more than two thoufand troops, who were quickly driven back to their fhips; but in the attack of Drake in 1586, confiderable buildings were deftroyed; and the terrible earthquakes of 1684, and 1691, threw down almoft all thofe that Drake had fpared: fo that towards 1700, there were to be feen at Santo-Domingo hardly any thing but ruins and rubbifh, intermixed with great trees, which teftified its depopulation.

Thus the island, the first discovered in the fourth quarter of the globe, contained only a handful of inhabitants, whose poverty alone prevented them from flying from it. The houses tumbled down for want of occupiers; the lands were often without proprietors, and the boundaries of many possessions having ceased to be visible, it was almost impossible for one to distinguish his property from that of another. Public contributions became, in a manner null, and the treasury had no other source than the sale of a few reams of stampt paper, and ecclesiastical bulls that were issued. They were obliged to defray the expences of government, and send annually sums of money from Mexico. In a word, the poverty of the colony was so extreme, that the greatest day of rejoicing for the city of Santo-Domingo was that on which the money arrived for the payment of the officers of government, and the garrison. Its entrance into the town was announced by the ringing of all the bells, and the huzzas and rejoicings of the people. The delay of this remittance, on the contrary, produced consternation and despair; and such has been the fate of the colony, that for a century past, it has cost the state more than twenty-two millions of dollars. A census even of 1737 shows, that the total population at that time, did not surpass six thousand souls, and the capital contained hardly five hundred.

It was in order to people this immense territory, that the Spanish ministry sent, at the close of the last century, a few distressed families from the Canaries, of whom the major part deserted, or perished, either by their own misery or by the sicknesses produced in the clearing of new lands.

At last, however, the colony emerged from its lethargy. Several new settlements, of small and large towns appeared in different parts of the island; the old ones augmented in population, or extent; the houses were rebuilt in the city, where it was even become difficult to find house room. In its jurisdiction appeared the settlement of St. Lawrence, consisting of Mine negroes, and that of St. Charles or of the Ileignes (islanders) was augmented. This latter formed by the assembling of several families from the Canaries, and known more commonly under the name of Ileignes town, is about two hundred fathoms from the western side of of Santo-Domingo.

This re-establishment was a natural effect of the augmentation of the French colony, the advancement of which bringing along with it a call for cattle, produced also an object of commerce, and a resource for the Spanish colony. This latter was now able, with its profits to procure things necessary for cultivation, and especially negroes, and this rendered the lands once more productive.

The greatest part of the trade between the two colonies was carried on by smuggling, and so was that between the Spaniards and other foreigners; in consequence of which, the government, to put a stop to that which was carried on by sea, authorised the fitting out of several privateers. The desperate boldness of poverty then showed itself, and a number of Spanish creoles enriched themselves with the spoils of those who came to bring them the means of existence. During the war of 1740, the president Horrilla, seeing the colony totally unprovided, invited foreigners to it, and at their presence plenty revived. The rupture between Spain and England in 1761, again encouraged the fitting out of privateers, and brought riches into the island; agriculture received considerable aid; the negroes augmented its produce, and enabled the proprietors to obtain fresh hands; the profits made by sea were laid out on fertile land, and a great number of sailors, at the end of the war, settled in the capital, there to enjoy the sweets of peace.

Don Joseph Solano, one of the presidents best calculated to be useful to the colony, found that it was advantageous to the colonists to employ the product of the sale of their cattle in the French part, in purchasing negroes there, who became so many cultivators.

Persuaded that it is from the land that true riches must come, he formed a society of agriculture at Santo-Domingo, after having asked, in the month of January, 1773, an account of the nature of that established at Cape-François.

After this digression, which was not totally unnecessary here (though it may seem to belong more particularly to the history), and the facts contained in which are cited by Valverde himself, I return to the description of Santo-Domingo.

Though the Spanish creoles love theatrical entertainments, they have none, not even in the capital;

unless we give this name to bull-fights, which may for them, be called a national entertainment, since Spaniards are every where fond of it. There are sometimes represented here operas of buffoons, a sort of farce that the French taste could hardly tolerate; but these are on the public square, and by the light of flambeaux. Some comedies, however, have been played at the Count de Solano's, during his presidency.

There is a commissary of the inquisition at Santo-Domingo, who is generally a canon of the cathedral. His commission is rather a form than otherwise. He dared, nevertheless, some years past, demand an examination of some books belonging to an envoy of the French governor, who complained of the measure. The archbishop, informed of this violation of the law of nations, and solicited, perhaps, by the canon himself, the excess of whose zeal had changed into alarm, sent one of his grand vicars to make excuses to the envoy, alledging at the same time, that his public character had been misunderstood. Thus the hideous features of this office do not show themselves in the island; though, as I have already observed, the colonists do not want for superstition. They even tore the handkerchiefs from the heads of the negro servants of the same envoy, and threw them on the ground with indignation, because they wore them in the church, according to the custom of the French part of the island.

The streets of Santo-Domingo are paved: there are a few carriages, such as we call chaises: they have shafts, and are drawn by a horse or a mule, on which the coachman is mounted. The movement of these carriages is analogous to the character of those who ride in them. It is looked upon as polite, when in them, to give the right hand; but this custom does not extend to the president, and *his dignity* forbids him to observe it. This constraint renders it impossible that he should dance also, while in that office, with any other woman but his wife.

This circumstance, ridiculous as it appears, proves what importance is given to the place of president, whose annual salary is forty thousand dollars. On the anniversary of the royal family, and on the days fixed for the *gallas* of the court of Madrid, the president, sitting under a canopy, receives the visits of the several bodies, each individual of which kisses his hand, as an homage due to the representative of the monarch. I shall mention hereafter the power that this post confers.

There is no company at Santo-Domingo; because the Spanish creole women, like those of all other nations, are little inclined to it; and because the women, whose fathers or husbands are of some profession, visit only women whose families are of the same profession; it is often the effect of certain laws even, which prescribe such a whimsical prohibition. The women are, however, agreeable enough during breakfast, to which the men are admitted.

The etiquette of Santo-Domingo makes it an act of politeness to visit strangers, instead of waiting for a notification from them. This custom is founded on the embarrassment that the new-comer must have in forming acquaintances, and in announcing himself to all those whom he visits. Whoever, then, wishes to be of his circle, makes the first advances.

The inhabitants of the city carry on no commerce whatever. Almost the whole of them have plantations, the greatest part of which are only hattes. The richest of them eat little or no bread.

It is at Santo-Domingo that the post-office is kept. It is on the king's account, and has three mails, one for Dahabon, another for St. Raphael, and the third for Neybe. They set out from Santo-Domingo on the first of every month, arrive at the places of their destination on the eighth or tenth, and start, on their return, in two days after. The mail of Dahabon takes in at Monte-Christ the letters brought each month by the packet coming from Spain, which remains three days before it proceeds for the Havanna, and which takes the letters and dispatches for Europe.

The agricultural society of Cape-François proposed, in 1785, to establish a regular mail, between that city and that of Santo-Domingo; the French ministry had even approved of the plan, by a letter to the administrators of the colony, dated the 11th February, 1786, but the tardiness of the Spaniards rendered it abortive; so that, to write from the Cape, or any other part of the French colony, the letter must be carried to

Ouanaminthe, from whence it is taken to Dahabon on the first of every month, and is sixteen days on the way between the Cape and Santo-Domingo. If the letter is for any other part of the Spanish possessions than Santo-Domingo, it must be post-paid as far as Oanaminthe.

The Spanish capital is about ninety leagues from the Cape, going by the road through St. Raphael, Azua, &c. and about one hundred leagues, by that of Dahabon, St. Yague, and la Vega; it is reckoned seventy leagues from Port-au-Prince; and is situated in 18 deg. 19 min. and 30 sec. north latitude; and 72 deg. 37 min. west longitude, meridian of Paris.

The arms of the city of Santo-Domingo are, an escutcheon of gueules, having in the superior part, two golden lions, and in the inferior, a key of Azure, on the side of a silver cross and a crown of gueules in the middle; the supporters are, two lions rampant; the crest is, a crown imperial.

Santo-Domingo is the birth place of many estimable men, among whom we ought to rekon Alonzo de Spinosa, a Dominican, and a celebrated writer. Gratitude as well as justice oblige me to mention among those who are now living there, Don Antonio Valverde, to whose inquiries I am indebted for a great part of what I advance with respect to the colony.

What I have hither described of the capital, comprehends, strictly speaking, only the city itself, and the establishments which ought to be considered as its suburbs; but much remains to be said as to its territory.

Santo-Domingo stands in an immense plain. The land lying between the city and the Jayna, is level, well watered, covered with bushy trees or smiling meadows.

The woods and savanas come almost to the walls of the capital, where we do not see, more than any where else, either pleasure or kitchen gardens; except it be in the monastries where such have been begun.

Between the Nisao and the Ozama are eleven sugar-mills, worked by oxen or mules, in a commodious situation for land or water carriage; but, though they may be easily approached by wheel carriages, the usual conveyance is on the backs of animals. The most distant of these eleven sugar-mills, which is Cumba-Chiqua, is situated on the banks of the Nisao. Some indigo and cotton manufactures are begun in this quarter.

There are also some sugar-manufactures on the banks of the Isabella and the Ozama. These two rivers serve to transport to the capital the produce collected along their borders, as well as those which are brought in carts from the plantations of Barbaroja and St. Joseph, which are situated higher up. Besides, they are, in the like way useful to parts still more remote from them, and lying towards the *east of the island*, by the intermediate aid of several little rivers, such as the Yavacao, Mont-de-Plate, Savita, Guavatree, Callabash-tree, Duey, Jaynamosa, Orange-tree, Cassavium, Dajao, and others, many of which might rendered navigable.

Of the nineteen or twenty sugar-manufactures, in the district of the capital, the most considerable is that of St. Joseph, where seventy negroes might be employed. That called Jagua, wnich is also distinguished, has fifty negroes; half the number that it contained when belonging to the Jesuits.

There are yet to be seen at this place, simple *trapiches* for melasses, the greatest part of which employ eight or ten negroes: provision plantations producing rice, Indian corn, cassavium, and other roots, with a few garden vegetables; they employ from two to six negroes. We see at times, a plantation of scrubbed cocoa-trees, while there might be fifty or sixty, each producing more than twenty-five thousand weight of cocoa. Fifty more sugar plantations and as many of indigo might be formed between Jayna and Isabella.

All that I have hitherto remarked of the southern coast of the Spanish part lies to the west of the capital: we must now follow the road of communication hence to the north of the colony; stopping only to add, that the land of the plain of Santo-Domingo is generally good, but that it is much to be regretted that it has been granted to the towns-people, who are even the lords of it; this was done, undoubtedly, that Spanish pride and poverty should ever be found under the same roof. Near the city the land is let to free negroes or day-labouring slaves, who work on it only enough to procure a subsistence, and who raise a few things for the consumption of the capital.

To go from Santo-Domingo towards the northern part of its jurisdiction, we must go out of the New Gate, or the Gate of Conde. From the foot of the rampart we begin to ascend the little hill of the Ileignes, and it is hence only that the city is to be seen when approached in that direction. At two hundred fathoms there is a road turns off to Jayna, Bani, Azua, &c. and at a short half league, the road forms a fork; the northern branch leading to the town of St. Charles, or of the Ileignes, by which one may also leave the capital, and come back to the fork I am speaking of.

This town of St. Charles, or of the Ileignes, has a few streets cutting each other at right angles, and running from the four cardinal points of the compass.

At the end of a good league and a quarter from the city, there is a road, which, turning to the left, leads to certain hattes and plantations in the neigbourhood. Half a league further on it passes on the left of a plantation, situated on a little eminence, at two leagues from Isabella, were there are sugar-canes and cocoa-nut trees. After this, having first passed by several hattes on each side of the road, we enter the wood leading down to the Isabella, which is crossed in a canoe, and which may be ascended in the same manner to within four or five leagues of its confluence with the Ozama, according to the times when it has more or less water. It is three leagues from this confluence to where the road crosses the river.

In leaving the Isabella we enter a wood, which continues for a league and a half, leading away toward the north-east, as far as the passage of the river Gribbe-Plate; a name, which, it appears to me, signifies that it bears silver along, or that it comes from a plain where there is silver. We may say, that, from Santo-Domingo, the country is all woody as far as the Gribbe-Plate; for, in all this extent, there are no openings, except such as are made by some scattering hattes and plantations.

After the little river of Gribbe-Plate, comes the savana of the Monge, which continues for a quarter of a league, and at the end of it the road arrives at the river, called *Guyacusa, Guacuara,* and even *Goyaconasi,* but oftener *Guyacuara.* Quitting this river we enter the savana Cansamanceu, which continues on to two little brooks, pretty near each other, called the brooks of Cassavium (Yuca). From these brooks the road runs towards the east, and winds round a little hill near the cerre de Prieta, which it leaves on the left hand, and the side of which is covered with wood. At the foot of this cerre lies the savana of Prieta, across which the road passes. It is about a league wide, and ends at the little river Ycaque, a league and a half distant from the Guyacuara by the windings of the road. This river Ycaque is followed by the savana Sanguine, as extensive as that of Prieta, where the road, turning away to the right, comes to the Ozama, which receives from its right bank, the rivers Gribbe-Plate, Guyacuara, and Ycaque, of which we have just been speaking.

The Ozama is commonly fordable at this place; but in the rainy seasons, a fording place must be sought higher up, and one must even wait several days, till the water falls; an inconvenience common to almost all the rivers of any confequence in Saint-Domingo.

After croffing the Ozama the road enters the favana of Louifa, at the end of which, it leaves on the right the hatte of the fame name, which is fituated on the border of the wood by which the favana is furrounded; then it paffes the ravin of Cavoa, and afterwards a little favana before it comes to the river of the Lemon, which is at a good league from the Ozama. Arrived at this point the traveller has paffed the fixth chain of mountains which I have fpoken of, the flope of which is almoft infenfible.

From the river Lemon we come to the favana of the Guite, which is preceded by the hatte of the fame name. This hatte is hardly feven leagues from Santo-Domingo, and yet, by the road, it is twelve. This difference is produced by the impoffibility of croffing the Ifabella and Ozama in favourable places, and by the neceffity of avoiding fwamps and marfhes, which are continually interrupting the road. Foot people may, indeed, venture to crofs thefe laft in the dry feafons, and to go over the Ozama in pirogas, or to fwim acrofs it, as is often done; but this is impracticable for travellers on horfe-back.

At a good quarter of a league from the hatte of the Guite, is a ftrip of woodland which feparates it from the fine, long favana of San-Pedro, which is not however, fo wide as the favana of the Guite, fince it is, at moft, not more than a quarter of a league in width. The hatte of San-Pedro, is in the middle of the favana of the fame name, from which it is two leagues to Red-river (Bermejo), the banks of which are covered with wood.

It is at this diftance to the north, but on the banks of the Jayna, where the commander Ovando built, in 1504, the town of Bonnaventure, which its vicinity to the mines of St. Chriftopher foon rendered confiderable; and which was erected near Bonao, a hamlet bearing the name of the lord of the manor, formed of itfelf round thefe mines from the time of their difcovery.

Bonao, at the end of the fixteenth century, abounded in all the productions of the country. It was founded by Columbus, in 1494, and had for its arms, in 1508, an efcutcheon, argent, filled with wheat ears of gold, at the foot of the finople; and by a fingular hazard, this place was forgotten, when, in 1512, the fettlements of the colony were divided between the two bifhopricks.

It was in the territory granted, fince at Bonnaventure, and on the river Jayna, that was found the famous lump of gold, fpoken of by the Spanifh writers, and efpecially by Oviedo, who fays that it weighed three thoufand fix hundred Spanifh dollars; without mentioning many others which were alfo of a remarkable fize. There were annually run at Bonnaventure, as many as two hundred and thirty thoufand dollars, and at the time of when the coat of arms was granted, that of this town had an efcutcheon, finople, with a golden fun appearing through a cloud, from which fell a fhower of gold.

Bonnaventure and Bonao, fell into decay soon after their establishment, and were both abandoned in 1606. I have already observed, in speaking of Jayna, that the district of Bonnaventure now makes a part of the cure of St. Rose, or Jayna. A number of poor inhabitants there find employment in washing gold, the standard of which is above twenty-three carats and a half. Valverde even says, on this subject, that in 1764, it was asked at the control-office, from whence came the gold of the buckles that were brought hither to be weighed, and that it was asserted, that none had ever been seen so pure. This gold, adds he, is not found on the surface, but it is borne along by the water in grain or in lumps, in detaching it from the great mass which was first worked, and the excavations of which are yet visible. In 1750, instruments were prepared in order to work them again, but the death of Don Jacob Cienfugos, who directed the enterprise, and who was looked upon as an intelligent man, caused it to be given up.

The Bermejo, or Red-river, is followed by the savana of Don-Juan, where there is a hatte of the same name. After this the road passes through a little wood, and comes to a wide ravin with high banks, which is at a long half league from Bermejo.

From this ravin the high road ascends the chain of Pardave, or the seventh chain, becomes crooked, very heavy, and difficult of access; but the fatigue here encountered is amply compensated by the magnificent prospect that is beheld from the summit of the mountain. Hence the delighted eye sweeps round over the peninsula of Samana, Cape Raphael, the Pointe-de-l'Epee, all the settlements of the immense plains of Seybo and Higuey, Santo-Domingo and its environs, and finds no end of its variegated pleasures, till it arrives at the east of the group of Cibao. In this extensive view there are a thousand spots, which, for a time, charm the sight, and withhold it from the general picture, by a display of more pittoresque and striking beauties. All is regular confusion, and majestic simplicity. Here the sea, the shining surface of which appears through the intervals, forms a contrast with the blue hills at a distance, while the sight is revived by the verdure of the neighbouring plains and groves. The rivers, too, of various width, add their limpid and winding streams to the enchanting scene, while the lofty dark-browed mountains of Cibao, crown the whole with a sort of awful sublimity. What sorrow must the beholder of all these riches feel, when he considers, that Nature has lavished them in vain! That they have served only to awaken the drowsy Spaniard a moment from his torpidity, in order to sink the unhappy Indians to the grave, in labouring to satisfy his guilty avarice, his thirst for gold, to him superior to all but his indolence!

The traveller is too much delighted to quit this summit without regret; and, as he departs, he looks back to have a last glimpse of what has so long rivetted him to the spot. But all in a moment disappears; and he has now to descend the other side of the mountain, on a steep and difficult road, through a wood, the openings of which present nothing pleasing to the sight. After having passed this wood, he enters a fine savana, called the savana of the Emerald (Aguacate), at the end of which he comes to a wide ravin, at the foot of the north side of the chain of Pardave, and which is a league and a half from the other ravin, at the foot of the south side of the same chain.

At the ravin the road again enters a wood, and, continuing on a short half league, comes to the crossing place of the river Yaffe, which falls, like the Lemon, or Red-river, into the Ozama, from its left bank. Having crossed the Yaffe, which is never dry, the wood continues on, but becomes narrower, till the road arrives at the river Arainos, which is but a short quarter of a league from the last river. After this river also the road has to pass through a wood, intermixed with glades, which are so many little savanas, at the end of which comes the savana of the Palience, nearly a league and an half long, in its direction north-west quarter-north; and a quarter of a league wide. This savana is closed by the Orange-tree river (Naranjo), which, as well as the Arainos, is never dry. These rivers are but two leagues asunder.

After Orange-tree river, which is also called the little Sevico, or Cevico, and which falls into the sea at the bottom of the bay of Samana, the road enters the savana of Sevico, very extensive, and diversified with little clumps of trees, having away to its right the hatte of the same name, to which there is a path leading from the road. This hatte is at about five or six hundred fathoms from the crossing place of the Orange-tree river. Passing the path, the road continues on about another half league, before it comes to the river Sevico, or Cevico, the banks of which are very high, its stream deep, and its borders covered with wood. From hence to the Little-White-River (Blanco), which comes from Cibao, and is never dry, the traveller has to go a long quarter of a league, partly woodland and partly savanas.

Departing from this last river, the road begins to ascend the second chain of mountains, or the chain of Sevico, which is, at least, as steep and lofty as the seventh chain. In general, it is covered with wood, though there are here and there a naked interval, or a little savana. The road is here extremely bad, and difficult to pass, and is much lengthened by the turnings that it is obliged to make on account of the nature of the land; but, arrived at the top, the sensations enjoyed on that of Pardave are revived. Hence, are seen, all the country stretching from the bottom of the bay of Samana and forming the Vega-Real, a plain of astonishing extent and beauty. Each point is here dwelt on with pleasure. The eye measures, calculates the distances, runs over the whole again and again; and the contemplative beholder, after having poured out his heart in gratitude to the Author of so meny blessings, is ever brought back to the unpleasing reflection of their being bestowed almost in vain on the present possessors.

But as we are now arrived at the point which is the real separation of the eastern and northern parts of the Spanish colony, and which ends the territory of Santo-Domingo, let us leave the traveller to repose, or satiate his view and his imagination, while we direct the reader's attention to an extent of country of about seven hundred square leagues, forming the eastern part of the island, and of which more than six hundred leagues are in plains. This vast tract is bounded to the north by the Round-Mountain, which might almost be considered as a prolongation of the second chain, and the north side of which falls down towards the southern part of the bay of Samana; to the east and south it is bounded by the sea, and to the west, in nearly its whole length, by the Ozama and several other rivers, which running on the south of the chain of Sevico, and falling successively into each other, carry the tribute of their waters, thus united, to the Ozama, or to the western side of the bottom of the bay of Samana.

In this immense extent of level and open country, which even takes the name of *the Plains*, and which is interspersed with only a few hills that seem to be the gentle extremities of trifling ridges coming from the groupe of Cibao, there are to be seen but a very few insignificant settlements or villages, the greatest part of which are hardly worthy of the name. This fine country is, of all the Spanish part, the poorest and most neglected.

St. Laurent-des-Mines.

On the left side of the Ozama, and opposite Santo-Domingo, is a little settlement, which has something of the appearance of a village. The vicinity of the city was the original cause of it. It stands in the place where the capital was first founded, and where the road from Santo-Domingo to Seybe begins. If we go from this settlement towards the north, we find, at about a league (after a passing a brick-yard), the little town of St. Laurent-des-Mines, situated at two hundred and fifty fathoms from the eastern bank of the Ozama, and about a quarter of a league from its confluence with the Isabella, and not on the western bank, as laid down in the greatest part of the maps.

Saint-Laurent-des-Mines, which can be considered as no more than one of the dependencies of Santo-Domingo, contains three hundred inhabitants, all free negroes, forming a cure. These negroes are the descendants of negroes, taken from the northern part of the French colony, in the invasions of 1691 and 1695, and other French fugitive negroes, which were assembled at Santo-Domingo in 1719, in order to return them, according to the orders of the king of Spain. But the Spaniards having opposed this by force of arms, in place of departing for the French part, they formed this settlement, which has taken the epithet of *Mines*, because the leaders among these negroes were of the kingdom of the Mines on the coast of Africa.

Continuing on still towards the north, we come to the second settlement of the east; which is that of Monte-de-Plate. It is about sixteen leagues to the north-east of Santo-Domingo, and is situated in the direction, north and south of a line, which, setting off from old Cape-François, would come at the mouth of the river Macoriz, from which Mont-de-Plate is about fifteen leagues. I have already had occasion to observe, that the settlement of Mont-de-Plate was formed by the inhabitants of Port-de-Plate and Monte-Christ, when they were obliged to abandon these latter towns. Originally, Monte-de-Plate flourished, but it fell rapidly to decay, and has become, for more than fifty years past, a miserable place, to which the name of *city* seems to have been given in irony. The parish of Mont-de-Plate contains about six hundred souls.

At two leagues, or thereabout, to the north-east of Mont-de-Plate is the wretched settlement of Boya, to which the cacique Henri retired with three or four hundred Indians, the remnant of those who had remained faithful to him, when the cruelties of the Spaniards had driven him to a revolt. He chose this asylum after the emperor Charles V. had, to make use of the expression of a Spanish writer, granted his pardon. The unfortunate people thus retired, were not more lucky than the other Indians of Haïti: they successively perished; so that there now exists not one pure descendant of their race. There would not even remain a vestige of a settlement in this place, if it was not for an image of the blessed Virgin with the title of *holy waters*, in a handsome vaulted church, for which a community of Santo-Domingo supports a chaplain. After the extinction of the Indians, the promulgation of miracles had attracted several persons coming from the Terra Firma, to settle at Boya with various designs; but they also have disappeared, leaving only twenty-five or thirty people of a mixed race, who enjoy the privileges, at last conceded to the cacique Henri, to whom the emperor deigned to grant the title of *Don*. It is asserted, that, for a long time, the chief of the Indians at Boya, took the title of *Cacique of the Island of Haïti*, and that a tribunal, composed of Indians, was empowered to pass sentence, even of death, with an appeal to the royal court at Santo-Domingo. Thus Boya must be dear to every feeling mind, as being the last spot of the island, where the Indians found a place of shelter from their ferocious conquerors, and as yet containing a few individuals who have a drop of that blood which flowed in the veins of a peaceful people, extirpated by European avarice.

At about four leagues to the south-east of Boya, is the city of St. John the Baptist of Bayaguana. It owes its foundation to the same cause as Mont-de-Plate, and was first formed by the inhabitants of Leogane and Bayaha. All that I have said of the different state of Mont-de-Plate may be applied to this city. The parish contains, however a thousand souls.

In the country lying between Mont-de-Plate, Boya, Bayaguana, and Santo-Domingo, there are two chapels of ease, built about twenty years ago, under the names of St. Joseph and Tavira, where mass is said to the inhabitants living too far from the first mentioned places.

It was on the heights situated in the district of Bayaguana, and which are called *Haïti de Roxas*, that Valverde saw, after having long sought it in vain, a little quadruped, which in make and size resembled a sucking pig of a fortnight old, except that its snout was a little longer. It had, according to this author, but very little hair, which was as fine as that of the dogs called *Chinese*. It had no tail at all, was perfectly mute, and lived but a short time. " I know not," adds Valverde, " to which of the four sorts of little quadrupeds " found in the island at the time of its discovery, this " animal could correspond; because Oviedo has de- " scribed them in a jumbling confused manner, in which " he has been followed by the new encyclopedia, with " the addition of other dubious expressions, accord- " ing to custom."

Twelve leagues, or thereabout, to the north of the little island of St. Catharine, we find Seyvo, or Seybo, which is not that founded in 1502, by John of Esquivel, but a settlement formed in the same canton, about sixty years ago, by several graziers living round the spot, and who wished for a place of assembly to hear mass. Towards 1780, this place had augmented, like many others of the colony; but since that time it has been on the decay, and is now fallen into a state that leaves no hopes of re-establishment.

Seybo, however, is very confiderable, compared to the reft of the eaftern territory. The parifh contains more than four thoufand perfons, the greateft part of whom are graziers or herdfmen, free negroes, and people of colour.

The grazing lands in the canton of Seybo are daily diminifhed by the immenfe quantity of guava and icaco trees which fpread over them, and which, befides their encroachment on the land, form a retreat for the cattle, and caufe fuch as are attacked with the maggot, or any kind of difeafe, to perifh for want of aid.

On a line from north to fouth, and running towards the middle of the Saone, at fix leagues from the fouthern coaft of the ifland, is the city of Higuey, which is alfo known by the names of *Salvaléon de Higuey*, and *Alta-Gratia*. This city has been very confiderable, and its territory was renowned for its fertility, and the fugar produced on it. Salvaleon was founded by John of Efquivel, in 1502, 1504, or 1506, (for the authors mention thefe three years), and, in 1508, it obtained a coat of arms, being an efcutcheon, argent, a purple lion, with two mens' heads below uncovered. There are even fome hiftorians who feem to believe that Higuey and Salvaléon of Higuey were two diftinct fettlements, and that the latter was near the fea. Higuey, which is the moft eaftern of all the fettlements in the ifland of Saint-Domingo, gives its name to a river, and to a bay into which that river falls. The bay is alfo known under the denomination of the bay of Yumba (callebafs-tree). Higuey was originally dedicated to St. Denis. At the time of the decay of the colony, it was reduced fo low as to contain no more than fifty inhabitants. During the prefent century a new church has been erected, and the population now amounts to five hundred perfons, defcended from the moft ancient families of the colony. All that now remains of the place where was once the court of the moft powerful cacique of the ifland, is the fertility of its environs; an advantage, for the future ufelefs to thofe who know not how to turn it to account. There are three roads from Higuey to Santo-Domingo, which places are at about forty leagues from each other: the firft, which is direct, runs along at about three or four leagues from the fea-fide, and croffes all the rivers that run down to it; but, till this road comes to the place where it is joined by that which leads from Seybe to Santo-Domingo, it is little better than a rugged path. The fecond goes throngh Seybe; and the third through Bayaguana and Boya, till it comes to the road going from Santo-Domingo to Cotuy, between the river Arainos and the Yaffe.

From what has been here faid, it is obfervable that Seybe has two ways of communication with Santo-Domingo. That by the road which comes out on the eaft bank of the Ozama oppofite the capital, is only about twenty leagues; but that leading through Cotuy, muft be extremely roundabout.

The inhabitants of Bayaguana, Boya, and Mont-de-Plate have their choice to come to Santo-Domingo through Seybe or through Cotuy; for, from Boya there is a high road which goes to Bayaguana, and from the latter there are two roads, one to Seybo and the other to Higuey. The latter of thefe roads leaves the river Higuey on the right, while that going from Seybo to Higuey leaves it on the left.

From Seybo to the bay of Semana there is a path, which was formerly paffable on horfe-back, but which is now acceffible to foot paffengers only.

One may go from Santo-Domingo to Samana by the eaftern part of the ifland. The Ozama being croffed oppofite the city, the traveller leaves the river on the left, and goes to the fugar plantation of the Dominicans, - - - 4 ¼ leagues,

From that fugar plantation to Los Nunos, - - - - 5

From hence to the Mata à la Carba, 3 ¾
From hence to the ftream Bruxelles, 7
From hence to Foffas (large ftream), 1

Here the road divides itfelf into two branches, one going by the Purgarin, and the other by the paffage of St. Jerome.

From Foffas to the Purgarin, 2 ½
From hence to Maffas Moras, 2 ½
From hence to Ouverture-du-Mort, 1 ¼
From hence to Grand-Savana, 1 ¼
From hence to Savana-la-Mer, 4 ½

33 leagues.

All this road is over a level country. In going by the paffage of St. Jerome inftead of the Purgarin the road is about three leagues longer, but nearly as good.

When I have added here what I have to fay relative to the coaft and the foil of this eaftern quarter of the ifland, I fhall have completed this part of my defcription.

After the mouth of the Ozama, the coaft runs in an eaftern direction as far as the point of the Little-Palm-Tree, which is oppofite the little ifland of the Saone, without the land's advancing perceptibly towards the fouth, except at the Pointe-de-Caufedo, where it runs out a good league into the fea. On the eaft of the mouth of the Ozama the land forms a little elbow, called the Anfe-de-la-Retraite (or the Cove of the Retreat), with a narrow point, commonly called the Petite-Pointe (Little Point), or the Tourelle (Turret); becaufe there was formely a little fortification which defended the entrance, the ruins and fragments of which ftill exift. In the part of the coaft lying between the Ozama and the Pointe-de-Caufedo, is the Callete, or Petite-Rade or (Little Road), where there is good anchorage for floops, and barks of a middling burden. Even fhips may approach near the land without danger along this flat fhore; and troops may here difembark under fail, which renders it a dangerous fituation for the inhabitants in war-time.

The Pointe-de-Caufedo once paffed, the coaft runs directly eaft quite to the point of the Little-Palm-Tree. In this fpace, more than twenty-five leagues, the fhore, from which falls feveral rivers of different dimenfions, is entirely open. Little barks and launches may everywhere come clofe in; and merchant fhips may approach very near, and even find anchorage in the mouths of the Macoriz, Soco, Comoyazu, Romaine, and Quiabon. The rivers are capable of being made navigable in different degrees, efpecially the Macoriz, up which the floops already go for feveral leagues. The mouth of this river forms a real port, before which is the bay of Andrez.

From the Little-Palm-Tree to the Pointe-de-l'Epee, which laft lies in 18 deg. 15 min. north lat. and 71 deg. 13 min. weft long. the coaft ftill continues open. In this fpace we find the mouth of the river Yumba (callebafs-tree), or Higuey, with the bay of the fame name. This bay admits of the entrance of little floops, and other veffels of a like burden. Its eaftern extremity is formed by the Pointe-de-l'Epee.

Doubling this point, and following the coaft towards the north, we come to Cape-Trompeur (del Enganno) or Falfe Cape, which is the eafternmoft point of the whole ifland, and which is fituated in 18 deg. 25 min. north latitude, and 71 deg. weft longitude.

After this cape comes Cape-Raphael, or St. Raphael, or the Round Mountain, lying in 19 deg. 3 min. north latitude, and 71 deg. 25 min. weft longitude. From Pointe-de-l'Epée to Cape-Raphael, the coaft is easy to approach, and furnishes good anchorage for launches, particularly in the mouths of the Nisibon, Maymon, and Macao, in all which there are fish in abundance.

The reader will undoubtedly remember, that in describing the plains of the Spanish part, I observed, that the tract of land extending forty-nine leagues from the eastern bank of the Ozama to the Pointe-de-l'Epée, and being about twelve leagues wide, is level, except between the rivers Soco and Romaine, where there are little hills susceptible of cultivation. This land, composed of woods and meadows (like the plain between the Nisao and the Ozama), is smooth, and watered by numberless rivers; especially by the Macoriz, which is in the eastern mountains, near the town of Bayaguana, runs south-south-west, and falls into the sea between Pointe-de-Causedo and the mouth of the river Soco; by the Soco itself, which has its source towards the same point; by the Cumayare; by the Romaine, which running along at about fifteen leagues from the Macoriz, but with less water, comes, like it, from the eastern mountains, and falls into the Bay des-Chevaux (Horse-Bay); and lastly, by the Quiabon and the Yuma or Higuey.

Each of these rivers receives others of less note in its course; among which we may name the Sanate, the Seybe, the Cibao, the Magarin, the Mayorazgo, the Mojaras, the Casui, the Amirale, and many others. All these may become the means of watering and fertilizing the land, of transporting its produce, of moving the necessary machines, &c. Indeed, we see, between the Casui and the Amirale, the ruins of a stout water-mill.

It would be an easy matter to establish in the plain, between Santo-Domingo and Pointe-de-l'Epée many hundreds of sugar plantations; and especially along the Macoriz, which invites the inhabitants by the commodiousness of its pleasant banks. The fertile and well-watered space lying to the north of Higuey, would also admit of a great number, while plantations of another sort would meet with a ready and advantageous reception on the neighbouring hills.

The mountains, which bound to the north the vast plain that I am describing, are full of game, invite the sportsman, and ever repay his toil. Some of these mountains are, indeed, difficult of access; because the ways over them are, at best, but paths; and because their fertility augmenting the bulk of the trees and the thickness of the underwood, leads up such a number of wild bines as, by their climbing and twisting from branch to branch, form a sort of web that is often impenetrable.

We are now come to the northern part of the Spanish colony.

In speaking of the two first chains of the mountains of Cibao, which extend from Cape-Raphael to Port-de-Paix, I have observed that the second sinks considerably from the point corresponding to the bottom of the bay of Samana, nearly to the Round-Mountain, though very high and steep at quitting the group.

Such are the conformation and fort of obliqueness of some spots in this chain, that, stretching along between the rivers Sevico and Yaqui (not either the great or little Yaqui), it does not prevent them, any more than the White-River, from falling into the Yuna, which, as we have already seen, falls into the bay of Samana. So that this chain, approaching the western extremity of the bay, leaves intervals or passages, by the means of which the waters, running from its southern side, fall into the sea at nearly the same place as do those running from its northern side; that is, at the bay of Samana. As to the other parts of the chain, the rivers that there rise, follow, during the whole of their course, the natural declivity of the two sides.

After this the reader will readily conceive that the northern part of the Spanish colony has for boundaries the sea to the north and east, the first and second chains of mountains to the south, and, to the west, the sea from Cape-la-Grange, to the southern side of the bay of Mancenilla, and afterwards a portion of the French colony as far as the upper end of the parish of Ouanaminthe.

But this northern part is itself, as it were, divided in two, by a chain of mountains, called *the chain of Monte-Christ*, which, from the bay of the same name, runs south-eastward to the bottom of the bay of Samana, near the little Ester, or salt-marsh, where it stops, as if to let pass the river Yuna.

This chain of Monte-Christ, is absolutely detached from all those which come from the group of Cibao.

Between it and the sea lies all the border of the coast, from Samana to Monte-Christ, and which I am first going to describe.

I shall afterwards come to the space between this chain and those of Cibao, setting off from the point corresponding with the bay of Samana, and going to that, where the boundaries of the two nations cut the first chain: a considerable extent of country, which I have as yet only glanced at in reckoning it among the level tracts of the colony.

Samana.

Opposite Cape Raphaël, but a little more to the north-west, lies Cape Samana, which is called also Cape Reson or Cape Grondeur. This cape forms the eastern point of the peninsula of Samana. Between these capes is the great bay of Samana, which was named by Columbus, *Bay of Arrows*, because he there found a great number of Indians armed with them. These Indians were subjects of the Cacique *Cayacoa*, who visited the admiral on board, and whose widow embracing christianity, was christened *Donna Inès Cayacoa*.

The bay of Samana may be about seven leagues broad at the mouth, which faces the east, that is to say, from Cape-Raphaël to that of Samana. Its mean breath is about five leagues, and it is twenty leagues long; though the north-east and south-west directions of the coast, running from Cape Samana down the bay, seems to mark its beginning at the little point, called by some *Pointe-du-Port-François*, and by others, *Pointe-à-Grappin* (Grapling-point), and which is at no more than thirteen leagues from the bottom of the bay. Other mariners reckon, as the southern point of the bay, the point called *Pointe-d'Icaque*, (Icaco-Point) which comes next after Cape-Raphaël, and lies in 19 deg. 2 min. latitude, and 71 deg. 35 min. longitude.

This bay offers a safe shelter to the stoutest squadrons. Lying to the windward of the island, it has an advantage over all the other places as a maritime post, which renders it capable of protecting the whole gulph of Mexico, to which it is in reality a key. But the entrance of this superb bay is very narrow; because from the southern side of its opening runs a breaker, which advances in a point towards *Port-Banister*, and between which and the northern coast, nature has placed the rock or shallow called *the rebels*. This rock narrows the entrance, so that between it and the land forming the north side in the interior of the bay, there is little more than a space of eight hundred fathoms. Thus a battery on shore, and another on the rock, *the rebels*, would, by their cross-fire, completely defend the entrance against even the smallest vessels. If, on the contrary, an attempt was made to enter between *the rebels* and the breakers, a battery on the latter, of which they would admit, would defend this passage still better, with the battery on *the rebels*, as the interval is still narrower. Besides these means of defence of the bay of Samana at its entrance, there are many others in its interior parts.

The difficulty of entering the bay of Samana, has been but too well proved by a great number of wrecks, since the Europeans have navigated in those seas. It is, indeed astonishing, that it should not be better known, and that Spain, which there lost, in 1724, two galloons of seventy guns (the *Guadaloupe* and the *Tolose*), under the command of Don Balthazar de Guevara, a lieutenant-general of the navy, and loaded with sugar for Vera-Cruz, has never ordered it to be sounded, and described so as to render the navigation safe. Perhaps this neglect is the effect of political calculation, for this science sometimes reckons misfortune an advantage. For my part, who cannot discover how this principle can be applicable to the bay of Samana, I shall cite the observations that a French inhabitant of Saint-Domingo, made in a voyage along the northern coast of the island, from Cape La Grange to the bay of Samana inclusive. The author has committed them to paper, and I publish them, that they may lead to a particular examination of this part of the coast, which is the terror of mariners.

According to these observations, it is a knowledge of the little islands of the rebels, called the Islands of Banister, that ought to serve as the only guide in entering the bay, on account of the breaker which continues from the Pointe-d'Icaque (which is, as I have already said, about four or five leagues further in than Cape Raphael) to these little clumps or islands. But as these latter, being about twelve leagues from the bottom of the bay, seem to be no more than a continuation of the land or of a point, the navigator muſt advance till he can perceive that they are ſeparated from it, and then he muſt take ſuch a courſe in the bay as will carry him through between the clumps and the peninſula, keeping very cloſe to the right of the former, and when they are once paſſed, he is out of danger. However, if he wants to advance further down the bay, he muſt ſtill follow the ſame courſe for ſome few cable's lengths, till the principle of the clumps called the *Caye-Elévantade*, is left to the north-weſt, when he muſt ſteer weſt-quarter-ſouth-weſt, or elſe towards the Point-Martiniquois, if the weather be clear, till he diſcovers the fort of Samana, which is on the northern ſide of the bay, and at ten leagues from its bottom. Veſſels may anchor at the fort by keeping the middle between the land and the little clumps of iſlands oppoſite it.

The name of *Iſlots-de-Baniſtre* and that of *Port-Baniſtre*, by which this anchoring place was formerly known, took their origin from a memorable engagement in 1690, between Baniſter, a famous Engliſh cruiſer, become a pirate, and two Engliſh frigates. Baniſter who had a little frigate, had formed a kind of partnerſhip with a French ſhip, commanded by one Lagarde. The frigates, knowing that they were anchored at Samana, entered the bay. Baniſter carried his guns a ſhore and erected a battery. With his 200 men, the crews of the veſſels, he killed more than 120 of his countrymen, and obliged the two frigates to retreat: not, however, till they had ſunk his own. As the pirates had now only a little veſſel capable of containing about 80 men, they fought, and many were killed, for the preference of embarking; ſo much did they fear to be taken and hanged.

There is an anchorage within the point Icaque. Towards this point there is a rock, amidſt the breakers, that may be ſeen at the diſtance of three leagues, and this rock is the mark for knowing the two paſſages, by which veſſels may enter and come to anchor ſheltered from the breakers, in taking care not to caſt on the White-bottoms which are a head, and where there is no hold. It was for want of knowing theſe circumſtances that Mr. de Grimouard, a captain of ſhip of the line, was wrecked here. He had had, on the 17th of October, 1782, an engagement with the *London* of a hundred guns and the *Torbay* of 74, in the channel between Porto-Rico and St.-Domingo. Followed by them, he ſteered, on the 18th, towards the anchorage, called *English-Port*; which his pilot pretended to know. He doubled point Icaque, and entered the bay; but, ready to caſt anchor with ſeven fathoms water, his veſſel touched. This was on the 18th in the evening. The Scipio, his ſhip, ſoon took in water in every part of her, and in the night of the 19th ſhe went entirely to pieces.

A little before you come to the iſlands of Baniſter, you paſs the cove of Grapin, ſituated in 19 deg. 12 min. lat. and 71 deg. 39 min. longitude. Here one may caſt anchor, and land. Veſſels may alſo anchor under the lee of the *Caye Élévantade*, between it and a little rock more to the weſt.

Vol. I.   Z

Middling veffels find a careenage in a place, called the Little-Careenage (Petit-Carénage), under fhelter of the little ifland du Fond, but in the port of the town of Samana, any veffel whatever may run her bowfprit a fhore, on the greateft of the clumps before the port.

All the coves, from the town of Samana to within two leagues of the bottom of the bay, and on the fame fide, are fo many anchoring places, expofed to the fouth winds only; but the fineft port in the bay on this fide of the peninfula, is that under the Point-of-the-Martiniquois.

It is, however, at three leagues before this point, that the fettlement which the Spanifh governement has formed at Samana is fituated. This governement, from what it had feen in almoft all the writings on St. Domingo, as well as from the conftant defire of the French governors to get poffeffion of Samana, was convinced of the importance of that bay, and at laft, when events feemed to forbode the war of 1756, it endeavoured to furnifh it with inhabitants. Don Francifco Rubio, prefident of the Spanifh part, received orders to people Samana; in confequence of which inhabitants were brought from the Canaries for whom lodging places were erected. They were a fort of framed barracks, covered wirh palm-tree leaves, placed in the lines which were to form the ftreets and public fquare, at a future epoch. To this firft fupply were added another of cows, mares and different forts of fowls. But, whether from want of care, or of pasture, these animals, intended to provide a sure mean of subsistence for the colonists, and to raise them from a state of poverty, soon disappeared. They were replaced by a stock of pigs, which seem to be a sort of wild ones, again become tame.

A very small church, dedicated to St. Barbe, and the presbytery, are built in masonry, as is also a house, which the vicinity of a platform with a few pieces of cannon has honoured with the name of fort. This house has four appartments, two of which are inhabited by the governor, who is very often no more than a serjeant; the third is the barrack of a corporal and four soldiers, and the fourth, a prison where there are a pair of stocks.

A new climate and the clearing of lands, always hurtful to health, have diminished this weak settlement, composed at present of about 250 persons, whose appearance illy agrees with the proud title of, city of Samana. The people are, besides, thwarted by the governor, whose permission every individual is obliged to obtain, before he can go to any distance from the settlement. This chief imposes also a certain duty of anchorage on all vessels entering the bay, a good method to disgust whoever might be attracted there by the hopes of barter. The constraint of obtaining permission to retire back ever so little, has caused the neighbouring lands to be cultivated, notwithstanding they were not always the best. It is true this cultivation has done no more than produce a bare subsistence. The trifling quantity of cleared land gives not the leaſt idea of a preparation for producing objects of commerce. Thus the government, or its agents, take the moſt efficacious meaſures for the fruſtration of its own views. It muſt be confeſſed, that the indolence of theſe coloniſts is alſo a cauſe, and perhaps the moſt powerful one, of their want of ſucceſs. Hunting and fiſhing, theſe want obliges them to purſue, and that want which is combatted by idleneſs loſes great part of its power.

I have ſaid, that the Point-of-Martiniquois is about three leagues to the weſt of the ſettlement of Samana, on the ſame ſide of the bay. It ſeems that a vaſt and fine ſituation, healthy air, the proximity of ſtone and wood fit for building, water in abundance, limpid and purified by caſcades, and capacious anchoring place, had better claims to the honour of a ſettlement than the port of Samana, which was preferred to it for I know not what reaſon.

In continuing along this northern coaſt towards the bottom of the bay we find, in general, a fine ſandy beach. This interval is watered by eight rivers, which make 16 which fall into this ſide of the bay, there being eight before we come to the Point-Martiniquois.

One cannot get further down the bay than to within about two leagues of the bottom, except it be in a canoe, becauſe of the mud. At the bottom there is an oyſter-bed of vaſt extent, ſome parts of which are ſeen at low water, looking like a little archipellago of black rocks. Oyſters are here taken up by bushels, and with very little trouble. It is said that they are not so delicate as those among the mangrove-trees, and even that they must be roasted before they are eatable or, at least, good.

There are three mouths in this extremity of the bay. The nearest to the peninsula is that of the Little-Salt-Marsh; the next, that of the river Yuna; the southernmost, that of the Great-Salt-Marsh. Neither of these could be the cause of the error, so long credited, that the peninsula of Samana was an island; an error that the history of St-Domingo, published by Charlevoix (according to the memoirs written in the beginning of the present century by Le Pers, his brother Jesuit) ought to have prevented, or done away. But every thing is so soon forgotten at St-Domingo! It is not improbable that another great salt-marsh, which we see at the *eastern* extremity of the Bay of Cosbeck, between Jackson and the point of Matance, and which may be taken for one of the openings of the channel, may have led some to look on the peninsula as a real island, detached from St. Domingo in the west, as marked in the maps; always excepting those in the work of Charlevoix.

We may be assured, that, had this communication subsisted between the bay of Samana and that of Cosbeck, the Free-Booters, for whom it was always difficult, and sometimes dangerous, to enter the bay of Samana by its opening between Cape-Raphaël and Cape-Samana, would have found out the entrance by the bay of Cosbeck. To this convincing proof comes another, furnished by certain observation; it is, that the mouth of the Little-Salt-Marsh is often obstructed by the sand thrown up by the tide, and which shuts in the boats or canoes which have been able to get into it. When this is the case, the owners are obliged to dig canals in the sand, at low water, after which the water in the marsh forces away the sand as it runs out into the bay; a circumstance that certainly could not happen, if the Salt-Marsh had a communication with the bay of Cosbeck; because the water, finding an obstacle at one opening, would run off by the other, in place of remaining dammed up by the sand.

In leaving the Great-Ester, or Salt-Marsh, and going eastward from the bottom of the bay along its southern side, we find the coast more and more irregular and rough, till at last it becomes inaccessible both by land and sea. It is composed of hideous rocks bearing a few stunted shrubs. It is lined with a chain of little islands of rock, some of which are not less than fifteen fathoms perpendicular; and between these islands and the coast, from which they appear to have been detached, there are immense depths and a very little space.

Between the first of these islands, to the west, there is a cove of a demi-circular form, and a marshy soil, called the Cove of Bertrand, from the name of a Frenchman, settled there in the last century. On the right side of this cove is a grotto, in which a man may walk upright; and further to the west, are mangrove-trees and oyster-beds.

At the end of this ftring of little iflands is the Bay of Pearls, facing the weft, and bounded to the north by a tongue of land. This little bay, which is about eight leagues from the bottom of the great bay, is a good league deep from weft to eaft. The ftouteft veffels may anchor in any part of it, except on a fhallow which rifes in the middle. It is an excellent port, well fheltered from the winds. Ships may anchor on the right, the left, or below the fhallow.

Advancing eaftward from the Bay of Pearls, and croffing the mouth of the river, Savana-la-Mer, we come to the place of the fame name, the anchorage of which is fit for little veffels only. This circumftance fhould have induced thofe who fettled Savana-la-Mer to prefer to it feveral other fpots round the bay. The name of Savana-la-Mer is undoubtedly due to the nature of the fituation, which is a fine favana near the coaft. The fettlement, peopled from the Canaries, is nearly facing that of Samana. It has alfo its governor and rector. The city of Samana, and the town of Savana-la-Mer were both begun in 1756, and both together do not now contain more than five hundred fouls.

Savana-la-Mer is at the end of a plain, which is more than ten leagues long from eaft to weft, and four wide from north to fouth, lying to the weft of the Round-Mountain, and to the north of the prolongation of the fecond chain. Nine rivers run down this plain (which is fometimes called alfo the plain of St. Raphaël) and fall into the fea from the fouthern fide of the bay of Samana. Among thefe are the river Magua, between the river of Adders and that of Savana-la-Mer; then comes the Nicagua, &c. There are, befides, an almoſt infinite number of ſtreams, running from the ridges by which this plain is divided from that of Seybo, to the ſouth, and from that of La Vega, to the weſt: and theſe ſtreams ſeparate the tracts of land proper for different ſorts of cultivation.

A navigator muſt know the coaſt on the ſouth of the bay perfectly well, to be able to follow it from Savana-la-Mer to the Point of Icaque; becauſe the ſhallows and breakers render the navigation very dangerous.

After theſe particulars, in ſome ſort topographical, there remain many of a nautical nature.

It is eaſy to diſcern, after what has been ſaid, how important it is for the mariner to take care not to ſuffer himſelf to be driven too near the peninſula, as the proximity of the land would take from him the winds of nearly one half of the compaſs, and leave him without the poſſibility of getting off. He ought neceſſarily to ceaſe tacking at about two leagues from the peninſula, and ſteer weſtward, till in ſight of the little iſlands of Baniſter, which mark, in ſome meaſure, the extremity of the breakers, the diagonal of which, beginning at Point-Icaque, runs about ſix leagues, from ſouth-eaſt to north-weſt.

The great difficulty of entering is not the only one that mariners find in the bay of Samana. That of getting out is full as great. It cannot take place at all, but with the land breeze; this muſt be taken advantage of, then, as soon after it begins as possible, to get entirely out of the bay, if the vessel be anchored any where near the mouth, and, if not, to get to an anchoring place so situated. If the land breeze ceases, or if the vessel be in a place too low in the bay, it is often useless to weigh, for the vessel is obliged to return to anchor at the place from whence she sailed. At other times the sea-breezes blow so constantly, that they cause a detention for a long time.

It is easy to conceive, after these observations on the bay of Samana, that it would be indispensably necessary, in time of war, to have a sufficient naval force to protect the entrance of it, since it would be easy for a force very inferior to that which might be at anchor in the bay, to block the latter, and thus render it useless.

The bay of Samana might be a convenient place for the establishment of an arsenal, docks, and a cannon foundery; because the river Yuna, the most considerable, as well as the most rapid in the island, having been, since some time, rendered navigable thirteen leagues up for flat-bottomed boats or barges (in order to convey the tobacco of St. Yago, La Vega, and Cotuy), might serve to convey down the wood, with which all the neighbouring lands are covered. The river Camu, and many others that fall into the Yuna, would augment the facility of the carriage. All their banks are covered with mahogany, sabineers, cedars, oaks, pines, and other trees equally fine and useful, and of which whole fleets might be built. Iron, copper, end tin mines, all very near, wait for the hand of the builder: every thing, in short, seems to say, that this superb bay ought to have the honour of being a capital sea-port.

The advantage it possesses of being to the windward of the island, had not escaped the French, since, from their first attempt to share the island with the Spaniards, the Freebooters appeared at Samana. The chace also being easy and productive round the bay, attracted the Buccaniers to it.

D'Ogeron having sailed from St. Domingo in the month of February, 1673, for St. Croix (the rendezvous appointed by Mr. de Baas, governor-general of the American islands, for the attack of Curaçao), and having been wrecked at Porto-Rico, made his escape in June following, with three other persons, and arrived in the bay of Samana, where they found some French who gave them every kind of assistance, and furnished them with the means of returning to the Tortue. Returning with his little armament to avenge the inhuman treatment of the French at Porto-Rico, he stopped again at Samana, in the month of November 1673, and took a reinforcement and some provisions.

D'Ogeron was capable of seeing the importance of a solid establishment at Samana; a point of union for the French, who lived scattered about for twenty years, independent of one another, having nothing in common except a pastor, a secular priest, named Duval. He therefore thought seriously of the project, which he realized in 1674. He sent a certain number of men to this colony under the command of Mr. Jamet, since killed at the battle of Limonade, in 1691. The new colonists regretted the absence of the female sex, when a ship from St. Malo, carrying women to the Tortue, put in; thus furnished with help-mates, the population was soon greatly augmented.

Mr. de Pouançay, the nephew of Mr. D'Ogeron, and who suceeded him in 1676, looking, undoubtedly, on the settlement at Samana as at too great a distance from the other French settlements, gave orders to the inhabitants to quit the peninsula where they were settled, and go to the plain of Cape François. This order displeased the colonists, who obeyed it tardily and with regret. The greatest part of those that had indigo plantations remained; but, after the taking of St. Yago, by Mr. de Cussy, in 1690, the French at Samana were much tormented by the Spaniards, who killed a great number of them. The colony was not, however, entirely dispersed, and it was even become once more considerable, when, in 1693, it was annihilated by an action which Charlevoix has doubly disfigured, with respect to the fact, and with respect to the date, since he has made it take place in 1676. (Vol. 2, in 4to, page 115).

According to him, the French, after having received from Mr. Franquesnay, the order to quit Samana, wishing to show the Spaniards that they did not quit it out of fear, went and pillaged without resistance, the town of Cotuy, the inhabitants of which, afterwards informed by a deserter, that the French were on a hunting party, surprised in their turn, the hunters and the people in the settlement, and put the whole to death.

I shall now relate the fact, such as I find it in an examination, made by order of the administrators in the month of July 1713, before Mr. Robineau, attorney-general of the superior council of Cape-François, in which certain old inhabitants of Samana relate it in the following manner.

A Frenchman named *la Fontaine*, carrying on a traffic in the flesh of different animals, with the Spaniards of Cotuy, married a wife there. His wife, who did not like to live among the French at Samana, profited by the discontent of her husband at some ill-treatment from the commandant, and prevailed on him to go and settle at Cotuy. There he excited the Spaniards to pillage the French settlement, conducted them, and caused the whole of his country people to be murdered in one night, without distinction of age or sex, and all they possessed to be plundered. The few that had the good luck to escape, went to Bayaha, now Fort-Dauphin, and to Cape-François.

From that time the Freebooters alone, and a very small number of inhabitants, had the courage to retire to Samana; till 1699, when the news being received that the English were preparing to make attempts on that place, Mr. de Galiffet sent off, on the 24th of July, Mr. de Cugnac, a lieutenant of a detached company of marines, with four soldiers, and a certain number of hunters. This officer found there some few French, and among others Mr. Foëfon, to whom Mr. de Cugnac transferred his poft as commandant, when, after remaining feven or eight months, he returned to the Cape. Mr. Foëfon (one of the witneffes in the examination of 1713), having a commiffion from Mr. de Galiffet, hoifted the arms of France on peninfula. But the inhabitants quitted Samana, in confequence of an order of the minifter of the 13th of January, 1700.

There is, then, no doubt that the French have feveral times had a real poffeffion at Samana; that they had fettlements, commandants, and, in fhort, all that indicate a public enjoyment, and political organization. Among the French we may inftance Meffrs. Jacques Louis Varin, Thibault, and Madame Larèche, who went afterwards to fettle in the Quarter-Morin; and, at the Petit-Anfe, Meffrs. Maréchal, la Taille, Vauville, Bapaume, François Sauvaget, Antoine Toby, Nicholas-Laurent. Thomas, Jean le Flamand, la Fleur, Bertrand, Charles Foreftier, Denis Gouffier, Ollivier Foëfon (fince lieutenant of the company of Bayaha), Jacques Lamy, (born at Samana in 1666), and Madame Frances Louis, wife of Mr. Maffé, born at Samana in 1673.

At the fame epoch of 1713, the reft of the old French inhabitants of Samana, and their defcendants, ardently requefted to be protected in their return to that place, and it was to fecond their earneft folicitations, that Mr. Mithon, then intendant of Saint-Domingo, caufed the examination to be taken, and fent it to the minister in the month of October following, accompanied with a justificatory memoire.

However, since the beginning of the present century, there has not been one hundred French really settled at Samana; for we cannot call such, neither the *Brethren of the Coast*, which the fishery and the chase have invited to settle along the Spanish coast, since in their manners, they are as much unlike the French, as they are unlike the Spaniards, and perhaps more; nor an inhabitant who came from St. Vincent's about thirty years ago, and who, in the name of a Spanish relative, has formed a settlement in the peninsula.

But the possession of Samana has never ceased to be a desirable object, with those who know its maritime importance. I make mention, in the history of Saint-Domingo, of the endeavours of Mr. d'Estaing in 1765, to obtain from Spain the cession of Samana. A sea-officer, a man who knew how useful the possession of Saint-Domingo is to France, must necessarily have been fully convinced of the importance of such an acquisition. This thought struck Mr. Weuves also. He dwells long on all the advantages that the position of Samana offers. But the Spanish government will never (at least while it retains its present character) suffer the idea of making concessions of lands: to be convinced of this, we need only read Valverde, who almost falls in a passion at the reflections of Mr. Weuves.

Were we to consider Samana and the peninsula, as a spot for cultivation, we should find much less to extol than in considering them in a maritime point of view. The peninsula, which at the isthmus is reduced to two short leagues in width, is no more than fifteen leagues in length; consequently it could admit of but very few settlements, particularly of sugar plantations; although it is watered by more than twenty rivers, sixteen of which run towards the interior part of the bay. Many of these rivers have not a current always visible; sometimes they are buried among rocks, or, sinking beneath a sandy soil, follow a subterraneous and unknown course; at times they form cascades, at others more rapid falls, and at others they run along a level bed. Some of their waters are enriched with gold-sand. Besides there are mountains on the peninsula ranged in amphitheatrical order, which take up great part of the surface. Their elevation is not very considerable, and on their tops there are often flats; but at the eastern extremity, and almost during a third of the length of the peninsula, the country is uninhabitable; as you approach the sea it often becomes inaccessible, on account of the rocks which cover it, and which cut and divide it in every direction.

The peninsula abounds in fine wood, another advantage as a spot for an arsenal and dock: on the other side of the bay, there is only Savana-la-Mer that can offer any idea of agriculture. Nature does not seem to have formed Samana for this useful object; but rather for a union of strength and protection, a particularity, among others, in which Samana resembles the Mole St. Nicholas.

It is then, under this point of view alone that we muſt eſtimate Samana, which is as yet in a ſtate of nature, and has ſo few inhabitants, that its fine bay and the animals which enjoy the dominion of it, have all the appearance and indications of a place entirely new.

On the borders of the bay, and of the ſalt-marſhes and the river Yuna, which form the bottom of it, we find the mangrove-tree, which flouriſhes in all the low and acquatic borders under the torrid zone, where the induſtry of man has not oppoſed its progreſs, and with it, millions of cruſtacees which find nouriſhement among its roots, and innumerable ſwarms of mouſtique flies and muſquitoes, the frail exiſtence of which it ſuſtains by ſheltering them, from the winds; as if in gratitude for the defence their imperceptible but tormenting ſtings yield it againſts the approachs of the wood-man.

I have ſaid that, particularly in the bottom of the bay, there are great quantities of oyſters, which preſerve undiſturbed the almoſt-vegetative exiſtence allotted them by nature. Miriads of fiſh are ſeen in every part of the bay.

The neighbouring woods are the abode of wild hogs. It is true the hunters ſometimes come to diſturb theſe, but the loſs is ſoon reparied by a continual breed.

In many parts of this immenſe bay, and particularly on the little iſlands, are multitudes of birds of every kind, from the man of war bird, the cooling oil of which is excellent for the gout and the sciatica, to the smallest wood-pigeon, to which sensuality even affixes a value. All these republics of animals are friends, they all live in the neighbourhood of each other, and when by chance, for it is by chance, in the bay of Samana, man, the enemy of almost every living creature, brings death along with him into their retreat, fear hurries the feathered nations into the air, which they darken beneath them; but their quick return alone is sufficient to prove that they have yet to learn mistrust.

Yet, there are still mute proofs, even close round the bay of Samana, that it was formerly inhabited by the Indians. We yet find, in the caverns, wooden swords of which Herrera speaks, made of the palm-tree, which is well known to be extremely hard. In digging in the ground, we find vessels of burnt clay, the work of these unfortunate people, whose unpolished understanding is prefered, by all those who know their deplorable history, to the bloody genius of those who have extirpated them from their native land.

It would be wrong to quit Samana, without mentioning the singular circumstance of a hermit who lived in that retreat for upwards of thirty years. He was born at Nantz, and had the misfortune to become a pirate. He was suddenly seized with an unconquerable horror for this infamous profession, and at once conceived the project of quitting his companions, whom he had surpassed in cruelty, and of retiring into a corner of the peninsula, where he long remained totally unknown. His solitary abode was discovered, at the end of 22 years, by one of his old comrades. The Spaniards, struck with his resolution, and the perseverance and austerity with which he had adhered to it, affected by the privations he had supported, and by the thousand ills and hardships that a lone individual, without aid, without means, reduced to his natural faculties to provide for all his wants, must encounter, were for ever talking, and always with veneration, of John the hermit of Samana. His name, and the praises accompanying it, at lenght reached Santo-Domingo, to which city he was at last prevailed on to repair at the joint request of the archbishop and the president. But the hermit was not able to support the noise of the word, to which he had been for more than thirty years a stranger. He died in the capital, soon after his arrival, leaving, by his return to virtue, an idea to which the Spaniards add one of a religious nature; for the greatest part of them revere his memory as that of a Saint.

After passing Cape-Rézon, or Cape-Samana, situated in 19 deg. 15 min. 40 seconds, north latitude, and 71 deg. 33 min. 30 seconds, west longitude, the coast runs towards the north-west, as far as Cape-Cabron, which lies in 19 deg. 21 min. 52 seconds, north-latitude, and 71 deg. 38 min. 40 seconds, west longitude. Near about half way between these two capes, but nearest Cape-Cabron, is a little island under which a vessel may cast anchor, but she must at the same time lie exposed to north winds.

From Cape-Cabron, which takes its name from a manor of the cacique *Mayobanex*, the land runs westward, forming the northern side of the peninsula of Samana, as far as point Jackson. In traversing this interval, in which are the rivers Port-St-Lawrence, Lemon-River, &c. we first find, at a good league from Cape - Cabron, the little port called Little-Port-Gosier, which is an anchoring-place for small vessels. At a league further on, the Great-Port-Gosier, where large merchant-men may moor, but not without fearing the winds, from all the points between north and west inclusive. A good league hence we come to the little island of the Hermit, which takes its name from John of Samana, whose hermitage was near this place. This part of the coast also is dangerous.

After passing the Great-Port-Gosier, at a third part of the distance between it and the hermit's island, we meet with the mouth of the river Jayan, (which has been changed for that of St-John). This river is like those which run towards the bay of Samana; that is to say, its current presents falls, cascades, hollow rocks, and chasms, where it becomes subterraneous. This river, the banks of which are covered with reeds, is very full of fish.

A league westward beyond the island of the hermit, we come to Port-Citron (Lemon Port), where in the mouth of the river of the same name, is good anchorage for merchant ships. It is reckoned a league from this port to another anchoring-place, called Little-Port, after which, at the end of another league, we come to a third anchoring-place, known by the name of the Terrienne. Three thousand fathoms to the weſt of the Terrienne, are the Whales, a clump of little iſlands, a league and a half eaſt of Port-Jackſon.

There is a chain of breakers, running from Port-Citron to the Whales, and at about half a league from the coaſt. But there are chaſms in theſe breakers, through which ſmall veſſels get to Little-Port and the Terrienne. It requires, however, a perfect knowledge of theſe moorings to venture into them ; for, though thoſe of the Terrienne, for inſtance, are fine, the entrance to them is dangerous. This is one of the parts of the peninſula, where the land is fit for cultivation.

After the Whales, comes Port-Jackſon, the beſt on the north of the peninſula. It is capable of receiving veſſels of any burthen. As there are ſome ſhallows, to the north of the breakers, a veſſel muſt get higher up to avoid them, and, before ſhe approaches the land, which cannot be done without riſk, ſhe muſt get oppoſite a white roch very remarkable, and then ſhe muſt ſteer direct towards a little iſland laying in the port. The paſſage has a large *key* eaſily diſtinguiſhed, with a good depth on each ſide.

Almoſt immediately after Port-Jackſon comes the point of the ſame name, whence the land runs rather ſouth-weſtward to the Great-Salt-Marſh, which lies in the ifthmus of Samana, and which forms a port, opening to the north-weft. This port has fhoals and breakers on each fide. The entrance is, however, clear, the interior part of it fpacious and well fheltered, and it has fourteen fathoms water. The Great-Salt-Marfh ends the peninfula in this point, and it is it, as already obferved, which occafioned it to be taken for an ifland. Perhaps, indeed, it would not be impoffible, by fufficient means, intelligently employed, to open a communication between this marfh and the bay of Samana.

From the Great-Salt-Marfh, the land runs towards Old-Cape, forming a wide bay, quite open to the winds from all the points from north to eaft. Some maps call it, the bay of Cofbeck, others Scotch bay.

In this bay we find, firft, Port-Matance, into which merchant veffels may at all times enter. This port is known by a fteep hill, much more advanced than the reft. The entrance is, on both fides, bordered with breakers.

Four leagues beyond Matance we come to Grand-Lagon, and at the end of another league, to Salt-River. It is next to impoffible to anchor in either of thefe, both being furrounded with breakers. According to Valverde, however, there are fome parts of the bay delightful; he even compares the coaft of it, for this reafon, to that between Pointe-de-l'Épée and Cape Samana.

Before we come to Old-Cape, we find Pointe-des-Savanettes (Point of little Savanas), the fteep coaft of which would be very dangerous for a veffel, landlocked in the bay of Cofbeck.

We now come to Old-Cape-François, thus named by Chriftopher Columbus, but for what reafon is unknown, It lies in 19 deg. 40 min. 30 feconds; north latitude, and 72 deg. 22 min. weft longitude. After doubling the cape we arrive fucceffively at Pierre-Percée, the Falaifes, and the Trou-d'Enfer, anchoring-places which can be of ufe to fuch veffels only as are coming from the weft, and as the rapid currents prevent doubling Old-Cape. In this cafe they may put in here in the evening, in order to preferve the diftance they have gained during the day.

Next comes Cape la Roche, lying in 19 deg. 41 min. 32 fecondes, north latutude, and 72 deg. 31 min 30 feconds, weft longitude. Further on is the anchoring-place, called Grigri, then Port-de-la Soufrière (Port-Sulpher), faid to be one of the fineft on this coaft, and capable of receiving veffels of the line. Between the breakers a head of it are two paffages; the weftern one is for great veffels. The bottom is good in this port, and a fteep hill in its neighbourhood is well calculated as a land-mark for thofe who wifh to approach it. There are again anchoring-places in the Port-des-Ananas (Pine appleport), and in Port-de-la-Groffe-Pointe (Port of Thick-Point); but thefe are for boats and barges only, and they muft be well known before one can venture into them. Once in, however, the breakers are a good fhelter from without.

After these we come to the mouth of the river St. John, and, further on, to that of the Macoriz. Some maps call the space between these two rivers, *Balm-Bay*; but surely the name of bay is here improperly employed. Other maps, changing it into Bay-de-Baune, have extended it almost from Old-Cape to Port-de-Plate.

Several leagues from the river Macoriz, but returning towards the north, we find the point of the same name. It was for the convenience of the inhabitants of this canton, living two distant from the parishes of Cotuy and la Véga, that the chaplainship of Macoriz was created, about thirty years ago. These chaplainships are chapels or oratories, due to the zeal of the archbishops, or else to the devotion of the inhabitans. The founder, or founders pay the curate.

After the point of Macoriz, we come to Port-St-Yague, vulgarly called, Old-Port. It is small, and hardly merits any other name than that of anchoring-place. Between Port-St.-Yague and Port-de-Plate is the little anchorage of Padre-Pin, the entrance of which is under the lee of two little islands. Its bottom is bad, and it has no shelter when the wind blows towards the coast.

Port - de - Plate was discovered and visited by Christopher Columbus, in his first voyage. It is overlooked by a mountain, the top of which is so white that the Spaniards thought it covered with snow; undeceived, they called it the Silver-Mountain, and the port, Port-de-Plate (Silver-Port). In another voyage, Columbus, who came hither with Bartholomew his brother, traced the plan of the settlement, which was formed by Ovando, in 1502. The entrance of the port, which is not very good, faces exactly to the north; the bottom has three fathoms water, which diminishes considerably as soon as the entrance is passed; this is attributed in particular to the mud, brought down by the two rivers, which here fall into the sea. Besides, in some parts of the port, the bottom is of sharp rocks, capable of cutting the cables. The squalls from the north and north-west are to be feared also. A vessel must, in entering, keep very close to the point of the breaker, near the eastern fort; when in, she anchors in the middle of the port.

The canton of Port-de-Plate greatly abounds in mines of gold, silver, and copper. There are also mines of plaster.

At the beginning of the sixteenth century this place was very flourishing. It had a coat of arms granted it, like many other places of the Spanish colony. It is an escutcheon, argent, a mountain, sinople, capped with an F and a Y, in gold, crowned, and below, waved with gold and azure. The Spanish merchant-men came here in great numbers to take in sugar, because it was, at that time, one of the outlets to La Vega and St. Yago, to which places Ovando had made a fine road, the expences of which he was afterwards reproached for. Port-de-Plate was, however, pillaged by the privateers before 1543, since when, the decay of which I have already spoken, arrived; and this place being one of the smuggling ports, that supplied the want of commerce with the mother country, it was comprehended in the proscription of 1606, and in the order for the demolition of the maritime places in the north. The inhabitants, after the issuing of the order for retiring into the interior of the colony, joined those of Monte-Christ, and settled the town of Monte-de-Plate. But a new population of Monte-Christ having obtained, under Don Francisco Rubio, a royal permission to carry on, with all nations, a free commerce, during ten years, this commerce which was very lucrative, and which brought in a supply of negroes, and a concourse of foreigners, gave rise to the re-establishment of Port-de-Plate, which was begun with families brought from the Canaries. The present population of its territory may be reckoned at 2,000, or 2,500 persons. Port-de-Plate is unhealthy from the custom which the inhabitants have of drinking the water of a ravin. This water gives the fever, and particularly to persons newly arrived. In 1788 the construction of a handsome church was yet going on.

From Port-de-Plate the coast runs north-westward to the point, called Red-Cape (Cap-Rouge). Before we come to this point, we meet with Port of Marmosets, which may receive merchantmen, but the entrancy of which is rendered difficult by the breakers. This port is followed by two anchoring-places, very near each other, called Grand-Port-Berhagne and Little-Port-Berhagne, which, notwithstanding the denomination of Port, offer anchorage for boats only. Little-Port-Berhagne is followed by Pointe-du-Carrouge (Cas-Rouge or Cap-Rouge,) from which the coast runs westward. A little further on is Little-Port-Souffleur (Port Grampus) and after it, Great-Port-Souffleur. The first, for small craft, and the second, for merchant-men. A little island of rock guides to the entrance of the latter. A vessel may enter on either side the island, but it is better to leave it to the east.

After the two Port-Souffleurs, comes the Anse-à-Baleine (Whale-cove) and Port-Caballo, Port-Cavaille (Horse-Port). Columbus entered here on board the Caravelle, the *Pinte*, one of the three vessels with which he made the discovery. As Captain Francisco Martin Pinzo, who had separated from him several days before, joined him in this place, he named it Port-de-Grace.

Port Cavaille would be one of the finest and best on this coast, if there were sufficient water at the entrance; but there is but nine feet water, and in one part there is a shallow. Here is a careenage, in which the mariner is perfectly at ease; a rumbling noise which he scarcely hears at a distance, makes him suspect that a tempest is agitating the waves.

There is yet the point, called Pointe-de-Briseval, after Port-Cavaille and the Grand-Anse-du-Nord (Great North Cove), before we come to Point Isabella, lying in 19 deg. 59 min. 10 sec. north latitude, and 73 deg. 37 min. 5 sec. west longitude. It is after this point going fouthward, that we find the port, where Columbus formed the firft Spanifh fettlement in the ifland. He called it *Ifabella*, after the catholic queen then reigning. He entered in during the night, driven by a tempeft. Day-light difcovered to him all the beauty of the port, although a little expofed to the north-weft wind. It is overlooked by a very high mountain, flat at the top, and furrounded with rocks. Columbus gave the name of Ifabella to the river alfo which falls into the port. This river is confiderable. There are fourteen fathoms water to anchor in.

The fettlement of the town of Ifabella, hardly begun in 1493, was given up in 1496, when its inhabitants were carried to the city of Santo-Domingo, which originally was called New-Ifabella. Thus, by a feries of circumftances, as fingular as inexplicable, the fourth quarter of the world takes a name different from that of the man who difcovered it, and the name of the princefs who affifted him in the undertaking, and to whom he wifhed to give a teftimony of his gratitude, almoft as foon as he beheld this new country, has not been preferved on this firft monument of a glory, in which fhe, in fome fort, had a fhare.

To the weft of Old Ifabella, and between it and Pointe-la-Roche, or Point-Ruffia, (Rocky-Point), is a little port, called the Deep-Salt-Marfh, or the Marigot. After it, comes Petit-Trou, or Marfh of the Petit-Trou.

As foon as we have doubled Pointe-la-Roche, we come to Sandy-Ifland. Between this latter and the land there is a paffage leading to Port-de-Balza, or Port of Petite-Saline, which is acceffible in no other direction, on account of the breaker runnings from Sandy-Ifland to Cape Monte-Chrift, or Cape la Grange, before which is ftill another point, called Pointe-des-Mangliers (Mangrove-tree point). But all thefe three points, from that of Ifabella to that of la Grange, are no more than little anchoring-places, to enter which with fmall veffels even, requires a pilot, extremely well acquainted with the breakers and the coaft. Without fuch a guide, difficult to be found, any veffel muft run a great rifque of being wrecked on thefe breakers, with the lofs of crew and all on board.

Cape la Grange, or Cape Monte-Chrift is the extremity of this part of the coaft, as I have already faid. It lies in 19 deg. 54 min. 30 fec. north latitude, and in 74 deg. 9 min. 30 fec. weft longitude, meridian of Paris. The name of Grange (Barn) was given it by the French, on account of its form, and that of Monte-Chrift comes from Columbus, who named it thus on the 14th of January, 1493. It is a very high hill, fays Herrera, in the form of a tent. This promontary, which even feems detached from the ifland, when feen at a fmall diftance, is perceivable a great way off, and if the weather be ever fo little clear, it is plainly to be feen with the naked eye, from Cape-François, from which it is fourteen leagues. A ftrip of level land joins Cape la Grange to the territory of Monte-Chrift, and it is owing to this, that the cape has been taken for an ifland.

After doubling this cape, we find the bay of Monte-Chrift, running nearly fouth-weft. It is formed by Cape la Grange, on one fide, and Pointe-des-Dunes (Down-Point), on the other. Thefe two are about 6,500 fathoms from each other. The bay is about 1,400 fathoms deep, and its winding is nearly four leagues. At about 900 fathoms from Cape la Grange, defcending the bay, we find the little ifland of Monte-Chrift, 350 fathoms from the fhore. One may fail between the two with two, four, and five fathoms water; and about 250 fathoms further on is anchorage in fix, feven, eight, and even ten fathoms. A league and a quarter from Cape la Grange, is a battery intended to protect a landing-place of 100 fathoms wide, which is below, and oppofite the town of Monte-Chrift.

The town of Monte-Chrift, ftanding at 800 fathoms from the fea-fide, rifes in an amphitheatre on the fide of the coaft, which is very high all round this bay. The town is 200 fathoms fquare, which fpace is divided in nine parts, cut by two ftreets running from eaft to weft, and two others from north to fouth. Monte-Chrift, which alfo boafts of a coat of arms, was founded in 1533, by fixty labourers fent hither from Spain with their families, in confequence of a bargain made by the government with Bolegnos, an inhabitant of Saint-Domingo. It was evacuated in 1606 (as before obferved), when the inhabitants confidered as fmugglers, were forced back into the interior of the country, and became, in conjunction with the inhabitants of Port-de-Plate, the founders of the town of Monte-de-Plate. Monte-Chrift, as well as Port-de-Plate had been an out-let to the fettlement of la Vega and St. Yago; but during the war of 1756, between France and Spain, the government having fent fome *Canarians* hither, they formed a fettlement. I have faid, in fpeaking of Port-de-Plate, that Spain made a neutral port of Monte-Chrift, for ten years. The proximity of this port to the French colony, and particularly Cape-François, was the caufe of a contraband commerce from which the Spanifh part derived great advantage. Monte-Chrift becoming a point of connection for the two moft commercial nations of Europo, deadened all the projects of war, and, more than once, ferved to prove the love of gain ever prevails over that of war, and over every fentiment of patriotifm. Monte-Chrift became the medium of plenty for all the places near it in the Spanifh part. There brought fuch an influx of riches, that the piece of gold, called half-joe (worth eight Spanifh dollars), was become the moft common; and when Spain took a part in the war, the town of Monte-Chrift, fitted out, at its own expence, feveral privateers, and thefe alfo became a new fource of profperity. But thefe happy effects difappeared with their caufe, and Monte-Chrift is again become a very poor place, deftitute of every refource, but that of cattle raifed in its territory, and fold to the French. It was a little while in agitation, in 1779, to make that port free again, on account of the war.

The population of Monte-Chrift and its dependencies may be computed at three thoufand fouls. The houfe, called the Government-houfe, overlooks the town. The commandant refides in it. It is fituated a little towards the fouth. There are yet to be feen the ruins of another houfe in mafonry, having a balcony and a roof of hollow tiles, which is a clear proof that it belonged to a Frenchman, who had fettled at this place, while it was looked upon as a neutre. There is a trifling garrifon at Monte-Chrift.

At about a league from the battery, following the winding of the bay, is the river of Monte-Chrift, or to fpeak more correctly, the river Yaqui, which has two mouths, at 300 fathoms from each other, but which form a fingle ftream at a quarter of a league higher up. Columbus named this river the Golden-River, in 1493, when he firft faw its mouth, believing that its fands contained grains of that metal. But, having croffed it fince, in his journey from Port de-Plate to Cibao, and not knowing it to be the fame, he gave it the name of Reedy-River. The pofition of the town relatively to the river, obliges the inhabitants to fetch their water from a great diftance. For this purpofe they make ufe of affes, which are here, of courfe, very common.

The land, in the environs of Monte-Chrift, is fandy and very fteril. Its fituation, which may contribute to its falubrity, has nothing elfe agreeable in it. The river which runs in it contains great numbers of crocodiles.

It is 3,000 fathoms from the western mouth of the Yaqui to the Pointe-des-Dunes (Down-Point) which encloses the bay.

Nearly opposite the town of Monte-Christ, and at more than 5,000 fathoms to the west, lies the *Petit-islet de Bois* (Little-Woody-Island), one of the seven, called the *Seven Brothers*. From the western border of this island to the eastern border of that which is called the *Western-Island* (which name marks its situation relatively to the six others), and which is nearly in a line with the Little-Woody-Island, it is no more than about 4,200 fathoms. At about 1,500 fathoms to the north-west of the Little-Woody-Island, is the *Great-Woody-Island*. To the south of this latter, and almost opposite it, at the distance of about 3,000 fathoms, is the little Island of *Toirou*, which lies about 2,000 fathoms to the west of the Point-des-Dunes (Down-Point). At 1,200 fathoms from the *Great-Woody-Island*, in a direction nearly west-north-west, is the *islet-à-Dumoulin* (Dumoulin's Island), and to the south-south-west of this latter, at the distance of 1,000 fathoms, is the *islet-à-Garcin* (Garcin's Island). *L'islet-à-Dressel* (or Dressel's Island) is 2,000 fathoms to the south of *Garcin's Island*.

On the south side of the Great-Woody-Island, and that of Toirou, there is an anchorage of four, five, and six fathoms of water, on a sandy bottom; and on the south of Dressel's Island, on a bottom of weeds and sand. But on the east and north of this latter island, there is a shallow running across to the Western-Iſland. From this iſland alſo there is a ſhallow which runs towards the ſouth-ſouth-weſt. But, generally ſpeaking, one muſt know theſe waters exceedingly well to attempt a paſſage among a chain of ſhoals, forming a circumference of about ſeven leagues; the northern point is, however, leſs ſhoaly, for about 1,000 fathoms, than Cape-la-Grange. Beſides, as a mariner cannot be driven here but by northerly winds, or thoſe from the north-weſt, or weſt, or elſe to take ſhelter from an enemy, ſuch mariner, arrived within the *Seven Brothers*, would undoubtedly prefer making to Fort-Dauphin, or to the Bay of Mencenilla, rather than moor his veſſel in ſuch anchorage. In conſequence of ſeveral wrecks, and of the ſhelter that Perkins, a famous Engliſh privateer commander on the coaſt of Saint-Domingo during the war of 1778, found among the Seven Brothers, induced Mr. Bellecombe, to have a chart of thoſe iſlands taken by Mr. Delaage, a lieutenant in the navy, commanding the cutter the Pivert.

In doubling the Pointe-des-Dunes (Down Point), and going towards the ſouth, we find, at a little more than 2,000 diſtance, the Point-des-Mangliers-Gris (Grey Mangrove-Point), and, at 2,000 further, the Point of Ycaque, (Icaco-Point), which is the northern point of the Bay of Mancenilla.

The bay, opening to the weſt, is about 4,000 fathoms deep, from weſt to eaſt, and 2,800 wide, from north to ſouth, between the Point of Ycaque and the land, which, running eaſt and weſt, forms the ſouthern side of the bay. The general form of this bay augments its extent. The Point of Ycaque being no more than a tongue of land, the extremity of which is not more than sixty or eighty fathoms wide, the bay falls back on the north side, and runs more than 2,500 fathoms up this tongue. Here it forms, as far as a point, called the Point-du-Boucan-à-Voleur (Robber's Coooking Place), lying on the eastern side of the bay, the Ester-des-Moucles, which is marshy, and almost dry, and which communicates with the sea at the Pointe-des-Mangliers-Gris. From the bottom of this Ester, or salt-marsh, the south side of the bay, it is reckoned to be about two leagues and three quarters.

From the Pointe-du-Boncan-à-Voleur, the land at the bottom of the bay running nearly south-east, this part of the bay becomes still wider, and affords excellent anchorage, even for vessels of the first size; except it be in a little cove which lies behind the Pointe-du-Boucan-à-Voleur; in the Ester, or salt-marsh of Tapion, which lies nearly in the east of the Point of Ycaque; and in the Ester-des-Vases, larger than the preceding one, and lying precisely in the north-east angle of the bottom of the bay; because, in all these three places, the water is too shallow.

On the south of the Ester-des-Vases, the coast begins to run east and west, and, at 5,500 fathoms from the beginning of the Ester, we find the mouth of the river of the Massacre, which also is in the bay of Mancenilla, and which is now the point of separation of the French and Spanish colonies on the north of the island.

The bay of Mancenilla, though a very fine one, is not so useful as it might be, if its bottom were well-known. There are several shallows in it; a circumstance to be attributed to the overflowings of the river of the Massacre, which roll into it wood, sand, and stones, in great quantities. Perhaps these overflowings would render it necessary to sound the bay annually, after they are over. In general, it is prudent, on entering, to keep closer to the point of Ycaque, than to the south side of the bay; because the sandy point has no rocks. The bottom of the bay is muddy.

The river of the Massacre, the mouth of which, as already mentioned, lies to the north, is, during a league, from five to twelve feet deep, and pretty wide; but its bed is often full of the wood which the current brings down. This wood collects together in some places, and forms a sort of basons, and here the crocodiles make their abode. The river is very full of fish, an advantage that has but too often attracted the vessels of war to the bay of Mancenilla, and retained them there. It is here that are found those enormous mullets which are the pride of the table at Cape-François. In the times of the floods, these fish are driven towards the bay, where negroes, well practised in the business, fish for them.

Fishing in the bay is difficult enough, on account of the wood, of which I have spoken. The negroes must be good divers; because they are often obliged to go to the bottom and difentangle the feine; but when it gets near the beach, it is a fingular and ftriking fpectacle, to fee the negroes, the fifh, and the crocodiles, all flouncing about in the water together. The boldnefs of the negroes feems to ftrike the crocodiles with ftupidity. They tamely fuffer themfelves to be killed with clubs or ax-handles. The negroes knock out their teeth, which they fell to make corals, the garniture of which ferves to mark the degree of luxury or pride of thofe who hang them to the necks of their children.

The reader would undoubtedly be aftonifhed that Frenchmen fhould go to fifh in the Spanifh territory, did I not inform him that the Spanifh prefident ordinarily grants permiffion to fuch perfons as are recommended to him by the French governor. Thefe permiffions, however, do not always fhelter them from the vexations of a Spanifh advanced poft, which is ftationed in the neighbourhood, and which fometimes ftops both the fifhermen and the boats. But, intelligent proprietors know, as it is faid, that thefe interruptions only mean, in plain Englifh, that it is high time to renew certain little prefents, to which they attribute the power of operating a perfect reconciliation.

I fhall return to the river of the Maffacre, when I begin the defcription of the French part.

Now let us take a general view of the coaft, from the Cape of Samana to the Bay of Mancenilla, comprehending an extent of more than eighty leagues, taken in a right line.

The most striking circumstance, and that, perhaps, which is the most proper to mark the character of the two nations, is, to see on the west side of the river Massacre, settlements where every thing bespeaks an active industry, and a degree of wealth that extends even to objects of luxury; while on the other side, all appears barren; for, here and there a spot, where the cultivator hardly raises what is necessary to the support of animal life, cannot be said to do away the uniform sadness of the prospect. It reigns, in some sort, from Samana to the eastern bank of the Massacre, and the height of the chain of Monte-Christ seems to add to it, if that be possible. Nothing but poverty presents itself, a poverty the most difficult to be cured, because accompanied with pride. Many parts of long extent are well adapted to settlements of divers kinds; but Nature waits for the aid of man, and man, if he appears here, is willing to do nothing, neither for her nor for himself. Hence the borders of the Bay of Mancenilla are useless; though it would be possible to drain them, and establish excellent manunufactures.

We have seen that, except the towns of Monte-Christ, Port-de-Plate, and Samana, to which the name of town is far from being due, the northern coast of the Spanish part is almost uninhabited. However, all the lands near the sea-side are granted, not in small lots, which would suppose a number of proprietors, and a design to cultivate, but in large grants. One of the objects in soliciting these tracts, is the fishery;

but a much more important one is, the hunting of the wild hogs.

The season for this hunting is that time of the year, when a sort of palm-tree bears bunches of a little grain, of which the hogs are very fond. The Spanish hunter, if alone, goes armed with a lance, a *machette*, and a knife, into those parts of the woods where the palm-trees most abound; He has dogs with him, which, upon sight of the wild-hog, fly round him and keep him at bay, till the hunter comes to kill him with his lance. The game is now opened and his entrails taken out; the head and feet are thrown away, and the hunter shoulders the carcass, which he sometimes divides, to be able to carry it home the more conveniently.

If, on the contrary, there are many hunters together, they choose a spot where they expect the chase to be productive; there they raise a little hut, or *ajoupa*, covered with branches, or palm-tree leaves. They then fix bars supported on forks, on which the flitches are salted and dried. When a good quantity are collected, they are packed together, and carried home; often by water, if the chase has been considerable.

When the hunters are furnished with powder, they hunt for other game at the same time; for, the ducks, teals, and wood-pigeons, fly in clouds, particularly in the Bay of Mancenilla and that of Cosbeck, of which the wild animals have a sort of exclusive possession.

Almost all the coast is lined with mangrove-trees, which always indicates a marshy soil. There are some of these trees big enough to make a good stout rafter. This plant is useful too in another way, its bark makes excellent tan; but the French only profit from this, and the neglected state of the coast, favours them in so doing. Perhaps, were care taken to cut the tree after having barked it, useful scions might spring out, whereas, the trunk left standing, rots, and the root perishes. This custom will, without doubt, oblige them to penetrate further into the island, which will augment the difficulty, and that sort of living martyrdom which the barkers suffer from the stings of the *moustiques*, and against which there is no defence but that of a thick smoke, well calculated to betray those, who are on so dangerous an errand in a foreign territory. These mangrove-trees form an abode for crabs without number, and an almost continued chain of oyster-beds. Some mariners have asserted, that the water, after remaining some time round the stems of certain mangrove-trees, becomes a good febrifuge.

The land along the coast bear also very fine woods, fit for different uses, whether for burning or building. Frenchmen venture to cut them down, at least for burning, and, in general, sell the produce of their voyage at Cape-François. These sort of adventures are not always without risk; for the noise of the axes and of the falling trees, may perchance awake some Spaniard from his apathy; he informs his neighbours, in hopes of seizing the woodmen, and in greater hopes of getting their shallops and provisions.

The breakers, so common along the northern beach, afford also a resource with regard to the fishery, for which those who go to fetch tan and wood through them are the best, and almost the only pilots, because the Spaniards rarely go from land. Several of these breakers are seen at low water, and discover madreporal, coral, sea-plants, and other substances, an examination of which would be interesting to the naturalist. Divers animals live in these aquatic abodes, some skim on the surface, whilst others remain sequestered in the clefts. There are lobsters of a prodigious size, and several sorts of shell-fish, such as the cockle and the sea-snail.

The cavities of some of these breakers, serve at low water, as reservoirs or fish-ponds. The fish may then be, as it were, laded out; but the French would destroy them, if they went more frequently, by their covetousness to take even more than they know what to do with. The little disturbance that the fish find in these retreats attracts, besides, numbers of sea-cows, (*manati, lamantin,*) and sharks. The former, notwithstanding their delicate ear, that advertises them of the most distant danger, do not always escape the harpoon; but, if struck, they plunge with the swiftness of an arrow, seek some cleft in the rocks, and thus rob the fisherman of his prey, and of the instrument with which they are pierced. The shark, rendered bold and obstinate by his voracity, is very hard to kill. Pierced, knocked, and bruised, completely skinned in a certain length of his body, and thrown up on the beach for dead, he sometimes, when the tide rises and sets him afloat, returns with ease and in triumph to his native element.

We must now turn to examin the settlements, between the chain of mountains of Monte-Christ to the north, and the first and the second chain of Cibao to the south.

In speaking of the territory of Santo-Domingo, I conducted the reader to the top of the chain of Sévico, which bounds towards the east, the territory which I am now going lead him over.

Cotuy.

With the northern side of the chain of Sévico, begins the territory of Cotuy. It is bounded to the east by the bay of Samana, to the norh, by the chain of Monte-Christ; to the west by the territory of la Véga; and to the south, by the chain of Sévico itself.

From the point on the summit of Sévico, across which the road goes, and which is about twenty five leagues from the city of Santo-Domingo, the traveller descends towards Cotuy, along a road full as difficult to pass as the one on the other side of the mountain. At the bottom is the river Yaqui, the third of that name in the Spanish part. It is never dry and is not, in reality, more than a league and a half from the White-River, which runs at the southern foot of the mountain of Sévico, but the windings of the road double, perhaps, this diftance. From the river Yaqui the road afcends pretty fuddenly to a flat covered with wood ; after which it again defcends to a deep-banked ravin. Here it enters a favana, a good league long from noth to fouth, and half a league wide. It is very uneven, being full of little eminences. A ravin, a league an a quarter from Maguac, terminates this favana, and divides it from an other, called the Grand-Savana, which is more than 2,500 fathoms from the river Yaqui, and which may be about a league and a half from north to fouth It is wholly furrounded with wood. After crofling the favana, the road enters the wood, where at the end of three hundred fathoms, we come to the Maguac. This river is never dry; the crofling place is at near a league from its mouth, which opens into the Yuna, and after having paffed it, we again enter the wood, continuing on to a little ravin, where we crofs a favana of about half a league wide, and bordered by a ftrip of wood-land. And now, at a league diftant from the river Maguac, we come to the town of Cotuy.

 This town is fituated at half a league from the right bank of the river Yuna, which becomes unnavigable near this place. Cotuy contains not more than 160 houfes, and thefe are fmall and fcattered, which gives it a very irregular appearance. It is in the middle of a little favana, of about a quarter of a league in extent, and furrounded with wood. The town of Cotuy is nearly thirty leagues from Santo-Domingo, and about twelve leagues from the bottom of the bay of Samana and the town of la Véga.

The settlement of Cotuy was formerly further advanced towards the north. It was at first called the Mines and Mejorada (the Privileged), when Roderigo Mescia founded it in 1505, by order of the commander Ovando. The name of the Mines was given to it, because there were mines in its territory, and several gold ones were working at that time. But from the year 1520, workmen began to be wanted here, as at the mines of Bonnaventure. In the mountain, of Maymon, whence comes the river of the same name, there is a very abundant copper mine, and this copper is so rish, that it is said, by refining it, eight *per cent* of gold may be produced. In 1747, Don Gregoire-Alvarez Traviéso, having formed a partnership with six other persons, began to work this mine, and Valverde tells us that his father, one of the partners, directed the undertaking during three years, and that he passed one year on the spot. In this mine there is an excellent *lapis-lasuli*, of which Mr. Charitte carried some pieces into France, in 1714, and a sort of chalk, or streaked plaster, that some painters think preferable to bole for gilding. Two mines of load-stone are found joining to the last mentioned one. Not far from the mountain of Maymon is another mountain, called the Emerald, because it contains of that precious stone. In the chain of Sévico and its neighbourhood, there is also pure iron, of the very best quality; which might easily be conveyed hence by means of the river Yuna.

Cotuy which had the avantage of being situated near the famous mines of Cibao, was not on that account less depressed and abandoned, like the rest of the Spanish part, at the beginning of the present century, at which time it contained hardly five hundred inhabitants. Since, it had revived, and had profited by the circumstances of wihch the colony had taken advantage, in the interval between 1744 and 1763; but both have since lost this advantage. However, in spite of its decay, Cotuy contains, at least, six thousand souls in its territory, from among whom have been taken, in part, the persons who form the parish of Macoriz, which takes its name ftom the river, that falls into the sea in the bay of Balm. There are, in this territory, a considerable number of poor inhabitants, who hardly ever stir from home, and who are not always included in the censuses; and at least as many others persons, descended from the first European proprietors.

According to Valverde, we may called these latter *stock-holders*, as they hold as they say, a stock or lot of land, by paying a quit-rent, estimated at from twenty to thirty reals (about three shillings and two pence sterling). There is a prodigious confusion in the same lands, on account of the great number of holders, who, without paying attention to the difference in the value of the land which has fallen to them, or which they have acquired, follow no other rule with respect to the number of flocks and herds they are permitted to keep, or with respect to number of days they are permitted to hunt in the mountains, than their own will.

The breeding of animals and particularly pigs, is almoſt the excluſive occupation of the inhabitants of Cotuy, and a very laborious occupation it is. It muſt, indeed, be very difficult to raiſe theſe animals in a country, where there are no ſwine-herds, and where they muſt be ſuffered to roam about in an extenſive ſpace. The people try, when the pigs are young, to accuſtom two or three ſows to keep together, and to remain near the houſe; and, in order to entice them, they feed them in troughs with Indian-corn, palm-tree grains, and plantains. When they pig, they are led, as often as it is poſſible, to lie in the parks, or *corails*; by placing food for them, or by feeding them in the morning, before they go out. But, once attracted to the woods, in ſearch of roots, fruits, and inſects, they do not return exactly in the evening. They often remain abſent till they become wild, and ſometimes in very great numbers. The ſows farrow in the woods, and the pigs, for want of care, periſh. In ſhort, he who breeds theſe animals, often loſes the fruit of his labour, and is even obliged to hunt for thoſe which he looked on as tamed.

This ſort of occupation prevents the inhabitants of Cotuy from applying themſelves to agriculture, except that of tobacco, ſince the king of Spain has thought it uſeful to encourage them to it. The ſoil of Cotuy is very good, the quantity of the tabocco is a proof of this; and it is thought, that it would be very proper for cocoa-nut trees, particularly, if we may judge from the beauty of those that now grow there, amongst which some are wild.

The plantain-trees, this plant so useful, this manna of the Antilles, here finds also a soil singularly agreable, and at all times, that fruit has been of so superior a quality at St. Domingo, that the Spaniards distinguish by the name of *sunday-plantains*, those produced in that island.

The inhabitants of Cotuy are accused of being clownish and of an unsociable character. Perhaps a life, almost solely occupied in the care of animals, is the cause of a rudeness which shocks those who are not themselves rude. Perhaps, too, prejudice may have some share in this opinion of their manners, entertained by Frenchmen, from whose minds a century has not been able to efface the recollection of the massacre of their countrymen at Samana.

After quitting Cotuy, by the high road leading to la Véga, we enter a wood which conducts us to the river Yuna.

We have already seen, that this river, which falls into the sea at the bottom of the bay of Samana, contains the greatest volume of water and runs with the greatest rappidity of any one in the island; and also that it has latterly been made navigable for the distance of more than twelve leagues, for the conveyance of the tabacco, bought on the king's account, in the territory of Cotuy, and in those of la Véga and St. Yago. On the banks of this river are a part of the woods proper for building, of which I have spoken in treating of the bay of Samana, and its water might be made to fertilize immence tracts of land.

The Yuna is too deep to be forded, at the place to which I have conducted the reader. A canoe must be had, that is to say, the passage here must ever be performed in a hide; a sort of passage that merits to be made known.

You take an oxe's hide, on which you place two sticks crosswise; you then turn up the sides of the hide in the form of a queen-cake paper; and, to keep it in this position, it is tied round with a cord, fastened at the points were the sticks meet. This sort of canoe is first launched, to see how it goes, and then the baggage is placed in the middle of it. If a man is to pass in it, it is brought to the shore, the passenger seats himself in the middle, with a strict charge to hold by the sticks. The canoe is again launched, and the passenger is told to fear nothing, but to take good care not to move hand or foot. All these precautions taken, the canoe goes off, a man going a head drawing it by a cord, and two others following to push it along in the proper direction. When the watermen can wade no further, they take to swimming, guiding and forcing the canoe, till arrived at the opposite banck; that is, at about a hundred paces distance, when passing the Yuna. The posture of one, who passes a river thus, is far from commodious, and persons unacustomed to it, repent of their undertaking, before they are half over; while the Spanish creoles, habituated to it from their infancy, think nothing at all of the matter.

The watermen also look upon this sort of navigation as the simplest thing in the world, and think of no danger; not even that of meeting the crocodiles, which seem to be struck with consternation at the boldness man.

These animals, which are far from being scarce, often lay hold of the oxen and horses, as they cross the rivers, which they drown by pulling them by the nose to the bottom. At first sight, the crocodile ever flies from a man; but, if he once attacks him, he loses all respect and fear.

As I am upon this subject, it is, perhaps, the most proper occasion to affirm, that what has been said of the sagacity of the dog with respect to the crocodile is actually true. When the dog comes to the bank of a river where crocodiles abound, before he ventures to cross, he sets up a bark for a long time; this brings to the spot all the crocodiles in the neighbourhood, and when that is done, the dog scampers off two or three hundred paces higher up, where he crosses in safety.

Having now passed the Yuna, we come to the chapel of ease of Angelina, the foundations of which were laid, about twenty years ago, by Don Joseph Salano. Here we enter a wood where there are two ravins. Hence we go to the savana of Guamitta, about twelve hundred fathoms wide, at the end of which is the river of the same name, which has always a little water. Its banks are rather high, and covered with wood. From this river the road comes to that of Voma, after crossing a savana of the same name, a good league in extent. The Voma crossed, the road runs over two other savanas (between which is a woody ravin), before it arrives at the river of la Caya, where there is always water.

The Voma joins the Caya: their confluence is at about two thousand and five hundred fathoms below the road, and at a small distance from where their waters united fall into the Camu or Camou.

From the Caya the road continues on over three savanas, separated by strips of woodland, where are several hattes and plantations of cocoa-trees. Here also is a little church, called Joma, situated in the hattes of Michel Villafame. After these three savanas, comes that of the mouth of Hyma (Boca d'Hyma), of about half a league in extent from east to west, being a little longer from north to south. This savana is followed by a wood for about a quarter of a league, in which runs the river Hyma, the banks of which are high. This river is crossed a little below its confluence with the Camou, by which junction it does not, however, lose its name, for it cuts the opposide bank of the Camou, and still bears its own name. After crossing the Hyma, the road goes on for more than two leagues in the wood, but during near a league and a half, it coasts the left bank of the Camou, then crosses it at about two leagues and a half from la Véga. The wood being quitted, the road comes into a little favana, to which feveral hattes with pretty plantations of cocoa-trees, plantains, and fome pieces of fugar-canes, give an air fo much the more pleafing, as, in all the interval between this and Cotuy, nothing is feen to recreate the view, and, in places fo little frequented, the traveller thinks that he has at laſt found what he has ſo long fought in vain.

At the end of the little favana, whence it is reckoned two leagues, or thereabouts, to the city of la Véga, there is a very high wood; then a long favana, very narrow, which leads to la Véga, along the right bank of the Camou, from the point where it was croſſed.

La Véga.

The name of Véga, which fignifies *Plain,* is one of thofe the beſt known in fpeaking of Saint-Domingo; becaufe it awakens the idea of la Véga-Réal, which is a fertile plain, and the moſt fpacious in the iſland. All who have written on Saint Domingo, have extolled la Véga-Réal of which, however, no one has fixed the extent: fo that, each author means, by this denomination, a certain fpace; but that fpace is not always the fpace meant by another author.

According to Charlevoix (book I. p. 91, quarto edition), la Véga-Réal is a plain, eighty leagues long, and ten leagues in its greateſt width. An eye witneſs, he fays, has affured him, that there run, in this plain, more than thirty thouſand rivers, among which there are twelve, as wide as the Ebra or the Guadalquivir; that more than twenty five thousand of these come from a great chain of mountains lying to the *west*, and that the greatest part of them run on a bed of gold sand.

If Charlevoix, before he hazarded these assertions, had made the least calculation, he would have found three hundred and seventy five rivers, in each league of two thousand, eight hundred and fifty three fathoms; whence it follows, that the rivers must be less than eight fathoms asunder, or sixteen fathoms, if we suppose them to enter the plain in equal number on each side. Now, what land could have remained between the rivers, after having deducted that covered by their beds, however narrow these may be supposed to be? And with what propriety could the fertility of such a plain have been extolled? It must of necessity have been overflowed in the rainy season, when all the rivers would have become united to one pond or lake.

In the next place, Charlevoix, speaking of an extent of eighty leagues in length, does not tell us where he begins or where he leaves off. If he begins la Véga-Réal at Samana, whence the level land goes, without interruption and without any considerable mountain, to the extremity of the plain of the Cape, there is a good deal to add; but if, on the contrary, he makes it end at the territory of the ancient city of the Conception-de-la-Véga-Réal, there is, as Valverde has observed, more than the half to be deducted.

In fact, it appears that, by the word Véga-Réal,

Columbus meant, only the level country between Samana, and Monte-Chrift; but as new settlements were formed, the sense of the word was narrowed, and applied to the land at, and near, the place, to which the name of Véga was more particularly given. At present, it is confined to the territory of that place, which is bounded to the east by Cotuy; to the north, by the chain of Monte-Chrift; to the west, by St. Yago; to the south, by the mountain of Cibao.

In 1493, Christopher Columbus having received an account of the mines of Cibao, from Alphonso, a brave capitain, whom he had difpached thither, he went himself, the next year, to verify the report; and it was on this occasion, that, in crossing from Isabella on the chain of Monte-Chrift, he discovered the plain, which he called la Véga-Réal. The beauty of this plain struck him still more, when seen from the top of the mountains of Cibao, and excited the highest degree of admiration in all the Spaniards who accompanied him. In 1495, Columbus had a fort constructed at la Véga, in order to maintain the tranquility of that place, where, as the historians relate, he defeated, with the affistance of Bartholomew Columbus, an army of a hundred thousand Indians. This post was the foundation of the city of the Conception-of-la-Véga. This city was built on the very spot where *Guarionex*, cacique of the kingdom of Magua, had resided. In the territory of la Véga also, and at three or four leagues from St. Yago, the fortrefs of Magdelaine was established, in 1504, by Ovando, in order to be a check on the Indians, who called this fortress, *Macriz-de-Abaxo*: an expression composed of the Indian word *Macoris* and the Spanish one *Abaxo*, which signifies, *below, under*. It is probable that the object of this epithet was, to distinguish this Macoris from that which we have seen on the coast of the southern part, to the east of the city of Santo-Domingo.

The Conception-of-la-Véga-Réal was the place where Don Bartholomew Columbus, agreed, in 1497, with the Aalcaïde major Roldan, the ring-leader of a revolt, that they would have an interview in neighbourhood; an interview which had so little effect in pacifying the troubles, that, the next year, the rebels came to attack the fort of the Conception, in which, however, they failed.

Eight years after, la Véga was already become a city of importance. Sometimes, during the year, there were two hundred and forty thousand crowns in gold, minted at this place. This gold was the products of the mines of Cibao, at a time when metallurgy was in no great perfection, and consequently when the loss was excessive. The persons concerned in the operation hid a great deal of gold, not counting that in grain. In 1508, la Véga had for its arms, an escutcheon, azure, with a castle of silver, crowned with an escutcheon, azure, with a crown of Our Lady, and two golden stars.

I have already said that, in 1511, Pope Julius II. established at the Conception de la Véga, a bishoprick which was to be the suffragan of the atchbishoprick of

Xaragua. But this archbishoprick not taking place, the bishop of la Véga was created to be suffragan of the archbishop of Séville, whose nephew Pedro de Deza, at first dignified as archbishop of *Xaragua*, was the first promoted. This bishoprick comprehended la Véga, Saint-Yago, Port-de-Plate, Port-Royal, Larez-de-Guahaba, Salvatiérra-de-la-Savana, and St. Croix; while that of Santo-Domingo contained, that capital, Salvaléon, Azua, St. John-de-la-Maguana, Vera-Paz and Yaquimo.

But the causes of depopulation, already often mentioned, did not spare la Véga. In 1525, the emperor Charles V. published an ordinance, to excite inhabitants to flock to St. Domingo, and this place in particular; promissing a passage gratis, and the liberty to each white person of having six negroes, in place of one only, which was before permitted.

This decay was the cause of the bishoprick of the Conception being joined to that of Santo-Domingo, which took place in 1627; from that time the city never returned to its primitive splendor. It was built at the foot of a mountain, at the top of which had been fixed up the cross which I have mention in description of the city of Santo-Domingo. The remains of this cross, of which almost every Spaniard would have a morcel, had been carried and deposited in the church of la Véga; the church in which the first high-mass was said at Santo-Domingo by Bartholomew Las-Cazas, since bishop of Chiapa, whose affection for the poor Indians has rendered him so justly celebrated.

In 1564, an earthquake overthrew almoſt all the town. From that time the idea was ſtarted of going to build another under the name of La Vega, two leagues ſouth-ſouth-eaſt of the firſt, and it was at this time that the croſs was, by order of Charles V. carried to Santo-Domingo. Towards the year 1724, as Charlevoix tells us, there were yet to be ſeen veſtiges of the ancient La Vega, ruins of the monaſtry of the monks of St. Francis, of two fountains, and of ſome of the fortifications. This city was on the left bank of the Camou; new La Vega is, on the contrary, on the right bank of that river.

V and B, having nearly the ſame ſound in the Spaniſh language, in which they are ſometimes employed indifferently, as in *Bani* or *Vani*, the Spaniards ſay alſo *Bega* or *Vega*, which has led many French to call the city of Vega *Bégue*. In 1724 there were but ninety miſerable houſes, and hardly five hundred perſons in all the territory, at the beginning of this century. Since, the city is enlarged and embelliſhed. It is ſituated at a quarter of a league from the Camou, in the middle of a fine ſavana almoſt circular, ſurrounded by the Camou to the weſt and north, but towards the eaſt, this river winds away from it. It is an open town with a large public ſquare in the middle. The ſtreets are very ſtrait, but the graſs, which Spaniſh indolence ſuffers to grow in them, makes them look like little meadows, and the inhabitants feed their cattle at their doors. The houſes are of wood, and are built ſeparate from each other. Their number amounts to about three hundred. La Vega is forty two leagues from Santo-Domingo, and about twenty leagues from the mouth of the Yuna in the bay of Samana, twelve from Cotuy, and ten from St. Yago.

The city of La Vega lies nearly to the north in face of the group of Cibao, that clump of mountains of the Spanish colony. The word Cibao, according to Herrera, Charlevoix, and others, is derived from *Ciba*, rock or flint, and this name, says Charlevoix, suits the frightful aspect of the entrance into this canton. Following the Celtic etymology this denomination would be still more curious, since, by resolving it, we should find *Ke-i-bé-aour*, which signifies *the mountains containing gold*. One thing is certain, the word *Cibao*, awakens the remembrance of very rich mines, celebrated ever since the discovery of America, by their abundant produce, and by the purity of their gold. Hence were dug the first lumps of this metal, presented by Columbus to Ferdinand and Isabella, who were then far from suspecting, how many tears and how much blood this gold would cause to be shed. These mines are generally in that part of the mountain lying towards the north, and near a river called by some, the Janico, and by others Cibao. During the first years it was sufficient to dig them, to draw hence immense profits. The neighbourhood also of Cibao has gold mines, and Valverde says, the mountains dividing the site of Constance, are known to be altogether mines so abundant in gold, that in digging the earth, it runs in sand and in grains, in every direction of the waters.

Spanish Part of St. Domingo. 233

This is not the only metal furnished by the mountains of Cibao. I have already mentioned other mines which are found in the prolongation of these mountains, in the territory of Cotuy, and in this, the canton of Garabacoa, has a mine of silver, which was worked formerly.

With respect to culture, that of La Vega is not very considerable, for it is not so in any part of the Spanish colony. Plantations of plantain-trees, cocoa-nut-trees, sugar-canes, resembling those of which I have already spoken of, employ a great part of the inhabitants; tobacco, and the breeding of cattle, the rest. What I have said, under the article Cotuy, of certain inhabitants living always in the country, spread about here and there, is applicable to la Vega also, the territory of which contains, in total, more than eight thousand inhabitants. We must add, that, in different parts of La Vega-Real, there are also, in pretty considerable numbers, vagabonds meriting an attention that the Spanish police is far from exercising.

Before I advance further with the description of la Vega, I must clear up a fact, the obscurity of which has already puzzled several authors, and if left existing, would rob my description of a part of the interest, of which I dare believe it to be susceptible.

We read in Oviedo and Herrera, and in Charlevoix who has followed them, that Columbus going, in 1494, to visit the mine of Cibao, set some pioneers at work, under the direction of certain gentlemen, at three leagues to the south of Isabella, to fill up the hollow

Vol. I. G g

of a mountain, where Ojeda had paffed in 1493, and to which he gave the name of *Chevaliers'-Gate*, (Puerto de los Hidalgos), and that hence he arrived at the top of the mountain, whence he difcovered La Vega-Real; that he croffed the latter, went towards the Green-River, and from thence to the province of Cibao, whence he afcended the mountains of the fame name, and that from Ifabella to Cibao he travelled eighteen leagues. The account of the journey of Ojeda fpeaks of the fame route exactly, and fays, that from La Vega to Cibao, there remain ftill about ten or eleven leagues to travel.

The fame writers relate, that, at the time of the difcovery, the ifland being divided into five kingdoms, and between five fovereign caciques, Cibao, which took its name from a province, or which gave its name to a province, did not belong to the cacique reigning on the north of the mountains of Cibao; that is to fay, at La Vega-Real, and which was *Guarionex*, fovereign of *Magua*; but that it made part of the province of Cibao, fituated to the fouth of the fame mountains, and which was under the fway of the cacique *Caonabo*, fovereign of *Maguana*, whofe capital was where *St. John-of-Maguana* now is.

In fpeaking of the eftablifhment of Fort St. Thomas, they fay again, that it was fituated on the fouth of the chain of Cibao, and, indeed, the plain of St. Thomé, is contiguous to the north of that of St. John of Maguana. With refpect to the foundation of Port-de-Plate, by Ovando, they afcribe it to its vicinity to the Conception of La Vega and St. Yago, to which it was to be a sea-port, and the desire he had of profiting from the neighbourhood of the mines of Cibao. In a word, we find at every step, in these historians, a proof of a communication between the level country bordering on the sea to the north, and La Vega-Real, separated from it by the chain of Monte-Christ; and again, between La Vega-Real and the province of Cibao, one on the north and the other on the south of the chain of Cibao.

Attentively reading these narrators, we find in twenty places, that people went from Santo-Domingo to the mines of Cibao, in the province of the same name, and that hence they went to La Vega-Real, or into the western part of the province of Cibao.

Facts so positive and corresponding ought never to have left an incertitude; but this incertitude itself is a proof at once very extraordinary and striking, of the state of decay of the Spanish part, since it had its rise in a want of knowing the communication here spoken of. Ignorance in this respect was carried so far, that the Jesuit Le Pers, who drew up at Saint-Domingo, in the beginning of the present century, the memoires from which, generally speaking, Charlevoix wrote his history, had no idea of this communication; and we have a proof of this in what Charlevoix says (Book 9, page 226), of the attack that Mr. la Boulaye wished to make on Gohave, where he believes that the hollow of St. Raphaël, called the *Gate*, is the same as the *Chevaliers'-Gate*, leading from

Isabella to La Vega Real. So evident a confusion would not have escaped one who had any knowledge of the colony, since the *Gate* of St. Raphaël is, at nearest, about fifty leagues from that of the Chevaliers.

But the communication between the mines of Cibao and La Vega Real was at last found again about forty years ago. It leads to that part of the ancient province of Cibao, now called the *Valley of Constance*, and which, though to the south of the chain of Cibao, is so near La Vega-Real, that it now makes part of the territory allotted to the city of La Vega.

Constance is nearly at an equal distance from La Vega and St. Yago, and is situated on the top of a mountain which is pretty extensive, since the valley is reckoned five leagues in circumference. The valley is fine and well watered by several springs always running. The pasture is good for all sorts of cattle. From this plain one may descend to St. John-of-Maguana, and some one, set out from La Vega, went to the top of the mountain, descended it towards St. John, and returned to La Vega in the space of two hours, on horseback.

A man named Victoriano Velano, built, about the year 1750, a sort of cow-house in this valley of Constance, where he kept some mares and cows, the propagation of which was very considerable. It is affirmed that horses become excellent here, and that oxen acquire a remarkable beauty. The fragrant slopes round this valley would be a delightful place for sheep and goats, the flesh of which must be exquisite.

The situation is so cold, that, during eight months of the year, thick blankets are necessary on the bed, and in the hottest season, meat keeps sweet several days. On the highest parts of the neighbouring mountains, there is often a sort of white frost, and in the valley, fire is wanted to render the evening comfortable. Wheat has been sown here, and succeeded perfectly well.

The communication between La Vega and the western part of the Spanish colony, would be extremely useful, were the settlements of the colony more productive: but in case of war it might become of great importance. It would be yet possible to re-establish the communication between La Vega-Real and the territory to the west of Santo-Domingo, by the chain of Constance, but it would require such labour that nothing could induce to the undertaking at present.

I now return to La Vega, after having made this slight excursion towards Constance, with the double motive of making it known, and the better to persuade the reader, because I appeal to him, of the state of nullity into which the Spanish colony must be fallen, since the points of communication between the former establishments were here unknown.

Quitting the city of La Vega, to go towards St. Yago, or St. Yague, we cross the river Camou, at the end of a quarter of a league.

Between this river and that of Yuna, is the eighth chain of mountains, of little extent or elevation, at the confluence of these two rivers; but the chain becomes more confiderable as it approaches Cibao. There are alfo ridges running from it, which, in the interval of the two rivers, form feparations between the intermediate rivers.

From Camou the road afcends a gentle flope, towards a flat, before it arrives at which it croffes two deep-banked ravins. This flat is not far from the level, but is, however, the higheft part of all the valley; that is to fay, of all La Vega-Real. The flopes from it run eaftward to the Camou, and weftward down to the Yaqui. This is the natural boundary of the territory of La Vega and that of St. Yago, making part of the ninth chain, almoft infenfible it is true, but which divides the rivers Camou and Yuna, from thofe of the Green-River and the Yaqui. This chain is a fucceffion of flats, little elevated one above another, running in a northern direction to the chain of Monte-Chrift, and rifing in proportion as they approach Cibao.

St. Yago.

Defcending from the flat, the weftern flope of which is the beginning of the territory of St. Yago, the road croffes three ravins with pretty high banks, and then comes to the little river Guaco, a league and a quarter after croffing the Camou. It now afcends again, then defcends and croffes the Green-river, fifteen or fixteen hundred fathoms from that of Guaco, which falls into the Green-river, and which, like the other and the Camou, is never dry.

After this the road comes to three hattes, with several plantations of cocoa-nut trees, called the plantations of the Green-river. At the end of another quarter of a league this river is crossed again. Green-river was the name given it by Columbus, when he visited the mines of Cibao, on account of the clearness of the water and rapidity of the current. Between the two crossing-places the road keeps along close to its left bank.

From the second crossing place of the Green-river, the road ascends gently, and afterwards descends in like manner to where it crosses the river of the Battle *(Pugnale)*, which is two leagues from the river last mentioned. The river of the Battle, which runs down a little valley, the slopes to which are very gentle, is sometimes dry. About two leagues from this river, the road is crossed by another high road, which runs away to the left towards Major-Hatte; not far thence, there is a guard-house to the left, and at this place, the wood, which has continued all along from La Vega, ceases. The road now follows the bank of the river Yaqui, which is very high in this part, and at the end of five hundred fathoms, or thereabouts, from the guard-house, it enters St. Yago.

Saint James, or Saint Yago, has the surname of the Knights, without doubt, in honour of an order of chivalry of Spain. It is one of the ancient towns of Saint-Domingo, since it was founded before 1504.

It owed its foundation to its being in the neighbourhood of the Conception of La Vega and Port-de-Plate, with which places it carried on a trade in cattle and hides. For this reason, the evacuation of Port-de-Plate, in 1606, was a cruel stroke for St. Yago.

Its arms, granted in 1508, were, an efcutcheon, gueules, two fcollops, argent, and orl, the fame, with feven fcollops, gueules.

The French of the Tortue, to be revenged of the Spaniards for the maffacre of feveral of that fettlement, committed near this place by order of the commander of a Spanifh fhip of war, who had taken them from on board a Flemifh veffel, in which they were going to St. Chriftopher's, went, under an Englifh flag, in 1659, to St. Yago, by the way of Port-de-Plate, and pillaged the town during twenty-four hours, not fparing even the churches. They brought off, as far as Port-de-Plate, the governor, whom they there releafed, though he had paid but a part of his ranfom, fixty thoufand dollars.

In 1667, d'Ogeron ordered an attack on St. Yago; the expedition was committed to four hundred men, under the command of a Freebooter captain, named Delifle. They arrived there by the way of Port-de-Plate. The inhabitants fled at the fight of the enemy; who did much mifchief, carried off all they could, and impofed a ranfom on the town of twenty-five thoufand dollars. After this vengeance, the confequence of the incurfions of the inhabitants of St. Yago in the French territory, the town was quiet 'till 1690. It was even increasing at this epoch, when, in the month of June, Mr. de Cussy marched from the Cape to attack it, with a thousand men, foot and horse. On the 6th of July an obstinate battle was fought at half a league from the town, into which the French entered victorious. Having made an immoderate use of provisions, drink in particular, they thought themselves poisoned, and, in a moment of fury, set fire to the town, excepting only the buildings consecrated to divine worship.

All was now to be rebuilt, but the remembrance of the attacks of the French, ceased not to animate the hatred of the Spaniards of St. Yago against them; and had it not been for the peace of Ryswick, the news of which Mr. Ducasse sent to the governor of that place in 1698, five hundred men, sent by him, and who had already penetrated into the French part, would have made great havoc.

St. Yago is situated on the right bank of the Yaqui, in a savana commanding the river. This river, the banks of which begin to be very deep in this part, is again overlooked by a height to the north-quarter-north-east, at the distance of a gun-shot, and covered with scattering wood. Another height, less considerable, which lies on the other side of the river, at half a cannon-shot to the south, is also more elevated than the town.

This latter is quite open, and has never had a fixed area. There is a pretty large square in the centre; the streets are very strait, and cut each other at right angles. It contains more than six hundred houses, which is a sign of great increase since 1724, when it contained no more than three hundred and eighty, according to a memoire of Mr. Buttet, printed at the end of the second volume of Charlevoix. This increase has been since twenty-five years. The houses are in wood, except about a hundred and fifty, which are in stone, or brick made in the neighbourhood. There is a brick-yard by the water-side, nearly in the south, and at a short quarter of a league from the town.

The territory of St. Yago is bounded to the east by that of La Vega, to the north by the chain of Monte-Christ, to the west by the territory of Daxabon and that of Monte-Christ, and to the south by the prolongation of the first chain of mountains. St. Yago itself is about fifty-two leagues from Santo-Domingo, thirty-four from the bottom of the bay of Samana, twenty-two from Cotuy, ten from La Vega, and about twenty-eight from Dahabon.

The air in the territory of St. Yago is reckoned as wholesome as any in the colony. This opinion is founded on the little sickness that appears, though there is a lazaretto, and on the longevity of the inhabitants. This has been a cause which has had a great influence on the population certainly, but it appears to have not been the only one; since, in 1724, the inhabitants amounted to but about three thousand, and, according to another document, I find but eight thousand in 1764. At present the population exceeds twenty-seven thousand souls, though Valverde affirms that St. Yago is less populous than before 1780, when they were obliged to establish the chapel of ease of Hamina, though St. Yago had already two parishes. The encouragement given to the cultivation of tobacco is most certainly one of the principal reasons of this difference.

This city is regarded by the colonists as a place of great importance. It has an Alcade-major, a sort of marshal, named by the king, and whose post is of great consideration among the Spaniards.

The territory of St. Yago is very fertile in mines. In the first place, the Green-river has grains of gold among its sand, and according to the account of Mr. Buttet, cited by Charlevoix, there was on the side of this river, a mine of gold, the principal vein of which had been worked, in part, by the person from whom Mr. Buttet had the particulars. This vein was three inches in circumference of gold, very pure, and unmixed with other matter. According to the same account, it was because Don Francisco de Lunæ, Alcade of La Vega, wanted to seize on the mines that were working along by the Green-river, and was opposed, that the president received an order to close up all the mines in the colony, which was executed. Much superficial gold was formerly collected on the heights near this river also, in the spot called *the Mesitas*, and which came from very abundant mines, never yet opened. Originally the town of St. Yago was peopled, in great part, with goldsmiths, which circumstance alone is sufficient to show the abundance of the mines.

The sand of the Yaqui also is mixed with gold, and according to Mr. Buttet, there was found, in 1708, a lump of nine ounces. Almost all the rivers that fall in from both banks of the Yaqui, such as Macabon, wash down gold from the mountains, which are as yet hardly known. Some individuals, however, have found the means of turning these circumstances to great profit, but this has been done almost by stealth.

Twelve leagues to the south of St. Yago, at Bishop-Stream, and in that of *Stones*, there are many mines of silver, which were tried at the end of the last century, by order of Don Roch Galindo, Alcade-major of St. Yago. To the west, in the cantons called *Tanci*, the abundance of such mines, caused these cantons to be looked upon as a second Potosi. Lastly, at Yasica, twelve leagues from St. Yago, on the bank of the river, there is, it is said, a little hillock abounding in silver.

There is copper also in the territory of St. Yago, and mercury at the head of the river Yaqui.

Since I am on the subject of remarkable things, I must not omit that Valverde mentions having found, some years ago, in the hatte of *Vrabo*, which takes its name from a neighbouring stream in the desert of St. Yago, a shell of a crustacee, on which is a cross perfectly marked in vermillion, placed on a pedestal, with two wax-tapers, and that these figures have increased in length and width, in the same proportion with the shell. Valverde adds, that he possesses one of them, the cross on which is three inches high, not including the pedestal.

We find in the territory of St. Yago as in that of Monte-Chrift, a tree, in great abondance, bearing a fort of grain, or cod, from which is extracted a very fine black dye. This tree ftill preferves the name of *guatapana*, given it by the Indians.

Quitting St. Yago to go weaftward, the road runs over the fine flat on the fummit of which the town is fituated. After this it continues on a quarter of a league through a wood, at the end of which it croffes the ifthmus of a little peninfula, formed by the winding of the river, where there are a few habitations. This ifthmus may be about five hundred fathoms acrofs, and at the oppofite fide of it we find the river Yaqui, at a league from St. Yago, the road from which, to come to the point were we now are, leads away to the left.

At this croffing-place of the Yaqui it is about fifty fathoms wide, and about four or five feet deep in the middle, pretty rapid and difficult to crofs. As this river has very deep banks, it is not without great pains that one is able to climb up the oppofite bank. From this place the road continues along the left fide of the river, in the lands called, the Continent-of-Lifon. There is a little wheat raifed on this land, the flour of which ferves to make the unlevened bread for all the churches in the Spanifh colony.

Immediately after croffing the Yaqui, we enter a pretty favana, bordered to the north and eaft by that river, being a quarter of a league wide from eaft to weft, and a little more in length. There is a very confiderable hatte in this favana. At the end of the favana, we again enter the wood, and continue in it three leagues to the favana, call Savana-Without-Profit (Sin-Provecho). It is in extent two leagues from eaft to weft, and nearly a league wide. It is bordered with wood, or, more correctly fpeaking, it is one of the natural glades of the foreft which are all along this part. To thefe glades we muft add the openings made by the clearing of land. Sin-Provecho paffed, we are in the wood, where we continue on weftward for near a league; then, making a little turn to the north, we come to the river Hamina, which has given its name to the chapel of eafe, founded here twenty years ago. In its neighbourhood is the hatte of the Bocca-d'Hamina. The banks of this river are nearly twenty feet deep, while the water is not above three or four. Its current is gentle and the croffing-place is not more than feven or eight fathoms wide. After croffing the river the road afcends to the Savana-Hamina, an exellent pafture for horfes. This was one of the places where Mr. the Cuffy encamped, on his route to attack St. Yago. This favana leads to a wood of a league and three quarters long, and near the middle of which runs, in a ferpentine direction, the river Maho, which is never dry. At the extremity of the wood there are two little ravins. This wood is lofty and thick. We now come to a very large favana; it is two leagues from eaft to weft, bounded by the river Gourabo, before we come to which there is a path, which leads to the left, and down to a hatte lying to the fouth-eaft.

After crossing the Gourabo we come to the Savana of the Pilot, which is followed by the Savana-Rompino. Three good quarters of a league from Gourabo, the road goes between two little eminences not far from each other, but that on the right is rather higher as well as steeper than the other. A good half league further and we come to Reedy-River (canna), a league and a half from Gourabo; these two rivers are mere beds without water.

A quarter of a league from Reedy-River, in the Savana of the Hospital, we see on the right, the hatte of the last name. Again in the Savana of Renchadere. A quarter of a league in the wood now brings us to the river of Guyabin, a short league from the hatte of Renchadere. This river, which is the same as the Rebouc, was long one of the bounderies between the Spanish and French colonies, as may be seen by the historical abridgement at the head of this volume. It receives the waters of Reedy-River, and sucessively those of Maguaca and Chaquei, and, thus augmented, falls into the Yaqui.

The wood *Rebouc* is a corruption of the Spanish word *Revuelto*, pronounced *Rebouelto*, and signifies *revolted*. As the Spaniards regarded the settlement of the French at St. Domingo as an usurpation, and their natural defence as a revolt, they gave the name of the *revolted* to the point which the French had fixed on as their boundary, and of which the ordinances of the administrators of the French colony, of

February 24th 1711 and December 3rd 1715, speak as of the frontiers of the two nations (*).

From the river of Rebouc the road continues a quarter of a league in the wood at the end of which it comes to the spacious Savana of the Canoe, a little before which there is a little path running off to the left, to the hatte of Antone, lying at a league distant. We now cross the Savana of the Canoe (de la Canoa), which is a league and a half wide, but the limits of which from north to south are not perceivable by the naked eye.

At about two thirds of the way over the savana, the road goes between two hillocks very near each other. From this part of the vast and fine plain down which runs the Yaqui, we may see Cape Grange, to north-west-quarter-north, and the long chain of mountain of Monte-Christ, which sink from the view in running down to the peninsula of Samana. The eye is astonished at this vast prospect which again inspire new reflections and furnish new subject of astonishment for the traveller, provided he be not a Spaniard. A little beyond the hillocks, we cross a fine road leading to Monte-Christ, distant about thirteen leagues.

From the Savana of Canoe, which is intersperfed

(*) See the laws of St. Domingo, Vol. I. P. 624, and Vol. II. pages 262 and 476.

with brush-wood, the road runs along a wood which is to the left, for a good quarter of a league, as far as a ravin. After this is a savana, of very little extent from east to west, terminated by another little ravin. The road is now bordered by wood again, till it comes to the little savana Scalente, surrounded with wood, and having in the middle a hatte bearing its name. Again the road enters a wood, and, at the end of two hundred fathoms, comes to the Maguaca, which is never dry.

First, after crossing this river, comes a wood, then a little savana, and after it, the Savana-of-Talenquera. This latter is a little hilly, and has two little ravins, which separate hillocks over which the road goes. This savana crossed, the wood is entered again, and the road continues along it till it comes to the river Chaquei, which is never dry, and which is, at this place, not more than sixteen or seventeen hundred fathoms from the Maguaca.

The Chaquei is followed by the wood, for about half a quarter of a league, as far as the Long-Savana, in which there is a little church; there are also several hattes on both sides of the road. It almost forms a point at its entrance, but it widens towards the north. At the end of the savana is a very fine hatte, towards the south, and at about a league from the road. The river Macabon, which is ordinarily dry, divides Long-Savana from that of Acouba, which is three leagues from north to south. After this last, the road crosses the hatte of Don Lewis de Tende, lying on the right bank of the Acouba, which terminates it. There is always water in this river, which is at no more than a league from that of Macabon. After the Acouba comes the Savana of St. James, which leads to the crossing-place of the river Gohave, half a league from the former river. After the Gohave which is dry except in rainy season, the road inters into the savana where we find the little town of Daxabon, towards which the road turns after have left the Gohave about a thousand fathoms.

DAXABON.

Daxabon, or Dajabon, or Dahabon, which the French made even Laxabon, is a settlement formed not forty years since. It is lies at four hundred fathoms from the right bank of the Massacre, which some call the river Daxabon, and the Indian name of which is *Guatapana*. It is the common boundary line of the two nations, in this part, since the treaty of 1777. This river falls, as we have already seen, into the bay of Mancenilla. Daxabon is to the south of the road. It is much augmented; but the augmentation has been at the expence of the colony; because they who come to settle here, are inhabitants of moderate circumstances who give up their hattes in order to profit from the little advantages offered to those who repair to Daxabon. This town is more than eighty leagues from Santo-Domingo, about twenty eight from St. Yago, ten from Monte-Chrift, about one from Ouanaminthe, fix from Fort-Dauphin, eighteen from Cape-François and about eighteen alfo from Hinche. Daxabon was formerly a part of territory of Saint-Yago, from which it has been detached to form a parifh, in which it is reckoned that there now are at leaft four thoufand perfons.

It is to its frontier pofition that Daxabon owes all its impotance, as will appear more fully prefently. It is commonly the place of refidence of the commandant in chief of the territories of Port-de-Plate, Monte-Chrift, Daxabon and St. Yago, and thofe who have the particular command of thofe places are under his orders. Then are here fome cavalry of the troops called Garda Coftas. Daxabon may contain a hundred horfes of little value; neither is the foil round the fpot very good.

Let us now take a retrofpective view of all that has attracted our attention, in what was originally called la Vega-Real; that is to fay, in the countrary from the bay of Samana to Daxabon. between the chain of Monte-Chrift and that of Cibao.

This immenfe level furface, the moft confiderable in the colony, contains four fettlements; Cotuy, la Vega, Saint-Yago, and Daxabon. Three great rivers run along the whole length of it, there are the Yuna, the Camou, and the Great-Yaqui, into which fall all the rivers coming from that part of the mountains of Cibao facing the north, and from that part of the chain of

Monte-Chrift facing the south. But nature, as if to grant still greater advantages to this delightful plain, has divided its slope in two portions, nearly equal. Thus the Camou falls into the Yuna, having itself received the Hima and the Caya, which, in their turn, had received the Voma and the Guamita. Thus the length of their currents united, form two-fifths of the length of the plain, from west to east; while the Yuna stretches along the other three-fifths, running from the east towards north-west-quarter-west, that is to say, in almost an opposite direction. I have several times repeated, that the Yuna is made navigable for twelve leagues up; it is even said that a little boat or piroga went up this river into the Camou, and afterwards, within a little of La Vega. The Yaqui also might be rendered navigable for more than twice twelve leagues. So that La Vega-Real, already watered by a great number of rivers, which are capable of being made navigable for flat-bottomed boats, and from which the hydraulic air might profit, in many ways, by distributing their waters in different directions, is at once the most extensive, and most fertile plain in the island, as well as the one which might find the best out-let and the easiest carriage, if the hand of Industry could once lay hold of the means that Nature has here spread with such profusion.

But where is at present the utility of this celebrated Vega-Real? The description I have just given of the lands over which the road runs along this plain, would, alone, suffice to prove, that the major part of its surface is in wood and pasture land; and of course, that many and considerable spaces are given up to sterility. The rest is useful only in the breeding of cattle, which are sold to the French, some for provision, and others for their plantations and manufactures; such as mules and oxen to turn the machines, or draw the produce of their lands. With respect to sheep, there are hardly any bred in the Spanish part; and, besides, sheep-breeding could not have much success in a plain too-well watered. The greatest part of the Spaniards are solely occupied in the care of cattle, and many of them have no other property. These all the year long hide their misery in the depth of the woods, except when it obliges them to come out for the sale of their cattle, and to convert their pitiful gains into objects of the first necessity.

The rest of the inhabitants are, in part, employed in the cultivation of tobacco; the taste for which, now become nearly general, has rendered it a necessary article, and which, if we may believe what its warm admirers have said of it, ought to be considered as a remedy for several sicknesses, and even for two great maladies of the mind, grief and weariness. Other of the colonists cultivate the cocoa-nut tree, the neglect of which the Spaniards themselves reproach their countrymen. Indeed, these two articles of produce might become much more useful to the inhabitants of ancient La Vega, but then the government must not engross the whole of the tobacco trade; it must engage to take a certain quantity, at a reasonable price, to obtain the preference, and encourage the cultivator at ordinary times. All the monopolizing companies, which are but blood-fuckers with an exclufive privilege, muft be fuppreffed, and a free trade opened, which, in its turn, would give life to undertakings, the produce of which would augment the national riches, and confequently the public revenue. In a word, Spain, which appears to have learnt that the converfion of the produce of the land into gold is more ufeful to nations as well as individuals, than that of gold into produce, muft in reality prevent, by numberlefs prohibitions, what it would feem to have the intention to permit.

With regard to the cocoa-nut tree, the plain of which we are fpeaking, feems to be more particularly intended for it by nature than any other part of the colony, fince it is here fecurely fheltered from the hurricanes, which have made fuch dreadful havoc amongft the cocoa-plantations in the fouthern part. The cocoa of Saint-Domingo would be ftill more lucrative for it proprietor than that of Caraca; becaufe, particularly in La Vega, the humidity of the foil, the coolnefs of the woods, renders watering the cocoa-trees unneceffary, which is not the cafe at Caraca. This faving of labour is a real gain in a country where flaves are employed in cultivation, and when once the cocoa-tree is planted and bearing, the keeping it in order requires no more than half the number of negroes that was at firft neceffary, and particulary when water carriage can be employed. Befides, before the cocoa-trees begin to bear, tobacco may be planted between them; and when it is, as in this excellent land, both productive, and of a superior quality, it indemnifies the cultivator for the expence he is at previous to the produce of the cocoa-trees. However extensive the cultivation of these two articles might be, there would still remain vast tracts for those of another kind, if the inhabitants wished to undertake them, even if it should ever be thought of to establish real sugar plantations in lieu of those *little syrop shops*, which are a dishonour to a fine soil.

We have seen that the inhabitants of Cotuy seem to be more especially attached to the breeding of hogs: it is a subsistence for them, and produces an article of exportation from which the French profit still more than the peeople of Santo-Domingo, whither also many are sent. As hog's-lard is employed in most kitchens in the French colonies, this speculation is of real use to the Spaniards, whose idleness does not prefer repose to every thing else.

To omit nothing appertaining to La Vega, I must observe, that there are yet two other ways of considering its extent. The first consists in dividing it into three portions; one extending from the bottom of the bay of Samana to the western extremity of the territory of La Vega, and which, of course, comprehends the level part of Cotuy; this portion is called the plain of La Vega. The second extends from east to west in the territory of St. Yago, and is called the plain of St. Yago. The third contains the level surface of the territory of Daxabon, and this is called the plain of Daxabon. The three portions altogether, form a length of sixty-two leagues: the first is the widest; the second not only less wide but less level also; and the third is a sort of medium between the two.

According to the second way of considering its extent, the part lying between the bottom of the bay of Samana and the Camou, is called the *Plain of La Vega,* and the part between the Camou and the Massacre, about thirty leagues long, is called the *Desert of St. Yago*. The knowledge of all these different denominations, will do away every equivocal meaning, and will serve to explain other works on the island of St. Domingo, which abound in obscure passages, merely because these denominations are confounded, or unexplained; perhaps, because the authors did not know their real value.

In the road of eighty leagues, which I have traced from Santo-Domingo to the Massacre, we cross thirty-five rivers, and twenty-nine great or small ravins; the greatest part of which belong, in some sort, to the plain of La Vega-Real. The most considerable of these rivers are, the Yuna, the Hima, the Green-river, the Camou, the Yaqui, and the Hamina, all having their sources in the mountains of Cibao. The Yuna's is quite at the very top of Cibao. It first runs towards the north-east, as far as its confluence with the Camou, whence it turns to the east, and when arrived below Cotuy, it runs nearly south-east to its mouth. The river Yuna is the widest, but the Yaqui runs along the greatest extent of country. This latter takes in the Green-river, already swelled with the waters of the Guaco and the Battle; afterwards it receives the Hamina, the Maho, the Gourabo, Reedy-river, the Guayabin or Rebouc, the Maguaca, the Chequei, the Macabon, and the Acouba, all which, except the Green-river, come from the mountains of Cibao.

Of all the rivers of La Vega-Real, the Battle, the Gourabo, Reedy-river, and the Macabou, are the only ones which have no water in the dry seasons; except we add the Gohave, which falls into the Massacre. In every part of this plain the water is excellent. All the rivers have high banks; some more and others less so, from four to ten, or even twelve feet. Those of the Hamina are more than twenty feet above the surface of the water; in that part, at least, where the road crosses it. By the side of the Yaqui there are eminences more than forty feet high. Above and below St. Yago these are pretty steep; but opposite the town they are more shelving. When the rains fill up the bed of this river, it must be crossed by swimming, or in a boat or hide. When the Yaqui is seen, opposite Monte-Christ, one cannot conceive it capable of receiving so great a volume of water, since it is there but about ten fathoms wide, but its banks are, at the same time, extremely high. In canoes, or small boats, this river might be ascended for fifteen leagues, were it not for the limbs of trees which lodge in it, and which, besides interrupting the passage, make the water flow out on each side. All the rivers of La Vega are in the woods, or bordered with wood.

Port-de-Plate was formerly the outlet to La Vega and St. Yago, as latterly Monte-Christ has been. The communication with Port-de-Plate is not very good, while that which now exists with Monte-Christ is commodious enough. The navigation of the Yuna is a great resource to La Vega, and the settlement of Daxabon is another.

Daxabon serves the Spaniards as a point of observation with respect to the French, and when the character of the former is well known, it is easy to conceive that they must always have wished for this sort of advanced post, at the gates of a rich neighbour, whose movements they have always watched. It must be confessed, however, that they should have considered also, that by means of the bay of Monte-Christ and that of Mancenilla, there are two points (which may be safely called the only ones), by which the enemy may attempt any thing against the northern part of the Spanish colony, and that, in case of a rupture with France, the post of Monte-Christ might be of real utility. But in any case, the best military post is at St. Yago. Daxabon is, nevertheless, an advanced post, and is, besides, very well situated to prevent smuggling, which the government fears the more, as it does nothing to render it useless; and, in cases where its agents at Saint-Domingo find it necessary, from considerations of more than one kind, to augment the difficulty of fending cattle into the French part, Daxabon is well placed to fecond their views. . . ..

After the fpot where I am now arrived, I have nothing more to defcribe than the weftern part of the Spanifh colony, which, during its whole length, has the French part for its frontier boundary.

Daxabon may be confidered as the firft point in this weftern part, beginning on its northern fide. It is bounded on the eaft by the territory of St. Yago; to the north, by the extremity of the bed of the Great Yaqui, and the bay of Mancemna; to the weft, the river and little ifland of the Maffacre, bordered by a part of the canton of Maribarou, belonging to the parifh of Fort-Dauphin, afterward the Stream of Capotille, from its mouth in the Maffacre to its fource, and confequently the French parifh of Ouanaminthe, which lies along the weftern fide of the ftream; to the fouth it is bounded by the mountains of the firft chain over which the boundary line runs. Daxabon now comprehends, Trou-de-Jean-de-Nantes, and Capotille, of which I often fpeak in the abridgement at the head of this volume, and which made part of the French colony.

The boundary line between the two nations follows the firft chain of Cibao, running, if we fet off from the fouth-weft end of the territory of Daxabon, about thirteen leagues weftward in the French part, and in a direction nearly ftrait. From this point, which correfponds with the French town of Dondon, the line goes in the direction of fouth-weft, again entering the territory of the French colony for about seven leagues more. So that the westernmost point in the Spanish part, is more to the west than the bay of Acul, from whence, however, we may reckon twenty leagues to the mouth of the Massacre, which is the boundary of the two nations on the northern coast; and between this same point and the bay of Grand-Pierre, to which it corresponds, the French part is not more than eight or nine leagues broad. It is then, on the southern side of the first chain that lies what I have yet to treat of, as far as the boundary of the plain of Neybe and that of St. John, since I arrived at this part in describing the south-west end of the Spanish colony, and in speaking of the territory of Neybe and Azua.

By looking over the map, we see, that what I have now to speak of, is comprehended in a curvlineal triangle, the north side of which is the first chain of mountains; the west side, the line of separation of the two colonies; and the south side, the third chain of mountains. So that, the top of the triangle is at the group of Cibao.

The western and lower part of this space, is composed of plains, across which other chains from Cibao, and the secondary ridges run in every direction. These are of various lengths, as their slopes and the intervals between them, are various in steepness and in width. Sometimes these intervals are nothing more than narrow valleys, at the bottom of which are the beds of the rivers that water this part of the island. Let us now run over this extent, and see what settlements it contains.

SAINT-RAPHAEL.

As soon as we arrive on the south side of the boundary line on the first chain, we find the canton of St. Raphaël, which has the surname of, the Straits *(Angostura)*. It took this epithet from the nature of its situation; St. Raphaël being a hollow by which there is a communication between the French and Spanish parts. It is even necessary to remark here, that the name of Mountain of the Gate, was given to that part of the first chain, which approaches the French part, and that the French have long called the canton of St. Raphaël *la Porte* (the Gate), a denomination evidently produced by the position of the hollow, considered as a passage, or gate. The word *angostura* is at present doubly applicable to this canton; since, by the run of the boundaries, it forms a sort of tongue or slip of land, advanced, as I have just said, further than any other of the Spanish possessions, into the French territory. This configuration of the canton of St. Raphaël, gives it for boundary to the north, after Daxabon, the slope of the mountains in the parishes of Ouanaminthe, Vallière, Grand Rivière, Dondon, and Marmelade, and part of the French parish of Gonaïves.

St. Raphaël is extremely well watered by a great number of rivers and ravins which run from the Dondon to the Ibara, between the several ridges on the south side of the first chain, and which separate the rivers Bouyaha or Bayhala, Gohave, Bohorque, Couladera, Lag, and Samana. Further in the south there is a tenth chain of mountains, the ridges running from which separate the river Banique from the Ibara.

This tenth chain comes not from the group of Cibao, but immediately from the first chain, and its waters, like those of the first chain, all fall into the different branches of the Artibonite. The valley of St. Raphaël is, then, but quite narrow, and it is covered with wood as far as the boundary, of Dondon. However, if we consider St. Raphaël as formerly considered; that is to say, as a portion of the vast plain of Gohave, what has been said of its narrowness is no longer applicable. The land in this canton is, in general, good, and its savanas are fine and well set with grafs.

About thrity years ago, under the presidency of Don Manuel d'Azelor, a little town was formed at St. Raphaël. It is on the right bank of the river Bouyaha, in the valley of St. Raphaël, or of the Gate, and at about a quarter of a league from the narrow hollow, the sides of which are very steep, and therefore easy to defend, or to shut up, being master of the heights on both sides. The town of St. Raphaël is not very considerable, and its parish is an annex and dependancy of that of Hinch.

The air in and round St. Raphaël is very cool and salubrious; but the town, which is in the hollow is very hot. It has a little garrison, which ought to be considered rather as an advanced frontier-guard, and as a check on the fmuggling trade with the French.

It is fomething remarkable, that the Savana of Gohave, which is nearly on a level with that which follows it, and which goes to the Little-Yaqui, fhould alfo be on a level with the town of Dondon. The elevation of the fite of this latter may be reckoned at five hundred fathoms above the fea. There muft, then, be a capital difference between the temperature of the plain of the Cape and that of the Spanifh plains we are fpeaking of; and, indeed, it is very fenfibly felt by thofe who travel from one to the other.

Two leagues and a half fouth-weft of the town of St. Raphaël, is that of Atalaye (fentinel, or difcovery), which the wefternmoft town of all the Spanifh colony. This little town was alfo begun about thirty years ago. Its parifh is under the invocation of St. Michaël, and is, like that of St. Raphaël, and annex of Hinche. Atalaye was founded by Don Jofeph Gufman, in favour of whom it has been erected into a barony. Without ftopping to confider how whimfical a manner this is of recompenfing virtue, in the Spanifh part of St. Domingo at leaft, I am pleafed to be able to fay, with all the French colonifts, that the virtues of Don Jofeph Gufman, among which we may reckon his beneficence and generous hofpitality, merit the admiration of all good men, and a place in the memory of all who are grateful.

The road from St. Raphaël to the frontier is bad. It was propofed to render it fit for every kind of travelling and carriage, in 1762, an epoch when the two colonies of St. Domingo were afraid of a visit from the common ennemy of the two nations; but the peace of 1763 put an end to the works were given up. Three quarters of a league to the right of the road there is a guard-house, near which there are hattes, on both sides of the road. After passing the guard-house, the road crosses a ravin, very steep, but without water, whence it continues on to the river Bouyaha, and from it to another guard-house, being three quarters of a league from the first, and on the frontier line opposite Dondon. But, let us return to St. Raphaël, in order to turn towards what remains to be examined.

Quitting St. Raphaël we cross the Bouyaha, and, arrived at the ravin, called the Dry-Reed-Stream (Rio-de-Cagna-Seca), a little way above its mouth in the river Bouyaha, we get out of the hollow, or Gate, formed by the mountain of John-Rodrigo, which runs away to the south-west, and by that of Kid which comes from the north-west; it is between these two that lies the valley down which runs the river Bouyaha, or the Gate. From the ravin we see, to the right, the hattes of Caboye, at about half a league from the road, from which there is a path, which forms a fork a little further on, the right branch going away to the hattes of Caboye, while that of the left goes to *Pignon*, a canton of which I shall speak by-and-by.

After this ravin we enter into the plain of Gohave.

A good quarter of a league further on, we crofs the Dead-Water-Ravin (Mata-Agua), and at the end of another quarter of a league, we come to the hatte of Bonna-Vifte, on the left of the road. At another half league is a road leading off to the right to the hattes of the plain of Gohave. About two leagues and a half from the hatte of Bonna-Vifte, we arrive at the bottom of the flope of Cerre-des-Pins (Pignon), on the right of which we pafs the Cerre or Hillock of the Pignon, lying to the weft-fouth-weft. This little hill ftands alone, leaving between it and the mountains on its left, a fpace of about a quarter of a league wide, along which goes the road, which is croffed in this place by another going to Daxabon. A little after thefe crofs-roads, the road we are following is croffed by a path, which, away to the left, leads to the hatte of St. Jofeph in the Savana of Crocodiles. Advancing on a little, we come to the crofs-roads formed by the road which, turning round the right of the Cerre-des-Pins, leads, along by the hattes, to Cape François. All this canton is called *Pins* (pine-trees). After the laft mentioned crofs-roads a third of a league, the road croffes the Gohave. The banks of this river are very high. At a little diftance from it, on the right of the road, is the Hatte-du-Cayman (Crocodile-Hatte).

A league and a quarter from the Gohave comes the Bohorque. The interval is called, Savane-du-Pedal. It has three ravins, all which muft be croffed: the laft of them is called Jayna-Cayman. On the left side of the Bohorque and of the road are the hattes of the same name. Here ends the plain of Gohave.

Advancing a league and a quarter from the Bohorque, and crossing two rivers, the road arrives at the river of Little-Passage (Coladera). A quarter of a league further on, and upon the right, there is a road going to Hinche. From the Coladère to the Lag it is about a league and a half, in which space there are two ravins. From the Lag it is a short league to the Samana. This last river crossed, we come to a ravin before arriving at the first of the Hattes of Papayer (Papa-Tree), which is at a short half league. Five hundred fathoms after these hattes, we leave to the right another road going to Hinche, of which place we must now speak.

Hinchi.

Hinche, which was originally known by the name of Gohave, or New-Gohave, the name given to the canton also, as we have already seen, is one of the most ancient of the Spanish settlements; for, it was pretty confiderable in 1504; that is to say, twelve years after the discovery of the island. It was, like the rest of the colony, reduced to a state below medicrity at the beginning of the present century.

On the 20th of October, 1691, Mr. Ducasse ordered Mr. de la Boulaye, a lieuteneant of the king at Port-de-Paix, to come to the Cape, there to affemble the inhabitants, and go and burn St. Yago or Gohave, becaufe the ennemy menaced Leogane and Little-Gohave. Mr. de la Boulaye advenced, by the way of the Joli-Trou, as far as the upper end of the hollow of St. Raphaël, but his troops refufed to execute the orders of Mr. Ducaffe, left the execution might draw on the French colony new vengeance on the part of the Spaniards, who had committed devaftations in it in the month of January preceding.

The town of Hinche, which is confiderable, and whi' ɩ has a pretty church, built about the middle of this c⸝ tury, is about twelve leagues, in a direction nearly .outh-weft, from St. Raphaël. It is fituated at the confluence of the rivers Guayamuco and Samana, and on the left fide of the Guayamuco. In 1724 it continued a hundred and twenty houfes. At that epoque the diftrict of Hinche was the moft extenfive in the Spanifh colony; but, fince that, it has been divided, at leaft with refpect to parifhes and regulations of local police, firft by the eftablifhment of St. Raphaël, at which fince there were five hundred houfes in the town of Hinche, and in its dependancy four thoufand five hundred perfons, and five hundred men capable of bearing arms.

The population being much augmented, the little town of St. Michaël-de-l'Atalaye was fince formed, befides a chappelry of eafe in the other part of

Hinche, called the Oratory of la Roche; and though the colony has diminſhed ſince the laſt twenty years, the territory of Hinche is yet reckoned to contain more than twelve thouſand ſouls, including thoſe of St. Raphaël, Atalaye, and the Oratory of la Roche, which are, properly ſpeaking, no more than annexes to the pariſh of Hinche.

The canton of Hinche is bounded to the weſt by the boundaries ſeparating it from the French pariſhes, of Gonaïves, Petite--Rivière, and Mirebalais. The town lies nearly eaſt and weſt with that of St. Mark, from which it is about twenty-two leagues. It is about twelve leagues from little twon of Petite-Rivière of the Artibonite, thirteen from that of Verretes, and ſeven from the little town of Mirebalais.

From Hinche to Cape-François we may reckon twenty five leagues; ſixty four to Santo Domingo, by the road of Neybe, Azua, Bani, &c. and about twenty to Port-au-Prince, through Mirebalais. It is the place of reſidence of the commandant of all the weſtern part of the Spaniſh colony. There are ſeveral companies of militia, one of which is of cavalry, and, in the town-ſtaff, there is a lieutenant general, of police.

There is a very fine road direct from St. Raphaël to Hinche, running along the bank of the Bouyaha, conſequently on the right of the high-road that I am leading the reader in. This latter road is croſſed by others, comming from Hinche and going to Daxabon by the river of the Little-Paſſage (Coladera), or to Banique, running directly from Hinche towards the river Samana, where I quitted the description of the royal high road.

This is the place to mention a tract of land, where there was a settlement which has disappeared, and the excessive mediocrity of which had long before caused it to be passed over in silence by all who wrote on the Spanish colony. It was in the east of the plain of Gohave or Hinche. I speak of the old Larez-de-Guaba, or Guahaba, which, together with its primitive splendor, has left its name to remain with humility, simply Guaba. It is now no more than a canton of Hinche and its annexes, according to the proximity of the situation of those who inhabit it.

Larez-de-Guaba was founded in 1503, by Roderigo Mescia, who joined to the Indian word Guaba, that of de Larez, because Ovando had then just obtained the commandership of Larez. Guaba, which at first belonged to St. Yago, was so considerable in 1508, that it then had granted it a coat of arms, being an escutcheon, sinople, with an adder of gold, and orls, argent. And, in 1511, it was intended for the seee of one of the bishopricks, which were about to be established in the colony; but Santo-Domingo was preferred to it, and since that time, Larez-de-Guaba has partaken in the decay of the colony, and has been even one of the settlements which have disappeared. This town was situated at the foot of the south side of the first chain of mountains, and not far from the mines of Cibao.

From the point where the road to Hinche croffes that we are now travelling, we advance on by the hattes of Papayer, which are on the right, we go on a league and a half, croffing fix ravins, before we come to Pie-Hatte *(Paftel)*, at a fhort league from which, after croffing three other ravins, we come to the great ravin, called Deep-Waters *(Aquas Hediondas).* A league and a quarter hence we come to a very high-banked ravin, at half a quarter of a league from the fouth bank of which there is another road croffes going to Hinche. We go a league hence, croffing two deep-banked ravins, and after them a favana and hatte of Petit-Foffé *(Lagunetta),* fituated at fix thoufand fathoms from Aquas-Hediondas.

After this hatte, the road continues of the fame kind as before, fince, at the end of a quarter of a league, we have another wide and deep-banked ravin to crofs, and after it another ravin a league further on. Two thoufand five hundred fathoms from this laft, is the river Ibara, of which we crofs two branches at half a quarter of a league from each other, becaufe they form a little ifland at the place where the road croffes. After croffing the Ibara, the road runs towards the Banique, or Onceano. Half a league on, to the right, is the hatte of Onceano, and at a good quarter of a league further on, we crofs the river Banique, which is only three quarters of a league from the Ibara.

The name of Onceano given to the hatte and river, is alfo that of the valley of Banique. From this expreffion, which is corrupted, comes the valley of the

Ocean; without doubt, says Valverde, because this valley is extensive. In this valley are the ridges running from the tenth chain of mountains.

At a good half league after having crossed the river Banique, we come to the road leading to the mineral waters of Banique, and to Daxabon; after this we descend a quarter of a league to the Hatibonico, which the French have changed for Artibonite, between which and the Banique, is the eleventh chain of mountains, which, like the tenth, is a branch of the first chain, which stretches away to the west-southwest.

In crossing the Artibonite at this place, though its banks are very high, and though, in the rainy season, it contains a great volume of water, one is far from conceiving that it can be that great river, which traverses the fertile plains of the French part, where its capacious bed has, for more than eighty years past, been the subject of projects and calculations, which have produced hardly any thing; while at different epochs, Nature, which sometimes mocks the designs of man, has caused the waters of the Artibonite to devastate a plain, where they should second the efforts of industry. But this river augments considerably before it quits the Spanish territory; in the first place, by the rivers mentioned since I began the description of St. Raphaël, all which fall into the Guamayuco, which falls into the Artibonite; and also by many others which remain to be named, and which fall into the Artibonite, but on its left side. This river runs the greatest distance of any one in the island, on account of its windings.

Valverde, after having related what Raynal says of the advantages to be drawn from watering the plain of Artibonite, adds, with an air of sorrow, that the Spaniards might spare themselves the pain of mathematical calculation, by distributing with a great deal of ease, the waters of this river in their own possessions, before they arrive at the boundary line. But Valverde did not consider, that there is but about the distance of five leagues from the boundary to where the Artibonite receives the other rivers, and that, the banks of it being very high, this volume of water can be useful only to tracts situated lower down, and consequently in the French part. Besides, the nature of the land would throw more than one obstacle in the way of any useful application that could be made of the waters of the Artibonite (which is bordered by the tenth and the eleventh chain of mountains as far as the height of the town of Banique), and of the waters of each of the tributary rivers. Again, if the Spaniards formed great establishments for cultivation, those of the western part of their colony, would not certainly be the first, particularly in the lands across which the Artibonite runs, because they would not be the most advantageous, were it only on acount of the distant carriage. Thus, then, one may continue to calculate, notwithstanding the observations of the author I have cited.

BANIQUE.

From the Artibonite the road re-afcends to the little town of Banique, fituated in a favana. This town, which gives its name to a great plain, or which has rather received its name from it, is to the left of the Artibonite, and on the edge of its bank. Banique was founded in 1504, by Diego Velafquez, who commanded in the fouthern part of the ifland, who drove away all the Indians of Bahoruco, and who, after having conquered the ifland of Cuba, prepared for the conqueft of Mexico, in which he afterwards wifhed to thwart Cortez, becaufe the latter would not yield to him the glory of the conqueft. The favana which furrounds Banique is extremely fine, but little, bordered with lofty wood, and at the foot of one of the ramnifications of the eleventh chain; fo that its pofition is a good deal overlooked. It has ufually a fmall detachment of troops.

The plain of Banique, or Ocean, is fubdivided into feveral portions, in its length from eaft to weft. As its extent did not permit of each inhabitant coming to the town for the difcharge of his religious duties, two chapels of eafe have been eftablifhed, in the eaft, the firft of the Chevalier *(Farfan)*, and the fecond of Peter the Short *(Pedro Corto)*. In fpeaking of their territory, we even fay, the Plain of Farfan, the Plain of Pedro-Corto. To the weft is the annex, called the Acajoux, formed about thirty years ago, where there is a chapel of eafe, and for the fame reafon, there is alfo the Plain of Acajoux. This latter extends quite to the French boundary, where it comes to a part of Mirebalais, the town of which is about twelve leagues eaft and weft with Banique. It is eight fhort leagues between Banique and Hinche. The parifh of Banique, in comprehending all the annexes that I have mentioned, contains, at leaft, feven thoufand fouls.

Quitting the town of Banique we crofs three little favanas, and at the end of a good half league, we crofs the river Toncio, at about five hundred fathoms from its mouth in the Artibonite. After the Toncio come three little favanas, and yet it is but half a league from the Savana of la Croix. In this favana are the hattes of the fame name, on the left of the road, and on the right fide of the ravin, which we now have to crofs. After this the road enters the wood, and at the end of fifteen hundred fathoms, we come to the croffing of the road, which, going away to the right, leads to Port-au-Prince. About fix hundred fathoms further on, we quit the wood, and traverfe a fpot, called the Paffage, or Hollow of Banique, formed by a chain of little hills. Here we meet, at half a league from the wood, with a wide ravin. From this to another ravin which has very high banks, it is a good league. After this we crofs four others, alfo rather high-banked, in an interval of not more than a league.

Five hundred fathoms from the laft ravin are the hattes of Hobbes, on the right of the road, and three quarters of a league after the laft of which, we come to the river of Hobbes. It is very high-banked, and bordered with wood, and it falls into the Artibonite, as does the Toncio.

Between the Hobbes and the Artibonite, is a twelfth chain of mountains, which end at the town of Banique, subdividing itself into several little chains, forming so many ravins, and separating also the Toncio from the Artibonite.

Fifteen hundred fathoms from the Hobbes are the hattes of La Matte, which are five hundred fathoms before the road comes to where it is crossed by that which, to its right, leads away to Port-au Prince. From the fork of the road, we go on half a league to a ravin, which is a league and a quarter from another ravin, called Ravin of Bagonay, which precedes, a good half league, the Stream of Nibaguana.

It is reckoned nearly fifteen hundred fathoms from this stream to the river Seybe, which we cross in the wood. At a good quarter of a league further on the wood ceases, and then begins the Savana of St. Rock, in which, on the left, distant half a league, we leave the Cerre of Pontacagne, from which, to Golden-Stream, it is half a league. This stream is preceded by some hattes, as far as which the Savana of St. Rock is a little hilly and stony.

Golden-Stream, or River, is deep-banked, and bordered with wood, and at three quarters of a league from the river Hyguera. Between them is a little clump of woodland, and on the left the little Cerre of Limaçon *(Caracol)*. At the river of Hyguera ends the plain of Banique, or of Oncean. The Hyguera and Rio-d'Oro, which have no water in the dry seasons, run into the Neybe as also the Seybe, in a current of west-south-west.

From the Hyguera we advance a short league to the crossing-place of the Neybe. This interval, at about the middle of which we come to a little ravin, and during which we have several hattes to the right, is a dependancy of the Plain of St. Thomé, or St. Thomas.

This name undoubtedly arose from that of a little assemblage of persons, which the construction of Fort St. Thomas produced. This fort Christopher Columbus had erected not far from the source of the Artibonite, in the province of Cibao, to the south of the mines of that name, to protect the works in them against the Indians. Every vestige of this settlement has long ago disappeared; I have, however, described its position, as near as can be on the map. But there is not the least reason to doubt, that Fort St. Thomë (thus named by Columbus, because people at first refused to believe in the riches of Cibao), gave its name to the plain; since the bottom of the plain leads towards the mountains where the mines were, and since Caonabo, one of the caciques, with whom the Spaniards fought for a long time, inhabited the country near the plain of St. Thomé, in the west, and interrupted the working of the mines.

The Neybe is one of the great rivers of the island, as has already been remarked. Between it and the

Hobbes, is the thirteenth chain of mountains, divided also into ridges, which end at the plain of St. John, and separate the river Heguera, the Oro, the Seybe, and many other ravins and springs, the two most considerable of which are the Bagonay and the Nibaguana.

St. John of Maguana.

After crossing the Neybe, the road ascends to St. John of Maguana, which many maps place on the right side of the Neybe, though in reality it is on the left. The surname of Maguana, recalls the idea of one of the five kingdoms, which composed the island at the time of the discovery; the capital was where St. John now is, and it disappeared with the unfortunate Anacoana. This canton was pillaged by the English privateers in 1543.

St. John of Maguana, founded by Diego Velasquez in 1503, obtained in 1508, a coat of arms, being an escutcheon, argent, with a black eagle holding a book, orl of gold, with five bleeding stars, but from the year 1606, this place was abandoned. The present town of St. John was not begun till late in the eighteenth century, and in 1764, it was still looked upon as a new place. At that time it was reckoned to contain but few houses. Now it is pretty considerable. It is situated at about three hundred fathoms from the Neybe, which, changing its direction at this point, and running weſt and ſouth, lies, of courſe, to the north and weſt of the town. The cauſe of its ſettlement was the multiplication of the hattes, and the diſtance at which the hattiers or herdſmen, were from their pariſhes. In 1764, the diſtrict of the new pariſh contained three thouſand ſix hundred perſons, of whom three hundred were capable of bearing arms. Now its population amounts to more than five thouſand ſouls.

Quitting the town, and ſtriking again into the road towards the ſouth, we come, at two ſhort leagues diſtant, to the river Hinova, leaving ſome hattes on the right. After croſſing this river, we continue on to that of the Yavana at fifteen hundred fathoms, leaving to the right the hattes of Puena. The Yavana, which the road croſſes at half a league from its mouth in the Neybe, has always water, as has the Hinova. From the Yavana, we come, after travelling a league and three quarters, to a little iſland formed by the river Migo, in the middle of which there is a path, leading away to the right, to the hatte of Elgorite, diſtant a quarter of a league. Leaving the iſland, the road croſſes three little ſavanas and two ravins, before it comes to the ſavana called *Savanette*, which is at the end of a good league. Then paſſing over five flats, and five little ravins which ſeparate them, we come, at the end of fifteen hundred fathoms, to the hatte of Louvenco, which is no more than half a quarter of a league from the croſſing-place of the Little Yaqui ; the very ſpot where I began the deſcription of the territory of Azua.

Between the Neybe and the Yaqui is the fourteenth chain of mountains, coming from the group of Cibao, either directly or by the connection of secondary chains. It runs in the direction of south-west-quarter-west, and divides itself into ridges, which separate the beds of the Hinova, the Yavana, and the Migo, all which fall into the Neybe. The plain of St. John is bounded to the west by the French parish Croix-des-Bouquets, and by the ponds. It was in its territory that Oviedo, the first historian of Saint-Domingo, and who wrote in 1535, had an habitation.

We must now return over what we have called the western part of the Spanish colony, in order to give way to some general observations.

The first, which we have already hinted at in speaking of St. Raphaël, is, that several points in the level portion of this part, which contains, at least, two hundred square leagues, are on a level with the site of the little town of Dondon, which is five hundred fathoms above the surface of the sea. This gives a particular cast to this part of the island, as its soil lies much higher than many of the mountains in the French part.

All we have traversed and described, from St. Raphaël to the Little Yaqui, and which is subdivided in divers plains, forming a space of two hundred leagues square, is at present for no other use than for breeding and raising cattle, intended, in great part, for the provisioning of the French colony; after, however, the several settlements of these plains, amounting to about twenty-five millions of perfons, have referved enough for their own fubfiftence. Yet, there were formerly fome fugar plantations in the canton of St. John, and the fugar was reckoned equal to that of Azua. The plain of St. John has, befides, in common with that of Azua, the advantage of having preferved a fine race of horfes. But to repay the care of which thefe ftand in need, the exportation of them muft be free; whereas, we fee but very few of them in the French colony, and efpecially of thofe fit for the faddle, which never find their way there but by contraband means. The leaft encouragement, in this refpect would rouze the Spanifh colonifts, who are extremely fond of horfes.

The vaft extent of the paftures, great forefts, rivers, ftreams, ravins, and fprings without number, the proximity of the mountains, all concur to give a mild temperature to the weftern part of the Spanifh colony, where the air is kept in continual motion by the evaporation of the humid particles. Oviedo fpeaks with admiration of the innumerable flocks and herds, of the plantations of all forts of merchantable produce, feen in this part of the ifland in the beginning of the fixteenth century, and for which the ports on the fouthern coaft were fo many outlets. Thefe muft be, too, the outlets again, if the cultivation took place, as the French boundaries, and the firft chain of mountains, leave no other iffue. But, in that cafe even, the facility of rendering the Neybe navigable for fmall craft, and the Yaqui alfo, would much diminifh the length, and consequently, the inconvenience of the inland carriage. What numbers of sugar plantations might find place in two hundred square leagues, thus watered! And how many other manufactures might be established in the intervals, not suiting the cultivation of sugar!

But, even in the extent of this vast plain, the temperature varies, as in other parts, with the sites, and the degrees of elevation. Thus, the valley of Banique is hotter than that of St. John; a circumstance that renders the cattle bigger and more robust in the former. In the valley of St. John it is pretty cold; so much so, that, during the greatest part of the year, one stands in need of good clothing, and good warm covering in the night; and this is more sensibly felt in the valley of Constance, which, as has already been observed, opens on one side towards the valley of St. John. In general, in this plain, as in almost all those of the Spanish colony, the climate is nearly that of the spring, during the night and in the morning, till after sunrise; after this, as the sun rises, the heat augments, and it also diminishes gradually as the sun goes down.

I repeat, that the canton of St. Raphaël is both healthy and fertile; which is applicable to that of Hinche also. With respect to Banique its soil is not so good; it is divided by hollows, ravins, &c. much covered with wood, and very hilly; accordingly, the cattle cannot augment much in number, on account of the mediocrity of the savanas. In the canton of St. John there are a great many cattle raised; but the canton is pretty frequently subject to long droughts, which deprive the proprietors of a great part of their profits. Their own indolence is still more against them; this is not, however, so very prevalent among the Ileignes.

The fine plain of St. John and St. Thomé are infested with the *lineonal* (toad-flax, called *grand-cousin*, by the French colonists), which already spreads over one quarter of them, and the propagation of which is astonishing. This is an unfortunate circumstance, and its effects must one day be still more forcibly felt, as this *lineonal* continues increasing. Another misfortune is, the plains of Hinche, Guaba, and St. Raphaël, are nearly over-run with myrtle, wild basilick, and other plants, which, in their turn, take so much land from the subsistence of the cattle. This diminution of pasture is but too general in the island.

The part we are at present describing has, in divers places, mines of different sorts. In the district of Guaba there are some very abundant; among others the Gilded-hill, which Valverde says, might be called the Golden-hill. Many persons, adds he, have there enriched themselves clandestinely, by the labour of their own hands, and those of a single negro; forbearing to take more assistants for fear of a discovery; and this fortune was acquired without having either the necessary talents or knowledge, a strong proof of the abundance of the metal.

Guaba partakes, with Banique and St. John, the advantage of having diamonds in its territory, and of producing, like them, jasper of all colours, porphyry, and alabaster. At Banique there are also some streams where we find those crustacees, the shell of which has a cross with the chandeliers. There was formerly a Date in this canton, the success of which ought to have caused a multiplication of that tree, at once useful and agreeable.

Mineral Waters of Banique.

Another great advantage enjoyed by the canton of Banique, are its mineral waters, the great utility of which merit a particular account. To give a full idea of them, I can take no better method than to take an extract on the subject, from a work entitled, *Journal de St. Domingue*, or, *Journal of St. Domingo*, for the months of February and March 1766.

"At two leagues from the town of Banique, and on the side of a hill, in the middle of a wood, are four springs of mineral waters, near each other, running along the neighbouring caverns and grottos. The first is called the Great Bath; the second, the Little Bath; the third, the Bath of the Woods; and the fourth, the Bath of Cantine. The thermometer of Reaumur, in the greatest heats at this place, does not rise to more than twenty-two or twenty-three degrees (eighty-two or eighty-four of Farenheit) at noon, and in the night it falls to fourteen, (sixty-three and a half). When plunged into

"the four springs, it rises, in the order I have mentioned them, seventeen, thirteen, ten and a half, and
eleven degrees, (thirty-eight one-fourth, twenty
nine one-fourth, twenty-three five-eighths, and
twenty-four three-fourths, of Farenheit) above the
temperature of the air. The analysis of these
waters has proved, that they have neither acid
salts, selenits, vitriol, nor iron. At the bottom of
them is found, in great quantity, the flour of sulphur,
which rises to the surface of the springs; but it is a
sulphur entirely divided, and unparticipated with
any mixture of acid. These waters, though very
clear, have a taste and smell extremely disagreeable,
and are smelt at a considerable distance. All the
four springs produce, in nearly the proportion of
twelve grains a pint, a true mineral salt, which har-
dens by the fire, and the grains of which are of a
cubic form, and half a saltish taste. These waters
are composed of a mineral, elastic, volatile, aërial
spirit, and contain a volatile-alcaline-urinous spirit,
which easily evaporates, and the dissolution of which,
produced by a sublimated corrosive, gives a yellow
colour, as also a bituminous, fat, and abundant oil,
besides a bituminous matter, but more thin and inti-
mately united to the waters, which, being mixed
with an earthy bottom, always sinks. The petrol
oil, which predominates, makes one of its greatest
virtues, as it does of all mineral waters, which run
over a chalky bed, and which contain a neutral salt
only."

The waters are extremely foft, penetrating, and melting. The ufe of them is forbidden in agues, inflammatory ailings, and in confumptions; for pregnant women, wet-nurfes, whofe milk they would dry up, and for perfons in the dropfy. They act with more vigour, according to the heat of one fpring relatively to another. They are ufed in ficknefles of weaknefs, long and intermitting fevers, obftructions, ficknefles which do but too much injury to beauty, particularly in the towns, or which fade and difcolour it, in the fcurvy, the phlegm, attacks on the ftomach, the vapours, the gout, the frigid rheumatifm, ailings in the loins, the afthma, and the palfy. They are a gentle purge, and, as a bath, are efficacious in ailings on the fkin. But, whether taken inwardly or outwardly, the ftate of the patient muft be confulted, and particularly to proportion it to the degree of warmnefs in the waters. In a word, here, as at all other mineral fprings, the produced effect muft be ftudied and followed, and it would be difficult to find wifer precepts, and more minute rules, than thofe laid down in the work I have quoted. I fhall clofe the medicinal article of thefe waters, in obferving, that the author points out, as the favourable feafon for taking them, the interval between October and May; becaufe then the fky is clear, and the ftorms and great winds are rare; the air is neither hot nor humid, but is as pure as in the fineft climates of Europe. All forts of food, meat, game, river-fifh, and milk, are then in abundance, and of an exquifite tafte. The reft of the year is very stormy, and we often see hail as large as in the southern countries of Europe. The mornings are so cool in this place as to require a winter dress.

More than forty years ago the reputation of the waters of Banique began to attract the French. The number that went hither became every year more and more considerable; and, in 1766, there were lodgings for more than sixty persons. Soldiers of the different French garrisons were also sent there. The waters of Banique had even their pretended patients, led by the love of good company; but, at length, the French travellers began to be interrupted, and tormented, sometimes under the pretext of smuggling, sometimes under other pretexts; and they were obliged to give up a journey, which promised nothing but fatigue and inconveniencies. When the Count of Solano came into the French part, in 1776, for the settlement of the boundaries, the Count d'Ennery, eager to procure an uninterrupted passage to this fountain of health, requested the president to remove the obstacles, and this was the cause of an article being inserted in the Gazette of the Cape, of 18th Sept. 1776, which article I copy:

" His excellency the Count of Solano, having ful-
" filled the wishes of the colony, conjointly with the
" Count of Ennery, has besides had the goodness to
" extend his attention to an object the most useful to
" humanity, to provide for the help to be derived from
" the mineral waters of Banique. Being informed of
" the abuses of every sort which have long prevented

" the inhabitants of the French colony to repair thither,
" through the inattention of those charged with his
" orders, he went to the spot, and during the little
" time he remained, he appointed a person of distinc-
" tion, who has all the qualities necessary to make to
" be respected and obeyed, with the greater exactness,
" the orders he gave concerning all the Spaniards,
" who should dare to disobey, or to avail themselves of
" their quality, as such, against any Frenchman what-
" ever. He has, besides, given orders for building,
" this year, four fine and capacious houses. He has
" caused woods to be felled opposite these baths,
" which will not only open the view, but will also
" afford a fine walk; and enclosed savanas, where
" there will be grass of all sorts, as also excellent gar-
" dens. He has further ordered, that all the French,
" who wish to go to the springs, on account of sick-
" ness, or for pleasure, shall be permitted to pass
" freely, with their servants and baggage, without the
" least molestation. The will have also liberty to hunt
" and fish, and all the conveniencies and aid, that the
" place can afford."

This advertisement, which I have extracted, because it proves what I have said of the interruptions given to the French, gave some persons encouragement to return to Banique; but, in 1778, two inhabitants were arrested in going thither, though furnished with a passport from the French governor. Some gold was found on the first, whence it was concluded that he was come to buy cattle underhanded; the other had some horses, and two negroes, and it was maintained that he came to sell them clandestinely. They were conducted to Santo-Domingo, where their effects and negroes were confiscated, and where they themselves underwent a long captivity. This last trait forced the French absolutely to give up all thoughts of travelling to so inhospitable a spot, and whither they were obliged to carry with them flour to make their bread, wine, and other heavy provisions, kitchen utensils, and all sorts of furniture. The mineral waters of Banique have since remained useless, like many other valuable things in the Spanish colony. I have had engraven in my atlas the abyss which is above the springs of Banique, such as it was drawn on the spot, the 27th of July, 1754, by Monf. Rabié, engineer in chief of the French part of the north of St. Domingo (who died in 1785), in gratitude for the influence of these waters on his health.

I must besides say, of this western part, that it affords, from the hollow of the Gate, or Porte, to St. John, no point susceptible of defence, unless it be the chain on the right side of the Artibonite, which is a good position to oppose any advances from the plain of St. John, since it has no other opening than the high-road. The same may be said of the chain on the left side, with respect to Toncio.

I shall now close my description of the boundaries between the two nations towards Banique and St. John, by speaking of the ponds.

PONDS.

The most considerable is the Salt-Pond, or Henriquille, or Lake of Xaragua, the whole of which is in the Spanish colony, and of which I have said a word or two with respect to the denomination Henriquille, in speaking of Neybe. This pond is about nine leagues in its greatest length, which lies nearly south-east and north-west, and about three leagues and a half in its greatest width. It may be reckoned twenty-two leagues about. The most remarkable singularity of this pond, is the little island near the middle of it, which is two leagues long and a league wide, where there is a spring of fresh water, and which is well stocked with cabritoes, which circumstance has caused the French to call it Cabrito-Island. It contains also lizards of an enormous bigness. This pond, which is deep, is the abode of a great number of crocodiles and land-tortoises.

The Spaniards assure us, that the pond of Henriquille contains sea-fish, and even that sharks have been seen in it, as also sea-cows, and a sort of salmon. If I believe several concurrent witnesses, and to whom I cannot well refuse belief, there are not now, at any rate, any one of these animals in this pond. The water is clear, bitter, salt, and has a disagreeable smell. The River of the Discovery, White, or Silver River, and the River of the Dames, fall into this pond.

To the south of this pond, distant a good league, and under the Cabrito-Island, is Sweet-Water-Pond, called by the Spaniards Laguna Icotea (Tortoise-Pond), which is nearly two leagues south-east and north-west, and half a league wide, varying in different parts. This pond has no communication with the two others, and its extent depends on the quantity of rain, and waters in the ravins, which feed it. It abounds in good fish, and in sea-fowl. From it there run some little streams, and it has a mountainous part between it and the sea, in a southern direction.

About two leagues north-west of Salt-Pond, or Great-Pond, there is another lying in the same direction, but being only five leagues long, and of various width, from a league and a half to three leagues. The French call it Brackish-Pond, on account of the acrid taste of its water, and the Spaniards, Pond of Azuei (Laguna de Azuei). The line of demarcation cuts it, in nearly equal parts lengthwise. It is surrounded with steep hills, except on the southern side, where is the little plain called the Fond-Parisien, which two proprietors have under cultivation in sugar canes, and which would admit of two more plantations of the same kind. The borders of this pond are very flat and shallow, it does not begin to be deep till you come to the middle; and even there it is much less so than the Great-Pond. There are crocodiles here also, land turtles, and three or four sorts of little fish, that are not good for much. There are tetards also, and a sort of eel. Very few springs send their waters to it, and there is no perceptible issue. It is a portion of the little plain of Verretes, which must not be confounded with the parish of Verretes near the head of the Artibonite, which lies between the Salt and Brackish ponds, and where there are springs of a strong sulphery smell.

The northern end of Brackish Pond is about six leagues from the sea, on the western coast of the island, and the south-east end of the Salt-Pond is a little further from the southern coast. To the south-west of this latter, is a mountain running down to the side of it.

The analogy of the waters of these two ponds with that of the sea, the proximity of the latter at two different points, and what has been said with respect to the fish found in the ponds, and also with respect to the movement, believed to be analogous to that of the tide, all has led to a belief that these ponds had a communication with the sea. With regard to the fish and the tides, the facts are far from being proved; and as to the taste of the water, it may be more easily accounted for by the vicinity of a mountain of fossil salt, the quick reproduction of which I have noticed, under the article Neybe. This salt is a very white, but is a little acrid, and corrodes the meat and fish which the Spaniards salt down with it. When in a mass it appears blue, but pulverized, it assumes the white colour, of which I have spoken. I do not pretend, however, that we ought to look on the question as resolved, by what I have just related, and I am of opinion, that motives, not of vain curiosity, ought to prompt some one to make such observations and enquiries as might determine fully, whether these ponds communicate with the sea or not.

The salt and fresh water ponds have crevices on their borders, some of which are even six feet deep. They are looked upon as marks of earthquakes, and particularly of that of the third of June, 1770. The mountains in the neighbourhood of these two ponds are fit for cultivation, and the Spaniards have hattes in them.

I have now explained, as minutely as I have been able, the several parts of the Spanish colony, and what now comes most naturally in turn to be described, appears to me to be, the manner in which these parts communicate with each other.

Roads.

The two principal communications of the Spanish part, not only as being common to the greatest number of the places therein, but because it is by the means of them that the relations of the two colonies are kept up, are those which I have followed in the description, and which go from St. Raphaël to Santo-Domingo, through Banique, St. John, Azua, Bani; and from Daxabon to Santo-Domingo, through St. Yago, La Vega, and Cotuy. But it is by these roads, the most frequented, the largest, and the most important to the Spaniards, that we may judge of the rest.

The first road, that from St. Raphaël to Santo-Domingo, runs over a length of about seventy-five leagues, which a traveller on horse-back cannot perform in less than ten days. This flow travelling is not owing to the soil alone, but to the necessity of so managing the journey as to find lodging places, which does not, however, render it unnecessary to carry with one all that is necessary for nourishment and sleep; since, the greatest part of the time, vast spaces must be travelled over, where there is no help whatever to be hoped for, and where the traveller must expect to sleep in the open air, if he has not provided a tent. Consequently he must regulate his pace by that of the animals carrying his provisions and bed, though composed of things the least luxurious. In the road from St. Raphaël to Santo-Domingo, there are thirty-three rivers, and more than a hundred ravins to be crossed.

The first day we can make but five leagues, from St. Raphaël to the hatte of St. Joseph, or of the Pines, going south-eastward. The road runs over the fine plain of Gohave, where there are several little clumps of wood and bushes.

The second day's journey is ten leagues, from the hatte of St. Joseph to the Lagunetta, east-south-east. In this space, the part lying between the Bohorque and the hattes of Papayer, not so steep and with a better road than that to the hattes of Lagunetta, because in the last mentioned portion the rivers and ravins have very steep and high banks, and are separated by little chains and elevations covered with wood, and which are ridges coming from the tenth and eleventh chains.

The third day we go south-eastward, from Langunetta to the hattes of Hobbes, nine leagues. The road bad, the land hilly; because the intervals between the rivers and ravins are so many diminutive chains of hills and flats, which render the road rough and crooked. Before we come to the Artibonite, the land is sterile, and is interspersed with savanas and clumps of wood.

From the hattes of Hobbes to the town of St. John, is the fourth day's journey. Eight leagues of good road, running east-south-east.

The fifth day, four leagues only, from St. John to the hatte of Elgoritte, lying a little way from the side of the road. The direction this day is, south-east-quarter-east. The road very good.

Eight leagues south-eastward is the journey of the sixth day, from the hatte of Elgoritte to that of Tavora. The road grows worse as we get from St. John; not bad, however, unless on the mountain of the Passage.

The seventh day also is a journey of eight leagues, from the hatte of Tavora to the savana of Sipicepy. This interval has many spots which are rough and stony, dry savanas, clumps of woody land, and a great many dildoe-trees. The road runs south-east-quarter-east.

The eighth day the road continues on in the same direction, over a good road, except on the strand of Ocoa. The distance is nine leagues, at the end of which we come to Bani.

From Bani to Nigua, nine leagues, over a good level road, running east-quarter-north-east, is the journey of the ninth day.

The close of the tenth day brings us to Santo-Domingo, along a good road of four leagues and a half; but the crossing of the Jayna takes up a good deal of time.

We shall have a better idea of the slowness of travelling here, when we know, that when it was proposed to send the regiment Enghien from the Cape, to garrison Santo-Domingo, in November 1780, this distance of seventy-five leagues and a half, from St. Raphaël to Santo-Domingo, was divided into eighteen days' march, in order to have hattes to lodge the soldiers in, and not to be obliged to encamp, which in the rainy seasons would have been attended with great inconveniencies. The route was as follows:

	Leagues.
1st day from St. Raphaël, the first halting place, to Bohorque,	$4\frac{1}{2}$
2d to the hatte of Papayer,	$4\frac{1}{2}$
3d to the Deep-Waters,	$4\frac{1}{2}$
4th to Banique,	$3\frac{3}{4}$
5th to Los-Jobos,	$5\frac{5}{8}$
6th to Seybe,	$4\frac{1}{2}$
7th to St. John,	$3\frac{3}{4}$

8th to Los-Bancos near the Yaqui,	5 $\frac{5}{8}$
9th to the Biahama,	4 $\frac{1}{2}$
10th to Tavora,	3 $\frac{7}{8}$
11th to Azua,	3 $\frac{7}{8}$
12th to Sipicepy,	3 $\frac{3}{8}$
13th to Savana Huey, after the Strand of Ocoa,	3 $\frac{3}{8}$
14th to Mantanza,	4 $\frac{1}{2}$
15th to Bosion de Palta,	3 $\frac{1}{2}$
16th to Great-Savana,	3 $\frac{1}{2}$
17th to the Mill of Nigua,	3 $\frac{15}{16}$
18th to Santo-Domingo,	5 $\frac{1}{16}$
Leagues	75 $\frac{1}{2}$

The other road, from Daxabon to Santo-Domingo, is eighty two leagues, and it is much more easily travelled, since it takes up but eight days.

The first day the traveller goes nine long leagues, from Daxabon to the hatte of Renchadère, a short league from the Guyabin, or Rebouc. The road runs south-east-quarter-east, is very good in dry weather, goes along the south of the first chain of mountains, and continually in view of the west side of the chain of mountains of Monte-Christ.

The second day's journey is about nine leagues and a quarter, from the hatte of Renchadère to the savana of Hamina. The road this day runs east-quarter-south-east, and among the same mountains as the day before. It is very good here; the savanas are interspersed thickly with wood, with brush-wood, and dildoe-trees.

The third day we travel nine leagues and a half, from Hamina to the town of St. Yago. The road is excellent, has mountains on each side, and runs eastward.

The fourth day takes us from St. Yago to La Vega, ten leagues. The road is good, still continues along the wood, and runs east-quarter-south-east.

From La Vega to Guamitta is the fifth day's journey, eight leagues. The road is prettty good, with wood on each side, except in the savana of the Voma, where we have the mountains again on each hand, and where we begin to see even the group of Cibao. In general the road runs eastward.

The sixth day is spent in going from the Gamitta to the hatte of Sevico, ten leagues. The road is not bad from the Guamitta to the Great Savana inclusively, and runs east-south-east; but from this savana to Sevico it is bad, and runs south-east-quarter-south. From time to time we may see the mountains of Cibao to the south-west-quarter-west.

The seventh day brings us from the hatte of Sevico to that of Guye, about eleven leagues. The road from the first, as far as the mountain of Pardavé, is not bad, and runs south-east-quarter-south; but from the foot of the Pardavé to the south, the road becomes fine again, and runs south-east-quarter-east. Here we see the summit of Cibao, away to the west-north-west.

The end of the eighth day sees us at the capital, after having travelled about fourteen leagues in a southern direction, but with many windings. The road is extremely fine from the passage of Isabella; nor can it be called bad, before you come to that.

Perhaps the reader will not be displeased to see how the eighty-two leagues of this road were distributed into eighteen day's march, in a route sent to the French governor by the Spanish president, for conducting the regiment of Enghien.

	Leagues.
1st from Daxabon to the Great Savana,	5
2d to the Hatte of Antone,	3 ½
3d to the Hospital,	4 ½
4th to the hatte of the mouth of the Hamina,	5
5th to St. Yago,	10
6th to the Ajoupas of the Crocodile, or Caysmin,	5
7th to La Vega,	5
8th to the Ajoupas of Michaël Villafama,	6
9th to Cotuy, by the road of Angelina,	6 ½
10th to the Ajoupas of the Great Savana,	3
11th to Oyo of Agua,	6
12th to the foot of the Louisa,	4 ½
13th to the hatte of Louisa, and Vemilian Stream,	4 ½
14th to the Ajoupas of Higuero, and Cana Mancebo,	5
15th to La Venta,	5
16th to Santo-Domingo,	3 ½
	82

I should observe here, that in a great many places, the route makes mention of ajoupas only, and that it contains obfervations fpecifying that the country is fo defert and lonely, from the Great Savana to the foot of the Louifa, that ajoupas muft be prepared for the troops. Hence we may form a pretty correct idea of the ftate of the Spanifh colony.

In returning to the beginning of the fecond of thefe great roads, we find a communication between Daxabon and Monte-Chrift, through the plain of Daxabon. We have already feen, that, from this laft place, there is a road to Hinche, and another to Banique. They go along the mountain of Sierra, which is a part of the firft chain of mountains.

St. Yago, befides the great road, has one which, from the plain of the Canoe, five leagues before Daxabon, leads to Monte-Chrift. There was formerly another, going to the fame place, along the right bank of the Yaqui; but it is long fince it became impaffable, except on foot.

I have noticed a fine road that was formerly between St. Yago and Port-de-Plate, and the expence of which had been a fubject of complaint againft the commander Ovando, but at prefent it is an extremely bad road, traverfing the chain of Monte-Chrift, through a fort of interval, which the mountains leave between them, forming in this part gentle flopes.

A road between Cotuy and Samana has had the fame fate. We go here, however; but it is an enterprife confined to few, and athwart hattes, and with many windings.

On the road from St. Raphaël to Santo-Domingo, I have noticed the roads leading to other places than thofe of the great road. There is one from St. Raphaël going to the upper part of the Gonaïves and the plain of Artibonite, through Atalaye; and another leading from Hinche to Mirebalais. This laft was, as late as 1754, the road of communication between Port-au-Prince and Cape-François. From Hinche the traveller went to the paffage of the Gate (now St. Raphaël), where there was even a fort of barrack, called the Tavern of the Gate; hence he defcended to Joli-Trou (Pretty Hole) of the Great-river, and went, through this laft, to Cape-François. This is the road, the very mark of which is now effaced in more than one place, that, by the treaty of the boundaries is referved to the ufe of the French, on condition of their keeping it in repair.

We muft alfo recollect the roads which go from the hatte of Tavora and its environs, towards the canton of Neybe, and which alfo ferves as a communication between the Spanifh colony and Port-au-Prince.

I imagine it is unneceffary to fay, that there are in the Spanifh part, other roads befides thofe I have had occafion to name in this defcription, as it is very eafy to conceive that, to go from the different plantations, whether to the parifh or elfewhere, to buy or to fell, there muft be roads, or at leaft paths; for any other word would give a wrong idea of these communications, which are simply marks, generally across the forests.

Woods.

These forests, some of which existed before the island was a Spanish colony, and others have been reproduced since the cultivation has been given up, contain the best trees for all uses. That which holds, perhaps the first place among them, on account of its solidity, and the ease with which it may be applied to all uses, and also on account of the polish of which it is susceptible, is the mahogany. It is also, perhaps, the most common, and particularly towards the eastern part of the island, where are the finest of these trees. Some are to be found of fifteen or eighteen feet girt, and of twice that length. But with respect to colour, those of Azua have the preference. Some of them have such beautiful veins, and so delineated, that one would be almost tempted to believe, that they were the effect of art rather than of nature. Every one knows the mahogany, and the uses it is put to, too well not to give it its just value.

Brazil wood is also found in pretty great abundance, in the canton of Azua. This wood was formerly much sought after in the island, on account of the yellow colour it produces.

The roble-oak, though less common than the mahogany, which it surpasses in height, is fit for the posts of sugar-mills. In buildings it would be very useful for pieces requiring great strength.

The walnut, the guaiacum, the iron-wood, the everlasting (bean tree), the sabine, the green balm, the pine, the cedar, the ebony, the marble-wood, and many others, are fit for buildings, either in shipping or houses, and for other rural and domestic uses. All of them have excellent qualities, and the iron-wood and everlasting seem to be worthy of their names, on account of their petrifying, when put into the ground in wet places. Formerly there were vessels which sailed out of the ports of Saint-Domingo made entirely of its woods, One of these vessels, says Valverde, gave occasion to a quarrel between Seville and Cadiz, touching the question, to which of these towns the exclusive commerce of America should belong.

We find here, besides, the tree, the fruit of which caused it to be regarded as the tree of the hesperides. It charms the sight as well as the smell, and its wood adds to its utility.

Less agreeable, but more majestick than the orange-tree, the mammee-tree, so beloved by the Indians, grows every where, and equally without cultivation. Among other uses, it is esteemed for canoes, as is also the mapou (cotton-tree).

There are shrubs which, like the trees, might be useful in all the combinations of colouring, and the seats made of the thorny acacia have great elegance on account of their various tints. I shall notice no more than that tree, the utility of which can never be enough extolled, which furnishes the poor African with plates and bowls, that he may renew at pleasure, without expence, and the means of carrying and preserving what he could not enjoy, without the vessels which the callebass-tree gives with prodigality.

The Spanish part is also loaded with palm-trees, the height and branches of which excite a just admiration. The tree, which nature seems to have made to give us an idea of the different sorts of colums, has a great variety, all more or less excellent, either for their wood, of which their boards are of long duration, or their fruit, which feed the cattle, or else by their leaves, which serve as a thick thatch, flexible osiers for baskets, or bottoms for a sort of bed. I shall hereafter return to these individuals of the vegetable creation.

Produce.

In speaking of the articles of colonial produce, it is narural to observe, that it was at Saint-Domingo that the cultivation of the sugar-cane began. This yellow reed came from the Canaries. Herrera tells us, that in 1506, one Aguilon, an inhabitant of the Conception of la Vega, transported and planted it; that a surgeon of Santo-Domingo, named Vellosa, applied himself to its cultivation, and that the success was due to his knowledge and zeal, as was also the first sugar-mill. I do not know why Charlevoix, who agrees with Herrera concerning Vellosa, names Pedro Alança in the place of Aguilon. It seems that, by a fatality attending Saint-Domingo, the glory of every thing useful must be torn from its true owner. If we may judge from what Oviedo relates, the success of the sugar-cane was very rapid, since towards 1530, there were twenty rich sugar-plantations, and in 1535, three others were begun. But, it is now more than a century since these have all disappeared, and I have already but too often repeated what miserable sugar establishments are at present found in the Spanish colony.

I have also related all that can be said of the coffee-tree, which is as yet weak and in its infancy there, and of the cotton, indigo, and tobacco. I have often arrested the attention of the reader on the cocoa-tree, the fruit of which was so dear to the Indians, who gave a very solemn testimony of its precious qualities, since, in the island, as in many parts of the continent, they made use of it as a standard in exchanges, and consequently as a sort of money. They highly esteemed the rocou also, (achiote), with which they rubbed themselves, thus imitating one of the follies or coquetteries of polished nations. But the Spaniards have abandoned all, even the ginger, which the inhabitants of the humid places only have retained the use of.

Valverde assures us, that there is real tea growing in Saint-Domingo, and that he has tasted of it, which came spontaneously in the interval between Santo-Domingo and Fort St. Jerome. He adds, that at Cape-François, they receive great quantities, brought from a hill near Monte-Christ. But if the existence of this tea is not founded on facts more exact than the cargoes sent to the Cape, the island does not rival Asia with respect to this plant, which custom has rendered a branch of very lucrative commerce, and which has lately been the eventual cause of the independence of a vast part of the continent of America.

I shall not enumerate here all the fruits of the Spanish part, because they are the same that are found in the French part, and because they will make, in speaking of this latter, the subject of some observations. I shall content myself with saying, that they are very common, that they are produced without care, and that they add to the means of subsistence.

Game, Fish, Turtles, &c.

Among the means of subsistence we ought to reckon the cattle and the game. The great ash-coloured wood pigeon, the ring-dove, and the violet-winged pigeon, are extremely delicate, and two other sorts of wood-pigeons, less in size, but not without a very good taste. These birds fly in clouds athwart the intervals undisturbed by man, where they may in security bill and coo, and propagate their species. The wild pintades (Guinea-fowls), so justly esteemed for their flavour, are equally numerous, and collected into flocks. Four or five sorts of turtle-doves, wild-ducks, tame-ducks and geese, among which there is a great variety, a sort of hern, spoon-bills, and many other birds multiply and diversify the garniture of the table, and are the cause, in some sort, of domestic fowls being neglected.

We find also covies of pheasants and flamingos, particularly by the sides of the rivers and watery places. It is principally at Neybe and Azua that they are numerous, like the royal peacock, which seems always to have preferred this quarter, as it was there that it was found, as soon as the island was discovered.

The parrots are also very numerous. Their plumage is not so brilliant as those of the Amazone, nor the elegant form of those of Senegal, nor the facility of imitating the human voice, like those of the coast of Africa; but, stripped of their feathers, which are quite green, they are a delicate dish, which may be prepared in different manners, and then the lover of the table will find them of greater value, than when they are flying in flocks through the air, stunning him with their hard and piercing garullity.

To so many sources of subsistence we must add those afforded by the sea, the rivers and streams. The mullet, the shad, the rouget (rot-fish), the besugo, the sprat, the dorade (gold-fish), the trout, and a multitude of other fish are here ready to pay a just tribute to the industry of man. We may, besides, make mention of the lobsters, crabs, oysters, and other shell-fish. Nor must the land and sea turtles be forgotten, the flesh of which, besides its delicate flavour, has the property of stopping the effects of the scurvy, that terrible scourge in hot countries.

But so many objects of utility united, prove, even by their profusion, the neglected state of the Spanish colony; for wherever man assumes dominion, all wild animals fly, or are destroyed. He spreads the effects of his destructive disposition far and wide.

It is not, perhaps, unnecessary for me to declare here, that, in so often repeating the negligence and indolence prevailing in the Spanish part, my reproach applies much less to the Spaniards of the colony than to the government, which has done nothing to raise them from their state of mediocrity, but has in a manner abandoned them. It would, without doubt, illy become a creole, to draw on himself the reproach of Valverde to Mr. Paw, who found it very convenient for his hypothesises, to lay it down as a maxim, that the American creoles, even of European extraction, are degenerated beings, from the influence of the country they inhabit. The state of the French colony sufficiently proves the value of this writer's dreams, and I have not the least reluctance to declare, that, with the same means, and equally clear of obstacles, the Spaniards of Saint-Domingo would yield in nothing to the French who inhabit the same land. After this acknowledgment I return to my subject.

Little Islands on the Spanish Coast of Saint-Domingo.

It is now indispensably necessary to lead the reader over the little islands on the coast of the great one. I shall follow the order adopted in treating of this latter.

The first we find on the southern coast, is the island of Beate. It lies about six thousand fathoms to the south-west of Cape Beate, or Bohoruco. From the southern side of the Beate there is a shelve, running towards the great island. Its direction is near about north-east, and it is covered, at most, with no more than about three fathoms and a half of water, a clear proof, according to Valverde, that the two islands were formerly joined together, as, besides, to the north-east of the Beate, opposite an acute angle, penetrating into the channel, there are four islands, running lengthwise south-west and north-east, and which go away toward Bahoruco. They are on one of the sides of the shelve, separated from one another, and take up altogether an extent of about two thousand fathoms. At a little quarter of a league, and to the south of the fourth island, there is another, called Table-Island, between which and the fourth island there is water of four fathoms and a half deep. These different obstacles narrow the channel still more, between the Beate and the point of Bahoruco, which has from six to nine fathoms water, as I have already observed. To the south of the Beate there is a shelve, which continues for a good half league with less than two fathoms water. In the month of August, 1504 Christopher Columbus was obliged to enter this channel. He had been opposite the same island in 1498, having overshot the port of Santo-Domingo.

The island of Beate, the middle of which lies in 17 deg. 51 min. north lat. and 74 deg. 1 min. west long. is two leagues and a half long, from east to west, by a mean width of two short leagues. In its north-west there a cove and anchorage. with ten fathoms water, and it is to be approached in small vessels in almost every point of its coast, the circuit of which is eight or nine leagues. The abundance and the quality of its woods, is a clear proof of the fertility of the land, and the multiplication of the flocks of wild creatures proves how favourable it is to them. Here might be plantations and hattes, as there were formerly.

Several vessels are known to have been wrecked on the Beate, and this has been attributed to its being badly defined by the charts, as well as to the rapidity of the currents, running westward on the coast, which renders this error very dangerous. Mr. Bauffan, then a captain of a ship, and since an inhabitant of Leogane, observed this difference in 1741, and made, in twenty-four hours, twenty-four leagues more than his reckoning, and this in consequence of these currents. Four leagues to the north-west of the island of Beate there is a clump of rocks, which rise above the water, and which are called the Brothers (the Monks, or los

Frayles), the position of which is particular in that they are nearly opposite the islands of the bay of Monte-Christ, called the Seven Brothers.

Two leagues south-south-westward of the island of Beate, is the little island of Altavele, so called by Columbus, in 1494. Between the two the channel is bottomless. Altavele took its name from its altitude, and its form, which, at a distance, gives it absolutely the appearance of a vessel under full sail. The greatest length of this island, east and west, is fifteen hundred fathoms; and its greatest width, north and south, is nearly the same. But these dimensions diminish a great deal, in different parts, on account of the coves and points. The land in this island takes a rapid rise towards the centre, and is covered with excellent wood.

From the northernmost point of the Altavele, there is a shelve, running about fifteen hundred fathoms towards the north-east. Three hundred fathoms to the south of its eastern extremity, is the rock of Altavele, very high, and stretching from north to south, a length of nearly five hundred fathoms. There is a channel between the shelve of Altavele and the rock, where there is three fathoms water. The rock also has a shelve running round the east end of it, from the middle of the north to the middle of the south side, in all two hundred and fifty fathoms. Altavele is opsite its middle.

There is no bottom between False-Cape, the Frayles, and Altavele. It is reckoned four short leagues from Altavèle to the Frayles, and a little more from the latter to Falſe-Cape.

Between the rivers Comayaſu and Romaine, following the ſouthern coaſt, is the Iſland of St. Catharine, or ſimply Catharine, thus called after a lady, to whom it belonged. Catharine is ſeparated from the land by a channel running eaſt and weſt, and which has ſeveral breakers, that the fiſhermen ſail along by without danger. Its productions are the ſame as thoſe of the Beate, and offers the ſame advantages.

To the eaſt of St. Catharine is the iſland of Saone, which, Valverde ſays, merits more attention than has been paid to it. Curaçao, which the Dutch have rendered well known by a conſiderable commerce, is neither ſo extenſive nor ſo fertile. It is no more than a very long league from Little Palm-Tree point to that which advances from the north of the Saone. It is ſurrounded with banks and breakers, except at the weſtern part. It is about eight leagues from eaſt to weſt, and two from north to ſouth, which becomes ſtill leſs in the narroweſt part. Its circumference is nearly twenty-five leagues. At each of its extremities, eaſt and weſt, is a mountain, and there is a third at point about the middle of the ſouthern ſide. Theſe mountains at once ſhelter and water it, and temper the air.

The Indians called this iſland Adamanoy. They had a particular cacique, who was the ſovereign of the iſland, independent of thoſe of Saint-Domingo. His ſubjects gave themſelves up to commerce with the

Spaniards, to agriculture, to the cultivation of grain, and of fruits. They furnished enough for the consumption of the city of Santo-Domingo, and for provisioning several expeditions going from hence. Some Castillians having caused the cacique to be eaten by a dog, this act of cruelty became the subject of a quarrel, and the Spaniards, after having destroyed the Indians, formed settlements on their little island, the success of which at once and excited their ferocious avarice. This island and its port are a shelter for the mariners sailing in this part, who here find water, wood, and wild cattle, all which are in abundance. It is almost impossible to have an idea of the quantity of birds, and particularly of wood-pigeons, that are seen here.

To the east of the Saone, veering a little more to the south, there are between Saint-Domingo and Porto-Rico, two little islands, called Mona (la Guenon), the Mone, and Monito, the Little Monkey (Monique). Monique, which is the nearest, is but very small, but the Mone is two good leagues from east to west, and a little more from north to south. It has several ports for little vessels, and all that would be necessary for settlements of culture, and the breeding of cattle. We may judge of its utility and value by this fact alone: it was the recompence of Don Bartholomew Columbus, the brother of Christopher, whom the king made a present of it, in 1512. It has been under good cultivation, and repaid well the proprietors' toil. Its fruit-trees, and particularly the orange, were much extolled.

Eight or nine leagues, north-east-quarter-north from the Mone, between the eastern part of Saint-Domingo and the western part of Porto-Rico, is the island of *Desecheo*, (Island of the Ramble), a Spanish word, which the French geographers have corrupted to *Zachée*. It is no more than a little hill covered with wood. Its real name comes from the circumstance of sailors being obliged, in order to double either of the islands, Saint-Domingo or Porto-Rico, in going from the western side to that of the north, to draw off from the land towards, though not too near, the island of the Ramble, or Zachée, to avoid the sand-banks.

Thus, the Beate, St. Catharine, and the Saone, are along the southern coast of Saint-Domingo; the Mone, Monique, and Zachée, on the eastern coast.

About twenty-five leagues north of point Jackson, in the peninsula of Samana, is a rock called the Silver Cayes. Nearly thirty-two leagues from Port-de-Plate, to the north, are other rocks or little islands, which the French call the Square-Handkerchief (Mouchoir Carré). The Spaniards at first called it *Abreojos* (the Thistles), from which it has been changed by corruption to *Abrojos* (the Eye-openers). To the west of these, and nearly in the same line, there are other groups of little islands, very low, called with a great deal of impropriety, *Ananas*, or Turkish islands, since they are the islands of Don Diego Luengo, thus called by him who discovered them. They are more than thirty-leagues north of the point Isabelique. Nearly at the same distance from Cape-Grange, are other islands, known under the name of the Caciques. But, as these islands of the northern part of Saint-Domingo, are the outlets of it, they are mentioned in another part of this island.

The reader, I imagine, will now expect me to speak of the administration of the Spanish colony; and I request, in my turn, his attention to subjects, which, though of a different nature from those hitherto treated of, will certainly not be found less interesting.

END OF THE FIRST VOLUME.

ENTERED ACCORDING TO LAW.

www.ingramcontent.com/pod-product-compliance
Lightning Source LLC
Chambersburg PA
CBHW030343230426
43664CB00007BA/516